Bomb Girls

BARBARA DICKSON

Bomb Girls

TRADING APRONS FOR AMMO

DUNDURN

A J. PATRICK BOYER BOOK

TORONTO

Editor: Dominic Farrell
Copy editor: Britanie Wilson
Design: BJ Weckerle
Cover Design: Sarah Beaudin
Cover Image: Female GECO war workers prepare fuses for shipping (AO1593, fonds F2082-1-2-24). *Courtesy of Archives of Ontario.*
Printer: Webcom

Library and Archives Canada Cataloguing in Publication

Dickson, Barbara, 1961-, author
          Bomb girls : trading aprons for ammo / Barbara Dickson.

Includes bibliographical references and index.
Issued in print and electronic formats.
ISBN 978-1-4597-3116-5 (pbk.).--ISBN 978-1-4597-3117-2 (pdf.).--
ISBN 978-1-4597-3118-9 (epub)

          1. World War, 1939-1945--Women--Canada. 2. World War,
1939-1945--War work--Canada. 3. Women in war--Canada--History--
20th century. 4. Weapons industry--Canada--History--20th century.
I. Title.

D810.W7D52 2015   940.53082'0971   C2015-902081-6
                                                                              C2015-902082-4

2   3   4   5   19   18   17   16

We acknowledge the support of the **Canada Council for the Arts** and the **Ontario Arts Council** for our publishing program. We also acknowledge the financial support of the **Government of Canada** through the **Canada Book Fund** and **Livres Canada Books**, and the **Government of Ontario** through the **Ontario Book Publishing Tax Credit** and the **Ontario Media Development Corporation**.

VISIT US AT
Dundurn.com | @dundurnpress | Facebook.com/dundurnpress | Pinterest.com/dundurnpress

Dundurn
3 Church Street, Suite 500
Toronto, Ontario, Canada
M5E 1M2

This book is dedicated to the brave Canadian women who left their homes and families — some from as far away as British Columbia — to fill munitions at "Scarboro" during the Second World War. Over twenty-one thousand people, predominantly women,[1] risked their lives filling munitions so that fellow Canadians living and dying on battlefields across the world had plenty of fighting power to put in their weapons, ultimately "speeding the victory" and bringing them home.

To my children and grandchildren, you are my joy. And to David, forever and for always.

To Those Women of All Ages
DEDICATED TO THE GIRLS BEHIND THE GUNS

"Give Us The Tools" ... Immortal words,
Were heard in darker days,
And answered by Canadians all,
In various fields and ways.
An urgent need — the guns to feed,
They heeded Scarboro's calls,
Those "Women of All Ages"
In "The Cleanside" shops and halls.

Both night and day, in spirits gay
To time clocks they make tracks,
Then journey to the Change House for
Their turbans and their slacks.
They cross "The Cleanside" barrier,
"All Clear" ... and without fuss
To ... "Keep 'em Firing" ... vital role,
"The Boys" to them entrust.

In spotless, air conditioned shops,
In to the fuse they pack
Explosive power ... pressing need,
The "key" to the attack.
They deal with primers, tubes and gaines,
They fill ... They press ... They stem,
To increase Allied might ... and save
The lives of valiant men.

They're soldiers of production lines
In uniforms of white,
The GECO Diamond is their badge,
They're workers in the fight.
While rhythmic music fills the air,
They seal the fate of Huns,
The songs they sing are "Preludes" to
"The Voices of the Guns."

When "Victory" trumpets sound the call,
For Gunners to … "Cease Fire!"
From ammunition-filling jobs,
They proudly can retire.
They'll hear … "They Kept 'Em Firing"
From Canada's fighting sons
Those "Women of All Ages"
The Girls behind the Guns.

— F.G. Brimicombe[1]

Contents

Foreword   11
Preface   15

1   In the Beginning   23
2   A Frozen Field of Dreams   33
3   A Mini City Tucked Behind an Eight-Foot Barbed-Wire Fence   41
4   Ramping Up   53
5   If You Can Walk, Talk, Creep, or Crawl — Apply Here!   60
6   A Day in the Life of a Bomb Girl   66
7   It All Depends on Me   88
8   Safety First Because Safety Lasts   155
9   Whistle While You Work: Industrial Relations and Personnel   173
10   Service with a Smile: Departments Serving Employees   181
11   Rolling Up Their Sleeves: Departments Contributing
      to Munitions Production   191
12   Nothing Less Will Do — Employee Morale   206
13   Disasters at the Plant   231
14   When "Victory" Trumpets Sound the Call   236
15   If You Build It, Scarborough Will Come   246

Appendix A: Layout of GECO: An Engineer's Sketch of GECO   257
Appendix B: GECO Management Chart   259
Appendix C: Typical Workshop Layout: Fuse 251, Shop 67C   263

Acknowledgements   267
Notes   270
Bibliography   271
Index   279

Foreword

When I first heard of Barbara Dickson's proposed book on the history of the A.W.S.C. Project No. 24, which was commonly referred to as the GECO Fuse-filling Plant or the GECO Munitions Plant, I was concerned. Was this author who had published several well-received romance novels about to produce a fictional romance story disguised as a documentary on GECO like some other recent works? Fearing this was the case, I prepared a memo that described my connection to GECO and the basic facts about its creation and operation. When the email of this memo was returned as undeliverable due to Barbara's website having been closed, I was dismayed and suspected that the book was being published.

This was not the case, however, and when we heard that Barbara was trying to contact relatives of the Hamilton brothers of GECO, my wife contacted her and we responded by sending her my memo.

This led to further communications and an invitation for her to visit us at our residence in Montreal. On July 17, 2012, when we finally met Barbara and her husband, my fears were allayed. Her book was not romantic fiction but an earnestly researched documentary of the General Engineering Company and its wartime project in Scarboro.

Barbara Dickson grew up in Scarboro (Scarborough) and lives south of the southern boundary of the GECO Plant. For years she has been interested in the site and the wartime history of GECO, and in her research she has consulted the documents that my uncle, R.M.P. Hamilton, donated to the Ontario Archives.

R.M.P. Hamilton and his brother, P.D.P. Hamilton, my father, were the owners and operators of the General Engineering Co. of Canada.

As the current patriarch of these two families, which our Montreal relatives always referred to as the Toronto Hamiltons, it gives me great pleasure to see that Barbara Dickson documents and praises the wartime effort of the Hamilton brothers. To my knowledge no other publication has ever done this.

During our first meeting, we discussed my background, history, and my wartime personal contacts with GECO Munitions, from the ground-breaking in the spring of 1941 to working on decontamination prior to its closure in 1945. I was able to show her some artifacts from the plant. At that time I was impressed by the depth and extensiveness of her research and the openness of her attitude. I learned a great deal from her.

It was toward the end of this visit that she did me the honour of asking me to write this foreword. I demurred at first, saying that it would be unconventional to write a foreword to a book that I had not read! Some discussion ensued and she agreed to provide me with the Table of Contents and the first three chapters of the book. I agreed to think about it.

Later in the summer, after I had agreed to her proposal, Barbara, her husband, and her daughter paid us a visit at our country home in the Laurentians when she delivered the Table of Contents and the three chapters, as we had agreed. Here, I was able to show her more artifacts from the fuse filling and more documents concerning the General Engineering Co.

Readers should be aware that this foreword was written for a book of which I have read less than 10 percent of the content, and that content being a typed draft that had not undergone a publisher's review and editing.

However, if this book is published and successfully documents the information described in the Table of Contents, it will provide a very readable and valuable account of a project and people that contributed to the winning of the Second World War.

Philip H.B. Hamilton
November 25, 2012

Preface

On September 10, 1939, Canada was thrust into a growing global conflict a mere two decades after the armistice had been signed for the "War to End All Wars." The First World War had left a legacy of human suffering and destruction that the free world hoped never would happen again. No nation, it had been decided, would be allowed to arm aggressively for any significant conflict. Tragically, promises were not kept, a failure that ultimately would cost a staggering loss of life — some estimates attribute the loss of fifty-five million souls to the Second World War, with more than eighty-one thousand Canadian casualties.[1] The greatest man-made conflict in human history would be fought — in the air, upon every sea, and on every continent except Antarctica.

On that fateful day in September 1939, Canadians knew that if they had any hope of beating Hitler and his belligerent bullies, the Allied forces would not only need every able-bodied man Canada could muster to fight, but a steady stream of ammunition as well.

Before Canada entered what was to become the Second World War, the only facility in Canada that produced ammunition was the Dominion Arsenal in Quebec City.[2] Opened in 1882, the plant turned out about

750,000 rounds a month of one type of ammunition.[3] The number sounded impressive for its time.

Hitler's relentless drive to rule the world forced Great Britain and her Commonwealth partners to ramp up production quickly. By November 1942, Canada had produced more explosives in six months than during the entire First World War.[4] Filled ammunition, from bombs and depth charges to rifle cartridges and heavy shells, left filling and assembly plants at the rate of millions of rounds a month.[5] By 1943, at its peak of munitions production, Canada produced more small-arms ammunition in one eight-hour shift than its peacetime facilities could have produced in two months.[6] In fact, munitions output reached an ultimate rate of nearly 1.5 billion rounds a year, with over thirty thousand workers employed in factories engaged in producing small-arms ammunition.[7]

Making this achievement even more impressive, the production of small-arms munitions was extremely complex. Even with far superior equipment and production methods than those used during the First World War, the assembly of a complete round required up to one hundred different operations.[8]

C.D. Howe, minister of Munitions and Supply during the Second World War, wrote in the foreword of *The History of the Department of Munitions and Supply: Canada in the Second World War*:

> Before the war, few thought of Canada as an industrial power and many doubted whether the manufacturing techniques, which had been perfected in other countries over the centuries, could be developed here in time to produce the war supplies required. It was a challenge that was splendidly met by the men and women of Canada.
>
> In the pages that follow will be found the record of one of the more important eras of Canadian history, the years during which the country emerged from its position as a producer of basic supplies to that of a highly industrialized state.
>
> The instrument knitting together this vast web of enterprise was the Department of Munitions and Supply where men and women, numbering several thousand, laboured to meet the

unprecedented demands of the greatest war in history. As a result of their work, the apparently insoluble problems of the early days were gradually resolved into a great orderly plan uniting the various phases of a wartime economy.[9]

The "key" to the attack, to ultimate victory, lay within vital complex military hardware. Fuses are devices used to arm and detonate explosive military munitions such as missiles, land mines, torpedoes, bombs, and explosive shells.[10] Made up of between twenty and fifty different parts, they are filled with explosive ingredients that explode quickly when exposed to a small spark.[11] The fuse, once detonated, lit a much larger projectile, causing it to explode, either upon impact, or at a certain time during flight.[12]

Fuses, the small but mighty heroes of war, are key to the flawless operation of a shell or bomb. However, unless the fuse is filled with combustible powder, it is as useful as a lampstand. "All the refinements of modern gunnery and highly developed methods of ranging and controlling fire power would be of no avail," W.H. Pitcher wrote in an article for *Canadian Chemistry and Process Industries*, "if the fuse failed at the crucial moment."[13]

The importance of reliable and efficient ammunition cannot be argued. Behind every man behind a gun in the Second World War stood a dedicated group of Canadians steadfast in their determination to ensure every fuse that passed through the combatant's hands reflected outstanding workmanship. From the transportation of raw materials to the manufacture of the ammunition, from filling the munitions with explosives to its transport to the theatre of war, brave men and women contributed directly to ensuring that ammunition found its proper place within a gun or war machine aboard a ship, tank, or plane. Courageous, trained fighting men willing to sacrifice their lives for freedom used those carefully designed fuses to trigger targeted massive explosions, stopping the enemy where he stood.

Lieutenant-Colonel H. Read, R.A., a British authority on ammunition, stated, "The whole national war effort is really nothing more or less than arranging for the contact between our ammunition and the enemy.

If at the very climax there is a failure, all has been wasted."[14] Continuing, he says:

> Think on the hunting and sinking of the *Bismarck*. Here the far-flung operation of sea power resulted in one vital bit of damage to her steering gear by a fleet (of Fairey Swordfish torpedo bombers.) This enabled the great ship to be caught and destroyed at leisure. But supposing the fuse of that aerial torpedo had failed, there was no opportunity to repeat the blow and the *Bismarck* would have escaped to prey with disastrous results on our Atlantic shipping. It is not too much to say that millions of tons of shipping depended on the correct functioning of one single fuse.[15]

W.H. Pitcher agreed. "The German battleship "Bismark" [*sic*] might still be afloat to harass Allied shipping if the fuse on the torpedo which first crippled her had failed in its action."[16]

Recognizing the vital necessity of supplying Canadian and other Allied forces with fuses and ammunition during the war, the Canadian government established Project No. 24 of Allied War Supplies Corporation (A.W.S.C.), a factory that would specialize in filling munitions, in 1940.[17] *Bomb Girls* tells the story of more than twenty-one thousand dedicated men and women who filled more than a quarter of a billion fuses for the Allied forces. Initially hired to build other wartime factories, General Engineering Company (Canada) Limited was given the responsibility of designing and building the shell-filling plant as well as selecting, training, and organizing its staff and overseeing its operation. Project No. 24 would come to be known simply as GECO, or "Scarboro."[18]

GECO's story is unique from its wartime counterparts in several ways. GECO was the only wartime plant in Canada dedicated to filling fuses, primers, tubes, and tracers.[19] When the war ended, the plant had filled more than 256 million units, providing the catalysts behind the greatest quantity of heavy ammunition manufactured in Canada from 1940 to 1945.[20] "Scarboro" became the largest fuse-filling plant in Canada's history. Incredibly, less than four months after the turning of the first piece of sod in February 1941, the first filling workshop was completed.[21]

Aerial view of GECO looking southeast from present-day Civic Road. *Courtesy of Archives of Ontario.*

The plant went into volume production in July 1941.[22] By September 1941, construction workers had erected more than 170 buildings on 346 acres of gently rolling farmland in Scarboro.[23]

Almost 99 percent of all production submitted to government inspection was approved and accepted into service — an extraordinary feat achieved by seamless teamwork.[24] Imbued with the resolve to reach maximum production without sacrificing quality, workers etched every filled fuse that left Scarboro with "Sc/C" (Scarboro/Canada) as a mark of quality. It was one recognized not only by fellow Canadians but also by Allied and enemy forces from around the world.[25]

Remarkably, GECO would suffer no fatal accidents, despite thousands of employees — predominately women — handling high explosives and gunpowder twenty-four hours a day, six days a week, for four years.[26] This accomplishment was truly rare in global arsenal practice. While there were no catastrophic disasters within the munitions industry during the Second World War in Canada, there were deaths, maimings, and other injuries recorded, with several deaths recorded at GECO's sister plant, managed by D.I.L. in Pickering, Ontario.[27] And finally, production was never interrupted by a single serious labour dispute.[28]

The world made its peace with Germany decades ago and the need for a munitions plant has long since passed, but GECO's legacy lives on, in its last surviving buildings and tunnels, buried under the city as an invisible reminder of a nation that went to war. GECO lives on, too, in the memories of those who worked at the plant, in the hearts and minds of children who remember their mom or dad faithfully serving their country doing war work, and in the memories of thousands of children who lived with their families in emergency housing set up at GECO after the war.

For reasons of national security, much of "Scarboro's" story was shrouded in secrecy during the war, and any discussion as to its existence was off-limits outside the plant. In fact, after the war ended, the government ordered Robert McLean Prior (R.M.P.) Hamilton, GECO's president, and Philip Dawson Prior (P.D.P.) Hamilton, his older brother and GECO's vice-president, to burn all specifications for Project No. 24. In a letter from the Inspection Board of United Kingdom and Canada, the controller general wrote, "All drawings and specifications should be destroyed by General Engineering … and a list of those destroyed should be forwarded … and should certify on the list that all drawings and specifications shown have been destroyed…"[29] From Air Raid Precaution Regulations to War Savings Certificates, all documentation was burned. All purchasing records for items from abrasives to linoleum, from sanitary pads to guard whistles, were destroyed.

The only proof GECO existed now lies in workers' personal keepsakes, and in the records saved by the Hamilton brothers. Both men felt it imperative that the "records of the design, construction, and operating of an ammunition 'Loading' plant should be kept available for future emergencies."[30] In fact, they recommended the Canadian government keep a contingent of expert ammunition personnel, provide munitions training to future "vocational" army reserves that could become and train munitions operators quickly, and, more ominously, maintain personnel who would work closely with Britain and Canada's allies "for the next war."[31] Hamilton's GECO records remained in his private possession until 1980, when he presented them to the Engineering Heritage Records Foundation. A year later, the foundation gave the records to the Archives

of Ontario. Elizabeth Hamilton — Betty — Bob's widow, donated additional material to the Archives in 1998. Phil's records remain with his
family. R.M.P. Hamilton, in a letter to John H. Fox, Esq. in April 1981,
forty years after the plant opened, stated that GECO "should be made
widely known to the Ontario Public."[32]

It is a privilege and honour to help Mr. Hamilton's desire come to
fruition. GECO's enduring spirit so aptly emulates the Canadians who
tirelessly worked there. GECO's ranks — the girls behind the guns — are
quickly dwindling. Unless their stories are told, how will future generations learn of their sacrifice, of their patriotism, of their resolve? This
book is part of GECO's one last song.

1

In the Beginning

The story of "Scarboro" begins as the curtain rises ... on a world teetering at the edge of war.

Canada Declares War

On September 10, 1939, Canada entered into a state of war with Germany, a week after Britain declared its own war on the Third Reich. Canada's prime minister, William Lyon Mackenzie King, did not see the need to conscript men for military service. King knew men were killed in war — men who would have to be replaced, drawing deeply from his country's workforce. Yet sixty-four thousand brave men immediately and voluntarily signed up in the first weeks after Canada's declaration. On December 17, Canada's first shipment of troops landed in the United Kingdom. Fifty thousand of the country's finest men were ready to fight, to offer their very lives, if necessary, to stop Hitler. With tens of thousands of souls now committed to the war, Canada had pledged its heart to the cause. As they say in the game of poker, the Commonwealth nation of Canada was "all in." There would be victory, or total annihilation.

With a strong majority Liberal government backing him, Prime Minister King appointed Member of Parliament Clarence Decatur Howe minister of the newly founded Department of Munitions and Supply. During the war years he earned the nickname the "Minister of Everything" responsible for all aspects of mustering Canada's resources — raw materials and manpower — to support the massive war effort.[1]

Wanted: One Mining Company, No War Experience Necessary

While Canada waited for Germany's next move, it quietly began building the infrastructure needed for a country at war by placing a moratorium on base metal mining and instead focusing all steel production on manufacturing instruments of war.

In February 1940, the Canadian government hired mining firm General Engineering Company (Canada) Limited — or "GECO" (pronounced GEE-KO) — to build No. 1 Elementary Flying Training School in Malton, Ontario, which would train young men to take to the skies over Europe.[2] The facility included hangars, barracks, mess halls, schools, a hospital, and other buildings. The government chose GECO for the project because, as a mining and metallurgical enterprise, it possessed the skill and experience to quickly erect temporary wooden buildings, similar to those used in mining endeavours.

Founded in 1906 in the United States by John Callow and Ernest Gayford, GECO had matured quickly, building an impressive reputation within the mining industry, opening a New York office in 1914 and a London, England, office in 1928.[3] In 1933, two GECO employees — brothers Philip Dawson Prior Hamilton and Robert McLean Prior Hamilton — launched a Canadian subsidiary in Toronto.[4] During the 1930s, the company expanded. Its main business involved designing and installing equipment to extract ore from the ground and process it enough to be shipped.[5]

GECO started construction of RCAF No. 1 Elementary Flying Training School on February 2, 1940, despite wintry conditions.[6] There was a shortage of steel, and constructing hangars large enough to house planes without steel support beams challenged GECO engineers. Hangar ceilings had to be freestanding, with no interior column support. Undaunted, the brilliant minds of GECO came up with an innovative solution. They created "wood trusses" — laminated two-by-eight-inch spruce planks stacked, glued, and nailed together side by side.[7] Government inspectors were wary of GECO's new "super structures," however. So, with inspectors present, engineers set the new laminated beam upon two concrete blocks and loaded it with cement blocks. The beam easily supported its expected "proof load," greatest "snow load," and "compression load."[8] Curious to know how much the beam could support, GECO engineers continued to load the beam. When the beam finally failed, it was well beyond government standards. Remarkably, while the wood fractured, the nails and glue held. More remarkable, engineers suggested these beams could sustain free spans of "at least" two hundred feet.[9] These super structures became well known within engineering circles as a good substitute for steel beams.

By June 1940, only four months after breaking ground, Malton's flying school opened.[10] With one outstanding military success to the mining company's credit, the Canadian government quickly hired GECO again, this time to build a larger enterprise, No. 4 Bombing and Gunnery School near Fingal, Ontario. Incredibly, by September, GECO had completed the school with top notch workmanship.[11] The Hamiltons were immediately asked to build an ordnance depot in London, Ontario, consisting of twenty-two large storage buildings. Under their leadership, the London project was finished in just 120 days.[12]

The Dynamic Duo

The Canadian government knew exactly who they needed to manage Project No. 24, a new, vitally important war project. Bob and Phil Hamilton had proven themselves in the past nine months. With GECO's amazing success to date, and with the Hamilton brothers' extraordinary reputation preceding them, C.D. Howe requested the dynamic duo design, build, and oversee the proposed munitions plant to be built in the area outside of Toronto.

Anticipation Swells

Speculation, curiosity, and press coverage seem to go hand in hand when a large "top-secret" wartime project is involved. Discussions between the Hamilton brothers at GECO, and the Allied War Supplies Corporation were ongoing during the fall of 1940 as construction on the ordnance depot in London, Ontario, continued.[13] The *Toronto Daily Star* reported on a rumour that an explosives plant was going to be built near the city. "Most of the 4,000 employees required to man the new government shell-filling plant being built east of Toronto, will be drawn from the city and suburbs," said T. Holmes Bartley, Toronto Industrial Commission's general manager, in the article.[14] Production would begin early in 1941. "The plant," Bartley said, "will cost between $5,000,000 and $8,000,000 and will be used to fill and fit fuses and shells produced in other Canadian factories. It will be one of the largest plants of its kind in the empire."[15] The article went on to say war work had "boosted employment in Toronto to an all-time high."[16] Companies within the city had employed 25,000 more men and women than they had on the same day a year ago.[17] Bartley said, "About 167,000 persons are now on the payrolls of Toronto Industrial companies."[18]

A.W.S.C. Project No. 24: Birth of a War Factory

On December 10, 1940, the Story of "Scarboro" — "Sc/C" as respectfully recognized by the Allied forces, and as "Project No. 24" within Allied War Supplies Corporation — began in earnest.[19] A.W.S.C. drew up a Document of Understanding (DOU) with GECO,[20] asking the mining company to take on the responsibility for design and construction of the plant, with the Canadian government retaining ownership.[21] The factory needed the capacity to produce top-quality artillery ammunition in perhaps unlimited quantities as the fortunes — or misfortunes — of war changed. If Britain had any chance of beating Germany, especially with its munitions supply already sluggish and ineffectual from Hitler's blitzkrieg against plants like Woolwich, GECO had to start immediately.

A tall order.

While Bartley speculated the cost to design, construct, and equip such a plant stood at between $5 million and $8 million, GECO's management team estimated construction would cost only $2.25 million, with an anticipated production capacity of 1.5 million units per month of seven different "natures" or types of fuses.[22]

A Few Good Men

Though exceptional design and superior construction were paramount to the GECO munitions plant's success, during its early days these responsibilities were only part of what was undertaken by Bob and Phil Hamilton and General Engineering Company (Canada) Limited. The plant also had to be tooled, prepared for production, and staffed with specially trained personnel, more than likely before construction of the plant was finished. Bob and Phil sought men of high calibre, and, in some instances, personally hand-selected individual candidates to fill engineering and administrative positions, choosing men specifically experienced in British munitions.[23] Finding such men was not easy.

This reliance on workers with foreign experience was due to the fact that there was an utter lack of expert personnel with technical experience in ammunition work in Canada.[24] Also, the machinery and tools required to fill munitions were virtually non-existent. These critical needs posed a serious problem, and called for ingenuity and improvisation of men skilled in mechanics. Mr. E.H. (Ted) Smith, originally from the Woolwich Arsenal in England, was helping at Defence Industries Limited — D.I.L. — in the Beloeil, Quebec, plant, which was about to go into production.[25] At the personal request of Bob Hamilton, Mr. Smith transferred from the Department of National Defence to GECO.[26]

Ted Smith's contribution to GECO was of incalculable value. He provided process specifications, several fuses, an old box of tools used in filling, and technical knowledge and experience that Canadians lacked.[27]

Bob and Phil Hamilton had the vital responsibility of selecting competent key GECO personnel, including department heads and supervisors, and establishing a complete organization that would enable

GECO's Executive Staff, as of June 1943, taken in front of the administration build-
ing. **Front Row from left to right**: Miss Grace Hyndman, D.A. Duff, E.N. Martin, H.L.
Tamplin, R.M.P. Hamilton, P.D.P. Hamilton, E. Flexman, E.H. Smith, G.M. Thomson, Mrs.
Florence Ignatieff. **Second Row from left to right**: J.P. Todd, J.H. MacLean, A.B. Taylor, E.
Littlejohn, Dr. A.H. Jeffrey, A.E. Johnston, T.B. Little, H.W. Little, D.E. Cumberland, C.R.
Avery, R.S. Segsworth, E.A. Williams, John Christo, J.C. Craig, A.J. Williams. *Courtesy of
Archives of Ontario.*

the plant to go into production as soon as a sufficient number of workshops were completed. Whoever was to manage the munitions plant
— the Hamilton brothers were not assured they would be retained as
management — they would take over the plant's operation for the duration of the war.[28] These chosen supervisors, affectionately referred to
as the "NCOs" of the fuse-filling production lines, would be responsible for training thousands of "operators," who, more than likely, would
be women, to undertake tasks that had not previously been attempted
in Canada.[29]

GECO's engineers worked tirelessly to plan and design Project No. 24.
The site's plans had to be ready to go as soon as a suitable physical site
was found. They examined plants, proposed sites, planned for founda-
tions, site grading, drainage, roads, and established standards for water,
fuel, steam, power, and sewage. They also helped determine suitable
locations for plant railway sidings. Two groups of men, mostly trainees

with engineering experience, sailed for England in December 1940 and February 1941, expecting to learn as much as humanly possible in eight weeks by gathering knowledge and experience of British arsenals in the manufacture of explosive munitions.[30]

Scarboro, Ontario, Canada: Farms, Fillies, and Fuses

By the time 1941's New Year rolled in, Canada had been at war with Germany for nearly a year and a half. Norway, Denmark, the Netherlands, Belgium, Luxembourg, and France had fallen. The evacuation at Dunkirk had been carried out, and the Battle of Britain was underway.

Time was precious. Like well-stacked dominoes, world governments were teetering and tumbling under the Axis's iron will. Hitler and his Huns were on a tear across Europe, and North America was in the crosshairs of their guns, too. If Canada and her allies hoped for victory, something needed to be done — and done fast. On January 9, 1941, members of GECO — including R.M.P. Hamilton and H.L. Tamplin — and the A.W.S.C. met in Montreal to decide on the plant's general layout, type of construction, and spacing of buildings, among myriad other macro and micro details.[31]

Bob and Phil Hamilton looked to history — the Great War in particular — to save time re-inventing the wheel. They chose National Filling Factory No. 7, situated at Hayes, Middlesex, England, built in 1915, as their model.[32] While twenty-five years had passed since that plant had been built, Hayes had done a lot of things right. General Engineering Company (Canada) Ltd. wanted to build on their successes and learn from their mistakes. Nine people died at Hayes due to explosions and tetryl poisoning[33] (a highly explosive powder used to manufacture fuses, tetryl is also extremely poisonous). The team at GECO were determined not to repeat such tragic accidents.

GECO's previous mining experience would come in handy, as well. For instance, the fire hall at the new munitions plant would include a tower, similar to a mine's "head frame" — a structure erected over the mineshaft to hoist men and supplies in and out of the mine, like an elevator. GECO's head frame would be used to hoist, hang, and dry fire hoses.[34]

Based on the criteria used to build Filling Factory No. 7, the site selected for Project No. 24 had to be within twenty miles of a large metropolis to access hundreds of construction workers and thousands of munitions operators who would be mostly women. A large city could meet the plant's other requirements as well, like providing transportation, having an available water supply and sewage disposal and hydro-electric power, and offering access to rail. Building on the outskirts of the city afforded access to large expanses of suitable, inexpensive acreage, as well as being far enough from nearby buildings or settlements to minimize damage or death due to explosion. Finally, the site had to be available immediately.[35]

The Hamilton brothers wanted to avoid building hostels, although this happened at other plants in both Britain and Canada, like at Defence Industries Limited in Pickering, Ontario.[36] Constructing housing for thousands of women would have delayed the start of production, in addition to adding significantly to government costs for materials and labour. As well, GECO wanted to avoid, if possible, taking women away from their homes, and incurring the moral responsibility of controlling a large number of women after working hours. Although war plants in Canada wanted to avoid importing labour from other provinces, as the war progressed many expanded their hiring radius to include women from as far away as British Columbia.[37]

Scarboro,[38] Ontario, Canada was a quiet rural community with gently undulating farmland when Canada entered the Second World War. Remarkably, the town, with its unsophisticated charm and a population of just over twenty-three thousand,[39] met Project No. 24's critical requirements. The township was only eight miles (ten miles by road from Union Station) northeast of Toronto, which provided easy access to a large labour force, including many men looking for work and thousands of women who were eager to work when their men enlisted and went off to war.[40] Toronto had an established public commuting service that could be expanded to accommodate GECO's workforce. Inexpensive farmland, sloping gradually toward the Scarboro Bluffs three miles to the south, was available in the Wardin [sic] and Eglinton Avenue area.[41] A small, local population minimized any risk due to explosion.[42]

The King's Speech

On January 27, 1941, His Majesty King George VI of Great Britain issued an expropriation decree for Lots 31, 32, and 33, Concession C, Scarboro Township, affecting seven proprietors.[43] King George's expropriation included "Hough's Corners," located at the southeast corner of Eglinton and Birchmount Avenues.[44] The Hough family had settled in Scarboro in 1804 and owned a substantial farming operation and blacksmithing business.[45] Other expropriated land included the W.T. Harris estate, along with Alexander S. Crichton and Elizabeth Jane Burke's land.[46]

In its final form, the future munitions plant comprised:

226.97	Acres in Lots 32, 33, Concession C, south of Eglinton Avenue between Birchmount Road and Wardin Avenue (Now spelled "Warden," with an "e," this road was spelled "Wardin" at the time.)
43.47	Acres in Concession D, Lot 32
77.20	Acres restricted in Lot 33, Concession C
347.64	(Total acres taken)[47]

GECO workers in Building No. 45 pack filled Primer 12 into containers for shipping.
Courtesy of Archives of Ontario.

Only forty-eight hours after King George issued his decree, a survey of the future GECO plant was undertaken, despite knee-deep snow.[48] By the end of January 1941, there were ten men on GECO's employment rolls.[49] In just over a week workmen would break ground and start excavation.

With a DOU signed, GECO engineers across "the pond" learning everything they could about filling munitions, and with about 350 acres of Scarboro farmland appropriated, the story of "Scarboro" was not only in motion, it was picking up speed.

2

A Frozen Field of Dreams

I f Bob and Phil Hamilton had felt any pressure to deliver their earlier Canadian wartime projects with haste, they would need to muster every bit of their collective experience and emotional vigour to manage the pace at which the Scarboro facility was expected to be up and running. With the land expropriation plan filed in the township's registry office at the end of January 1941, the month of February stormed in without reprieve. Construction had to start immediately. Workmen would have to find a way — and fast — to dig through one and a half to two feet of permafrost and snow. However, as problematic as the pending excavation was, breaking ground would not be the Hamilton brothers' biggest challenge that February. The war was about to hit a little closer to home — Bob and Phil found themselves having to handle a situation that had the potential to cripple not only Canada's fledging munitions industry but that of Great Britain as well.

Dead in the Water

An elite group of engineers who collectively represented the greatest minds in British munitions expertise sailed for England January 19,

1941, while another group of their esteemed colleagues, who had set out for Britain two months earlier, were well on their way home, with their arrival imminent.[1] Everyone involved in Project No. 24 assumed all was well. However, anxious days passed with no word from the returning gentlemen or their ship. Days slipped into weeks. GECO personnel and government officials feared the worst. Had a German U-boat sunk the vessel carrying many of the brightest engineering minds in the world? A year would pass before GECO's employee newspaper, the *GECO Fusilier*, would issue a small news item relaying the incident, after the secrecy surrounding the engineering mission had passed. The news clip read:

> One wintry day in February, 1941, a weather-scarred ship, grotesque in its camouflage paint, plowed its way into Montreal harbo[u]r and was berthed by fussy, panting tugs. Her arrival caused a stir in many hearts. She had left Scotland three weeks before and was long overdue. The worst was feared for she had picked her precarious way unconvoyed from Iceland across the sub-infested north Atlantic. So convinced were officials concerned that she had gone the way of so many good ships since 1939 that the terse, official forms used for notifying next of kin of passengers and crew had already been made out. Mercifully, there was now no need to send them.
>
> From the ship a group of Canadian men, some still recovering from the pangs of seasickness, disembarked. This group had been handpicked, mostly from the engineering profession, by Allied War Supplies Corporation months before.[2]

It was from members of this sea-tossed group — including several British personnel who migrated to Canada to consult on plant design and assist in fuse-filling methodology — and the second group, which followed (and returned without incident), that "Scarboro" recruited its start-up supervisory staff. Had these men truly been lost at sea, "Scarboro," and, in turn, Canada's entire munitions war effort, might have suffered a significant and perhaps disastrous delay.

Turning of the Sod — with a Little Help from Some TNT

Within two weeks of King George expropriating Canadian soil, lumber and materials were delivered to the future plant's home — a huge expanse of farmland covered in knee-deep snow. On February 6, without pomp or circumstance, without cheery speeches or a silver shovel, a handful of resilient Canadian construction workers set off dynamite to blast through two feet of hardened earth and snow.[3] Blasting agitated nearby livestock and farm families alike, and GECO personnel had to deal with the wrath of the latter. Their complaints were of little consequence, though. The war could not wait for Canada's spring thaw.

The Hamilton brothers had lots of experience coping with fierce Canadian winters in their earlier government war projects, and encouraged their men to remain steadfast in their mission. Bob Hamilton's clear mandate fuelled construction: the plant was to be in production by July, with completion of construction of some 130 buildings by September.[4] His goal was no small one; it had never had been attempted before in Canada's history, nor has it since. A.W.S.C.'s early production capacity of 1.5 million filled munitions per month seemed a reasonable goal for future employees of GECO to meet.[5] They expected the facility to cost $2.96 million to build.[6]

Bob Hamilton instructed his newly formed construction team: "Keep things moving as fast as possible with the best information we can obtain from any source, keeping A.W.S.C. posted so they can stop or change anything they do not want."[7] Despite bitter northerly winds and lots of snow, the patriotic and indomitable spirit of dedicated workers on GECO's payroll overcame anything the winter of '41 fired their way.

Loose Lips Sink Ships

On March 3, 1941, less than a month after breaking ground, Bob and Phil Hamilton leased space at 1218 Danforth Avenue in Toronto that would eventually become the first administration and employment office for the Scarboro plant.[8] They hired Project No. 24's first secretary, Miss Dorothy Cheesman.

The Hamilton brothers expected Dorothy, at just sixteen years of age, to type up top-secret engineering notes. She had her photo and finger-prints taken, and swore a solemn oath of secrecy. To be sure, she had never experienced the intrigue associated with such clandestine activities before. Forbidden to reveal anything she saw, heard, or learned, Dorothy was entrusted by GECO staff to lock the safe each evening with classified engineering notes safely tucked inside. Some might say Dorothy's young age and naivety subjected Canada's war effort to possible sabotage should she accidently "spill the beans," allowing delicate information to slip into treasonous hands. Bob and Phil Hamilton's gamble paid off, however. A steadfast and patriotic employee, Dorothy would accomplish great things at GECO.

The Gunpowder Plot

Prior to opening its Danforth office, the General Engineering Company (Canada) Ltd. conducted business from its longstanding offices situ-ated in the Concourse Building at 100 Adelaide Street West.[9] "Adelaide" became the birthplace of Project No. 24. During the winter and spring of 1941, planning, organization, and design of the new plant originated from these offices. GECO engineers, along with several of Britain's chemical experts, covertly transformed basement offices into a minia-ture machine shop and fuse-filling factory.[10] A year later, once GECO's production was well underway, the employee newspaper would comment on the "Gunpowder Plot":

> Piece by piece a 1,400 lb. ring press and facing lathe had been smuggled in and set up. A twelve-inch-wide pipe was installed to carry off smoke and fumes as unobtrusively as might be. Innocent looking packages that might have been mistaken for Sunday's roast, but were gunpowder, and primer components came next. A stranger "barging in" inopportunely might well have thought he had stumbled on a modern Guy Fawkes' plot.
>
> Everything was so "hush hush" that no one outside a small coterie of GECO principals, technicians, and a few operators had

the slightest inkling of the exciting things that were taking place in that downtown cellar — certainly not the office tenants of the building, which was fortunate for their individual and collective peace of mind — nor the "news hawks" not much farther than a good stone's throw away.[11]

Despite the best intentions and precautions of those involved, occasionally acrid black smoke escaped up the building's elevator shafts.[12] Amazingly, no one noticed. Explosives were stored in an old office vault at day's end.[13] The work accomplished in those cramped basement quarters with minimal equipment came to be known as "The Gunpowder Plot." Newly acquired Ted Smith felt this work "was instrumental in speeding Canada's ammunition[-]filling programme by six to eight months."[14] Engineer William Taylor acknowledged that "Between March and May, 1941, all of the secret doings in that cellar suite had some significance."[15]

Canadian history was made in the basement of that tall downtown office building.

Needed: 2,500 Good Strong Men

By early March 1941, GECO's construction "gang" was moving heaven and earth to turn pastures and wheat fields into a wartime ammunition plant. Bob and Phil Hamilton needed good strong men, and a lot of them. Business in Canada had not recovered from the Great Depression and a significant job shortage remained. If anything good could come from a world at war, perhaps it was full-time employment. Canada's unemployment rate fell from 10 percent in 1939 to almost zero by 1943 as wartime industry grew.[16] In 1941, GECO was one of the first large employers to offer work in over a decade.

Construction crews were working around the clock by early May 1941.[17] With over two thousand workmen employed, several buildings were well on their way to completion.[18] Staff opened GECO's first change house temporarily in an old construction shed abutting Building No. 26.[19] The change house was prepared in anticipation of GECO receiving its inaugural group of female supervisors.

Hartley Anthony French was a young man, twenty years old, attending the University of Toronto in its electrical engineering program in May 1941. Desperate for summer employment, Hartley discovered an advertisement for GECO in a local paper. He headed to the hiring office on Danforth Avenue on May 3, and signed up immediately as an apprentice electrician. By 2:00 that same afternoon, Hartley had hopped aboard the bus for the bumpy forty-five-minute ride to the GECO construction site amid the farmland of Scarboro. He would spend the next four months under the tutelage of an electrician, helping lay GECO's electrical foundation, primarily housed underground in an emerging elaborate tunnel system.[20] GECO, to Hartley, was not a top-secret munitions plant, but rather a large, roaming, and busy construction site. Buildings at the north end of the complex — near Wardin and Eglinton Avenues — had completed construction, while the more southern area of the site — toward Wardin Avenue and Comstock Road — was still under excavation.

In June 1941, GECO's construction rolls peaked at 2,681 men working around the clock.[21] The expected total cost to build the plant had increased, now expected to exceed $3.5 million up from an earlier $2.25 million projection.[22]

On the seventh of the month, engineers at the rapidly expanding munitions site filled and tested GECO's first few fuses, all for the "defence of the empire."[23] Media showed up for this important milestone to watch the earth-shaking demonstration of explosive might.[24] Engineers timed the explosions, and all was declared "definitely good," by Ted Smith, resident Brititsh munitions expert.[25]

With construction slowing and production beginning, it was now time to give thought to filling the many positions needed to bring the plant to full capacity. At the time, Bob and Phil Hamilton expected to hire 1,500 men and 2,500 women to work at GECO with an annual cost to employ these 4,000 civilians expected to reach $3 million.[26]

If there was some concern that potential workers might be afraid to sign up for a position at a munitions plant because of the danger of explosions, an article that appeared in the *Toronto Daily Star* helped to allay it. The reporter explained that filling munitions was safer than other types of manufacturing, "and much safer than general construction work."[27] He also stated that "production accidents" would be less than those experienced so far in the construction of the plant.

There are no accounts of construction "accidents" in GECO's records, although Hartley French recalls a construction worker falling twenty feet from the roof of a gallery, seriously injuring himself.

The news article ended with a stellar list of amenities to be enjoyed at GECO including a bank, post office, laundry, doctor, fire brigade, police, and living accommodations.[28] Many "perks" did come to fruition, but the Hamilton brothers already had abandoned trying to board their workforce, and there would be no police on site, only security guards.

Producing required tools and equipment for the different natures was done in tandem with construction. All engineering and experimental work was transferred from 100 Adelaide St. West to Building No. 4, the electrical shop, mid-June 1941.[29] Engineers used the first fuse-filling shop — Building No. 26 — that had been completed May 28, to work out the details of equipment needed for other filling shops nearing completion.

Miss Dorothy Cheesman, GECO's first secretary, transferred from 1218 Danforth Avenue to the plant site when the administration building opened.

Hitler's Fate Sealed

June 16, 1940, started like any other day at the flourishing GECO site. Bulldozers and diggers still took centre stage, while "Tony's" sandwich bar in the corner of a makeshift baseball diamond drew steady business from thousands of keen and dedicated workers.[30] Tradesmen and stenographers, technicians and accountants, engineers and "trainees" all dined in a "fresh air canteen" along the country roadside. However, there was one definitive difference this day. This would be a day Hitler and his hordes would live to regret. Not only were the first filling shops nearing completion, but the first batch of Danforth Tech "trainees" had arrived that morning — men and women who had been trained, ready to fill fuses in the now formally opened Shop 26D.[31] Production was underway.

Yes, GECO still had to iron out the kinks, but "Scarboro," as a full-fledged munitions factory, was in production. Over the course of a hot, hazy, humid summer, close to one hundred additional buildings would open, and hundreds upon hundreds of predominantly female fuse-fillers would be hired, trained, and put to good work, eager to join in the battle for freedom. That average sunny day in June held the promise of greater things to come.

3

A Mini City Tucked Behind an Eight-Foot Barbed-Wire Fence

The Hamiltons and their expert staff based Scarboro's design and layout on the No. 7 munitions plant built during the First World War in Hayes, England.[1] GECO needed to meet both quality and quantity targets, filling the greatest number of fuses in the shortest time, with the least wastage of materials, in the safest manner. GECO's design reflected these high ideals, ideals embodied in such details as the optimization of inter-building distances, the storage of explosives, the design of machinery, and the handling of personnel.

Isolating operations involved in filling a munition within one building minimized widespread damage should an explosion occur from handling high explosives.[2] Scarboro was split into two distinct areas: at the north end of the plant there was a "safe," or "dirty," side, where operations not specifically related to munitions were situated; at the south end of the plant, which encompassed the vastly larger portion of the GECO site, there was a "Danger Zone," or "clean" side, where munitions were filled.[3] Workers on the clean side wore special clothing and shoes that would minimize static electricity, and they followed stringent anti-spark rules in meticulously clean workshops.[4]

Aerial view of GECO looking southwest from Building No. 94. One of the ninety-ton coal bunkers can be seen in the foreground. "Pennsylvania Slack" fuelled boilers that produced steam to heat the facility, with the heating system's main line running throughout the underground tunnel system. *Courtesy of Archives of Ontario.*

Taking Sides

The administration building and many other buildings servicing the plant and employees were situated along the north end of the plant at Eglinton Avenue, running south to below present-day Civic Road. Service buildings on the dirty side of the plant included the administration building (No. 1), the guardhouse and clock house where employees punched in (No. 98), the time office and personnel building (No. 2), purchasing and a bank (No. 3), operating stores and engineering (No. 126), a garage (No. 89), a medical centre (No. 86), a fire hall and ambulance facilities (No. 90), the paint shop (No. 92), and inflammable stores (No. 141).[5] Service buildings situated below Civic Road included the massive cafeteria (No. 13), a textile shop (No. 21) and chemical lab (No. 144), seven large change houses (Nos. 16, 17, 18, 20, 23, 24, and 25), the power plant (Nos. 11 and 12), and laundry facilities (No. 9).[6] In addition, several workshops for site maintenance were housed on the dirty side of the site. Finally, the dirty side of the plant held two large water storage tanks and an excavated water reservoir as a precautionary measure against explosion or fire.[7]

The clean side of the plant encompassed the vastly larger portion of the GECO plant.[8]

Give Me a "U"!

Bob and Phil Hamilton based Scarboro's design and operation on British arsenal practice. Taking the view that "if it ain't broke, don't fix it," they followed British methods as closely as possible until Canadian conditions and actual experience warranted changes and improvements.[9] Under British practice, high explosives (H.E.) such as tetryl could not be handled in proximity to gunpowder (G.P.)[10]

Essentially, GECO engineers incorporated two separate filling lines at the plant through establishing two groupings of buildings on the clean side of the plant: the "H.E. Group" where operators used high explosives to fill munitions,[11] and the "G.P. Group" where gunpowder was used.[12]

Clean-side buildings and filling shops were connected by an extensive system of covered corridors or "cleanways" running southward from Eglinton Avenue in a U-shaped formation.[13] Directly beneath these galleries ran a complex system of service tunnels carrying steam, water, and power lines.[14]

At the base of the "U" sat the twelve-foot-wide North cleanway, providing access to employee change houses, as well as storage buildings for

GECO galleries, in which employees travelled from change houses to their munitions workshop were windowless — heated in winter and air-conditioned in summer. The galleries in this photograph probably spanned present-day Manville Road. Notice the "igloos" or "berms" that buried buildings. Also notice the small shed in the foreground, most likely a security booth. *Courtesy of Archives of Ontario.*

munitions components.[15] The two arms of the "U" layout offered access to the G.P. and H.E. filling lines via ten-foot-wide cleanways.[16] The two filling lines operated as separate munitions-filling plants — H.E. on the east side and G.P. to the west — complete with component stores, filling shops, bonded warehouses to store filled ammunition awaiting inspection, painting, soldering and packing shops, and shipping.[17] Offices, tool rooms, personnel and first aid quarters, washrooms, and canteens, which served refreshments during work breaks, met each line's non-production needs.[18] Eight- and ten-foot-wide secondary cleanways branched off from the main arms, running east and west, giving access to the various fuse-filling-related shops.[19] These secondary galleries were staggered, effectively preventing traffic congestion in the main cleanways during shift changes. Bulk magazines (structures built to house explosives), pellet pressing shops, and X-ray inspection served both H.E. and G.P. lines, accessed via two "crossover" galleries bridging the east and west cleanways between the open ends of the "U" in the southern section of the clean area.[20]

Employees were forbidden to enter the compound through any entrance other than the clock house at the north end of the site.[21] They walked to their respective change rooms, where they prepared to move to the clean side; they travelled to their respective workshops through the covered aboveground gallery system.[22]

Pick a Number, Any Number

Engineers commenced numbering GECO's buildings loosely, starting at No. 1 for the administration building at the most northerly area of the site, at Eglinton Avenue. Moving south, as an empty fuse moved toward the Proof Yard, the numbering on the buildings increased.[23] Many small "rooms" were added to the layout as the GECO site grew, sending the original numbered plan askew, causing some higher-numbered buildings to be out of sequence with surrounding lower-numbered buildings.[24] Some numbered buildings were neither recorded in the financial records GECO kept for construction costs, nor on the engineer's sketch of the site.[25] For example, the change room housed in building No. 18 was identified on the map but does not show up anywhere in GECO's financial records.[26] Obviously, the change house existed, but its cost to build wasn't included. Some building numbers were skipped on the map.[27] Building No. 13 housed the cafeteria, Building No. 15 housed component stores, but there is no location for No. 14, the clean-side laboratory on the site sketch.

Perhaps these inconsistencies are the result of the fact that, due to the secretive nature of experimental work taking place on site, information about the building was given only on a need-to-know basis. Or perhaps, while GECO kept meticulous notes, this oversight may indicate that the speed at which the plant was built overwhelmed its ability to keep up with ever-changing physical requirements. It's a fact that many buildings, while they appear on the engineer's sketch, had no identification as to how they were used.

Many unrecorded "rooms" were washrooms — there were many located throughout the clean side of the plant, attached to fuse-filling workshops, such as Nos. 27, 28, 31, 32, 36, 37, etc. — or were transformer vaults housed in the tunnels (for example, Nos. 109–114).[28] Note that Building No. 46 is a men's washroom; there is no corresponding women's washroom — women did not work this far south. Waste stations were located in Buildings 95, 96, 99, and 100.

A Fuse's Journey

Engineers at GECO determined that all plant materials entered through the main gate at the north or "dirty" end of the plant.[29] To minimize the chance of accident and maximize efficiency, munitions would travel in a southerly direction from Eglinton Avenue, undergoing all operations necessary for filling, until they reached the Proof Yard at the southern end of the site, ready for final quality testing and shipment.[30]

Explosives were stored safely in "magazines" (Buildings 157–161) at the south end of the plant until needed, then working quantities of explosives were transported and stored in smaller "expense magazines" situated alongside each fuse-filling building, such as in Buildings 116–125.[31] The amount of combustible materials allowed in each small magazine was proportionate to the material's level of stability — the more unstable the explosive the less could be stored.[32] From these smaller magazines, the explosives were supplied to the various workshops as required.

When empties — fuses that had not been filled with explosives yet — arrived at the plant, workmen delivered them to Building No. 15 to await

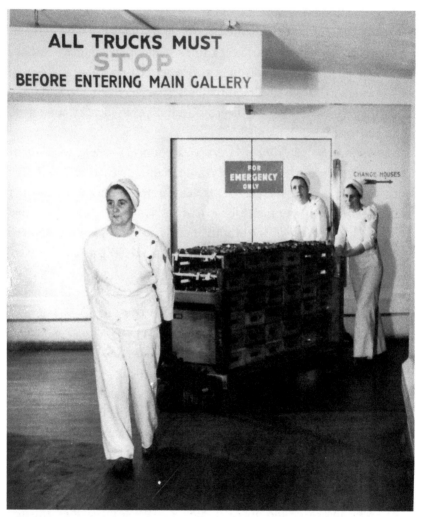

GECO workers transported munitions through the plant's gallery system. In this particular case, they are transporting a load of completed Fuze 720 to another plant for assembly into compete rounds of ammunition. *Courtesy of Archives of Ontario.*

filling.[33] The shipping containers in which empties arrived were taken to Building No. 44 or 78 for storage.[34] Empty components and filling compounds stored in expense magazines were brought together in filling shops.[35] Upwards of seventy separate operations were needed to fill one unit of munitions.[36] Once filled, "truckerettes" trucked fuses to Factory Bond where they awaited approval by internal inspectors.[37] The filled munitions then travelled to Government Bond where they awaited final inspection.[38] Following inspection, fuses moved to soldering and painting shops (Building No. 76 or No. 43), then to packing (Building No. 77 on the H.E. line and No. 45 on the G.P. line).[39] A representative sample of each lot filled — a lot contained two thousand units — were "proofed" in the Proof Yard to ensure accuracy, reliability, ease of use, and safety.[40] The last step in the filling process involved moving the packed munitions to the shipping area (either Building No. 80 or 47) at the extreme south end of the plant.[41] Filled munitions left by truck.[42] Some munitions were flown directly to battlefronts in England, India, North Africa, and South Africa.[43] A greater portion headed to other ammunition-filling plants in Canada, such as Pickering and Cherrier, where workers assembled filled munitions into complete rounds of ammunition.[44]

If munitions did not pass inspection, they proceeded to Rejection Bond (Building Nos. 72 and 34) then to the Reclaiming Shop (Building No. 71) for correction.[45] If the defect was irreparable, the defective stores ended up in the Proof Yard in Building No. 115 for reclamation of empties and filling components.[46]

What Lies Beneath

More than two and a half miles[47] of tunnels lay beneath GECO's gallery system. These tunnels carried service lines for electricity, water, steam, and compressed air; housed transformer vaults and switch rooms; and helped provide a simpler method for installing sanitary sewers.[48] Management felt the additional expense of excavating and installing this elaborate tunnel system was justified because erecting buildings and galleries could be done while laying facilities in newly dug and walled tunnels, shortening construction time.[49] Once the plant was in production, the tunnels provided easy access to carry out repairs and maintenance at any time without causing disruptions in production or introducing a hazard through "dirty" maintenance workers entering "clean" workshops.[50] Should an explosion occur in one building, having all services buried underground could minimize the impact to production. There may have been loss of life and property, but production in surrounding buildings could continue.

As noted, the tunnel system was big, equivalent to the distance from St. Clair Avenue at the north end of Toronto to almost Queen Street in its downtown core.[51] GECO's tunnel system was also byzantine, and construction workers were warned of the potential danger of losing their bearings while underground. Making navigating the system even more difficult was the fact that not all of it was laid out on the site sketch. According to the 1956 Fire Insurance Plan of Toronto, an additional tunnel not shown on the GECO engineering sketch ran at a diagonal south from the main east-west tunnel at the north end of the plant to meet the western part of the main north-south tunnel.[52] This tunnel created a triangle enveloping Building Nos. 101 and 109.[53] In order to avoid workers getting lost, construction crews were restricted to working on short sections of tunnel.

Hartley French's main tasks as an apprentice electrician included running wires and conduit to underground transformer rooms within the honeycomb of tunnels. The plumbing system for GECO was also housed underground and was installed ahead of the electricians' arrival. The summer of 1941 was terribly hot, and Hartley enjoyed working underground in the coolness of the tunnels. He recalled wiring a large warehouse on the GECO property, more than likely the site of the future cafeteria where eventually sixty-five thousand meals would be served every month.[54]

Life Happens: A Change of Plans

The outlook of war changed while GECO was under construction. Subsequently, the Canadian government thrust more responsibility in Bob and Phil Hamilton's direction to manage aggressive ammunition-filling schedules. The types of munitions to be filled and the revised monthly number of units required to be filled swelled. This meant constructing new buildings not originally planned, adding extensions to existing buildings, extending service accommodations, including expansions to the cafeteria, putting increased strains on water mains and sewers, increasing fire protection, and adding or changing heating, plumbing, electrical, and mechanical equipment for laundry and the cafeteria.[55]

Chief Engineer H.L. Tamplin responded competently to these ever-changing and strenuous demands, amending GECO's layout. Construction crews adapted well, too. However, on several occasions, construction of buildings occurred concurrently with various modifications to the design and engineering of said buildings.[56]

Can We Talk?

Bob and Phil Hamilton felt regular staff meetings, as well as taking advantage of frequent impromptu conferences when needed, helped to not only keep the lines of communication open and keep the project moving toward a rapid completion, but also to promote a heightened sense of *esprit de corps* among all departments of the plant. Good feelings imparted by these affable relationships trickled down to operators working in the fuse-filling workshops and helped employee morale plant-wide.

Regular staff meetings started early in the planning stages of the GECO project and continued during Scarboro's entire active production period.[57] Management, along with all department heads, reviewed the plant's progress and discussed problems, which ranged in scope from emerging explosive technology to designing women's underwear. Starting early in June 1941, these meetings developed into a weekly event.[58]

Minutes of early staff meetings detailed such topics as what special requirements were needed in the design for a truck to carry explosives, potential tray designs to carry fuses, how strict adherence to safety rules should be, what a cafeteria expected to serve several thousand meals a day would need, and whether women engaged in fuse filling would be allowed to wear bobby pins in their hair. Discussions surrounding the use of bobby pins and ladies' underwear might have seemed trivial and unimportant. This view could not have been farther from the truth. These discussions and the decisions made meant the difference between living another day to see family, or dying in a terrible explosion.

There Is No "I" in "Team"

By the end of July 1941, GECO's management and supervisory positions were staffed.

There were, of course, the Hamilton brothers, who served as president and vice-president. According to Philip Hamilton, P.D.P. Hamilton's son and namesake, his father, the vice-president of GECO, was the quiet brother, more technical, and concerned about everyday details of operations. Bob, on the other hand, was gregarious. As president he was eager to promote GECO, and comfortable meeting the public. Their complementary personalities melded into a powerful executive twosome.

Some of GECO's senior staff, including Dr. Jeffrey, GECO's medical officer; Major Flexman, operations manager; Mr. Duff, production manager; and Mrs. Florence Ignatieff, Cafeteria Services, lived onsite in six homes at the extreme northwest area of the site.[59] This dedicated staff was available twenty-four hours a day, every day, in case of accident or explosion. Good thing, too; their emergency services would be needed before the war ended.

A Squeaky Wheel Gets an Earful

In the ensuing months and years of war, when the early days of GECO's construction were but a sentimental memory for a handful of original, seasoned employees, there may have come the odd grumble from more recent operators over a squeaky door or a doorknob coming loose. These new hires had not witnessed the countless obstacles overcome or the dogged determination and fierce pride of the thousands of patriotic Canadians involved during construction. To anyone who complained the plant did not function perfectly — a squeaky door for instance — came these words of rebuttal, written in the company newspaper from Walter Campbell, one of those seasoned souls:

> You weren't there when caterpillars were completely buried in mud. You were not there when every night over a foot of mud was pushed off the construction road in order to bring in the material to carry on. You were not there when frozen ground had to be blasted so that footings could be rushed. You did not have the complaints from householders three miles away that the electric fixtures came down and marked their dining room table during the blasting periods. One walking around the plant now could not see why there were difficulties, difficulties that were encountered — and licked."[60]

When All Is Said and Done: Feeds and Speeds of a Top-Secret Munitions Factory
Financial Totals

Early estimates put the cost to build "Scarboro" at $2.25 million.[61] The actual cost reached $7,181,124 — more than three times the original projection.[62] The anticipated quantity of units — fuses — to be filled monthly fluctuated from early estimates of 1.9 million per month to 4,135,000 actually filled.[63] The Hamiltons originally planned to fill seven types of fuses.[64] The plant eventually tooled up for and filled forty-one types, almost six times its original plan.[65]

Construction Totals

GECO's construction program took approximately two million man-hours to complete.[66] The site contained more than 1.8 miles of paved roadway[67] on 345 acres of land, of which 121 acres were enclosed by an eight-foot-high barbed-wire fence that ran for nearly two miles.[68] More than three miles of "cleanways" and and nearly three miles of tunnels connected the buildings in the "Danger Zone."[69]

What did it take to build a top-secret munitions plant?

- more than one million board feet of lumber (the equivalent of 256 acres)
- 1,270,000 bricks
- 340,000 concrete blocks
- 292 tons of reinforcing iron
- 1,645,000 square feet of plywood and weatherboard
- 870,000 square feet of roofing
- 1,330,000 square feet of Gyproc wallboard
- 985,500 square feet of insulation
- 420,000 pounds of nails
- nearly 400,000 square feet of hardwood flooring
- more than 346,250 square feet of linoleum flooring
- 1,585,000 feet of electrical wire
- 184,000 feet of conduit, ranging in size from 3/8 inches to 4 inches
- 451 glued laminated beams or "super structures" comprising 605,000 board feet of lumber, 37 tons of nails, and 16 tons of casein glue.[70]

4

Ramping Up

Eight months had passed since dynamite had broken ground on rich Scarboro farmland for the future GECO munitions plant. By the end of September 1941, almost 100 percent of the munitions plant was complete. There were 170 buildings up and running, almost forty more shops than staff originally planned.[1]

However, while the Hamilton brothers, with the help of their dedicated team of engineers and management staff, had erected a huge, sprawling complex of munitions workshops and ancillary buildings, transforming the plant into a lean, mean, fuse-filling machine was another matter entirely.

In a summation written at the end of the war, Major Flexman, plant manager, stated that management was clear about the intent of "Project 24" from its outset: "Scarboro was conceived, constructed, organized, and operated for but one purpose — PRODUCTION — and to that end every department of The General Engineering Company (Canada) Limited made direct or indirect contribution. The success or failure of the project would depend upon the quality and quantity of its output and the ability to deliver the goods when they were required."[2] Major Flexman felt other achievements, while they may have been noteworthy, would be "incidental or secondary" to the plant's primary purpose.[3]

Even safety — "important and desirable as it might be" — could not, and would not take precedence over production of top-notch ammunition at a time when countless lives might be sacrificed for lack of dependable shells, grenades, bullets, and bombs.[4] "Costs could not be measured in dollars in a period when the survival of an empire was at stake," Flexman stated. "The comfort and convenience of employees would not be placed ahead of the needs of the men in the armed forces."[5] Quality production and output were always the first concern — that, and safety.

In hindsight, with GECO's incredible record in both production and safety — over 256 million munitions shipped without one fatal accident — its simple production decree seems straightforward, perhaps even simplistic.[6] Boiled down, GECO wanted to get the job done as quickly as possible, hopefully without blowing anyone up.

Talk Is Cheap: Bring on the High Explosives

Once production got underway, GECO planned to fill eleven natures.[7] Of these, four were to be filled on the H.E. side — Fuse 119, Fuse 152, Fuse 251, and Gaine 11 — while the G.P. side would fill Fuse 199, three Primers (Nos. 1, 11, and 12), Tube Vent Percussion 0.5", another Tube, and Tracer-Igniter No. 12.[8]

However, with any new undertaking comes the odd glitch. Factoring in the sheer size of an operation like GECO with its aggressive production schedule; the difficulty of keeping over twenty-one thousand employees[9] motivated, healthy, safe, and happy; and the pressure to supply the Allied forces with millions of filled munitions, it was a wonder management resolved every glitch, hitch, and snag so well. In fact, to expect new enterprises such as GECO to ramp up production without, as Major Flexman wrote, "…running into all kinds of grief and difficulties" would be unreasonable and perhaps deadly.[10]

Glitches, Hitches, and Snags

No matter how extensive the training or how thoughtful the foresight, nothing could replace real-time experience.

Wartime industry was new in Canada, a national enterprise that had to be put together not only brick by brick, but department by department. There was no precedent to go back to, to study, or learn from, other than the lessons learned from the British in the Great War two decades earlier.

Bob and Phil Hamilton recognized fully that they needed gifted and capable departmental heads who would drive GECO into production as soon as enough buildings were finished. The Hamilton brothers sought men and women of high calibre. Despite thousands of outstanding personnel already in war administration work from whom they could choose, Bob and Phil selected upstanding men and women from wide-ranging occupations and professions, with diverse backgrounds.[11] They were not of the mind that "birds of a feather flock together," but rather "opposites attract."

Bob and Phil did not know in July 1941 whether the Canadian government would ultimately keep them as joint managers of the GECO plant at Scarboro. At that point, they had only been hired to oversee Scarboro's design, construction, and staffing. They were concerned that if they were moved on to the next big thing — which was quite possible given GECO already had overseen the building of an R.C.A.F flying school, a gunnery school, and a large ordnance complex in London — the administrative staff they hired might be transferred to other plants once production started. Hence, they secured assurance from Allied War Supplies Corporation that they would honour employment arrangements made with key administrative officials when GECO's management was finally decided.[12] It was only after this assurance was given that Bob and Phil commenced hiring.

Securing talented personnel was not easy. Canadian wartime industries had had over a year to mobilize men for war production, employing thousands of competent men and women. Ottawa and the armed forces had absorbed thousands of men with administrative experience and ability for overseas duty. The success or failure of the entire GECO enterprise at Scarboro was contingent on the calibre of this select group of men and women. Everyone recognized that any administrative routine had to grow gradually since there was no background of arsenal experience on which to draw, and problems to be solved had had little existence in peacetime.

Once the plant was up and running, there were other problems, too. Scarboro was not self-sufficient, but was both aided and hindered by outside factors beyond company control.[13] GECO was dependent on supplies from a great number of other wartime factories going through their own growing pains. Fuse-filling workshops declared clean and ready for production sat idle because empties or other vital components had not arrived.[14] When materials did arrive, sometimes they were defective or unusable, or sometimes they broke upon filling, which further retarded production.[15] Another significant delay occurred when pre-assembled empties arrived at the plant.[16] The shells for Fuse 251, one of GECO's most commonly filled munitions, had to be broken down into their individual pieces before they could be filled; then they had to be re-assembled after filling.[17] This breaking down process hampered production, adding many, many operator hours to filling schedules.[18]

Then there was "proofing" — testing the dependability and accuracy of filled munitions. Caps and detonators were produced and tested first, then primers and fuses, then assembled shells, and so on. As GECO ramped up production, proofing developed into a frustratingly long, time-consuming, and cumbersome process.

Despite the vital need to test the quality of munitions in Canada with actual weapons, the Allied forces needed the guns more.[19] Therefore, early proofing was done on semi-assembled rounds that had to be shipped by air to the United Kingdom; after the testing, the results were then cabled back. Only then could the ammunition continue on its journey down the line to its next steps in filling, and another round of proofing.[20] This exasperating process was repeated until final shipment. A delay in "sentencing" — the acceptance or rejection — of any one component along its assembly held up the complete round.[21] This early production glitch had the potential to hold up hundreds of thousands of rounds of ammunition because samples of some small stage in the process were working their way to England or awaiting their sentencing.[22] And if the samples didn't pass? Those hundreds of thousands of lethal rounds sat and waited until they did.

Churchill's plea for international assistance could not be answered until GECO was up and running. The problems that confronted GECO's fledging Tooling Department were many, and none had straightforward solutions. For example, filling Time Fuse 199 was a high priority, but before it went into full production, tools had to arrive and glitches unforeseen in the days of the "Gunpowder Plot" had to be resolved. Machines and tools, never designed for wartime, had to be found and adapted. Ingenuity and the art of improvisation of men proficient in all things mechanical were called for, so that harmless workaday tools could be converted into instruments of war. Management wrote of the acute shortage: "Less than half a dozen men in Canada had any knowledge or experience of the technique associated with this special industry, and these men, experts on loan to the Canadian government from British arsenals, had no knowledge of Canadian conditions, customs, or industrial practices."[23] The climate in Canada — the "Great White North" — necessitated changes to materials and tool design, and sometimes warranted deviations from British specifications in fuse-filling practice.

Not only was inexperience a problem, because GECO was a government-owned enterprise, there were many persnickety fingers in the pot. Allied War Supplies Corp., the Department of Munitions and Supply, Federal Treasury officials, the Inspection Board of the United Kingdom and Canada, and the British Admiralty Technical Mission, to name just a few, had specific requirements that changed often.[24] Independent government inspectors (G.I.s) sought and ensured the quality of all empties and filled fuses at GECO. Government inspectors expected perfection, and rightly so. If the Allies had hit the *Bismarck* with a dud, that battle might have ended very differently. These inspectors had the first and last word on every aspect of fuse-filling. In fact, they held the power to stop all production.[25]

Lieutenant-Colonel H. Read, a British authority on ammunition, wrote: "It must be borne in mind that inspection does not make anything wrong, it only finds things wrong. It must be realized that inspection involves far more than the mere interception and rejection of faulty items. A good inspector should be the guide, philosopher and friend to production and by timely advice and instruction as to what exactly is required and in many cases how it can best be achieved, is able to effect a great economy in material and effort."[26]

Read went on to say that units filled and accepted for service "represented a vital part in a complete round of ammo for use on land, or sea, or in the air, in defensive or offensive action."[27]

Personnel from the Inspection Board were held in the "highest esteem" and GECO understood clearly that they were "bound by the limitation of a system in which there was little elasticity."[28] Nonetheless, the conflict between independent inspection personnel and the production team, including workshop supervisors and operators, was, at times, volatile.

The Girls Behind the Boys Behind the Guns

Despite growing pains, GECO rolled out dozens of fuse-filling workshops throughout the month of September, starting production on several different components. The complex was built in record-breaking time — just 236 days — a feat that would be entered into the annals of Canadian war history.[29] The extraordinary record is an everlasting credit to the thousands of men and women who worked so tirelessly through the winter, spring, and summer of 1941 with a united and steadfast goal: to get the biggest and finest munitions factory in Canada's history into meaningful production as quickly as humanly possible. By the end of September 1941, management declared that "practically all filling buildings were completed."[30] Bob and Phil Hamilton had remarkably surpassed even their own aggressive objectives of being in production by July 1941 and erecting 130 buildings by September.[31]

GECO would fill more than one million ammunition units each month throughout the war, its workers filled with an unconquerable spirit, arming the Allied forces fighting for the world's freedom with top-quality munitions. GECO's Bill Taylor of Building No. 126, engineering, said, "Scarboro was built in a hurry — and well built."[32]

The story at Scarboro had started with two humble, loyal Canadians — Bob Hamilton and his brother, Phil — along with a small company of equally patriotic men, buoyed by pride of personal achievement and

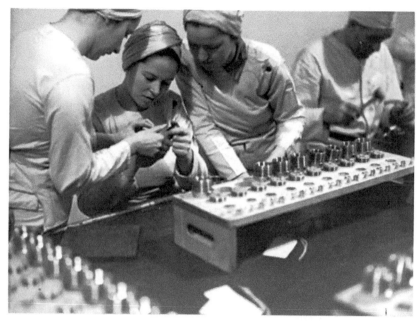

Three GECO fuse-fillers examine fuses. *Courtesy of Archives of Ontario.*

determination that only true "fuse-filled achievement" could satisfy the "ammunition needs of a nation and world at war."[33]

With the bombing at Pearl Harbor on December 7, 1941, and the fall of Hong Kong on Christmas Day, the world, more than ever, needed war plants, including munitions enterprises like GECO, if the fight for freedom had any hope of succeeding.

5

If You Can Walk, Talk, Creep, or Crawl — Apply Here!

It's in Their Blood

Thousands of women worked in wartime factories during the Great War in Britain. They toiled under distressing conditions, enduring long shifts and tolerating dirty, dingy, dangerous work. "Life may appear hard to us," a female war worker lamented, "but we go on. No one notices whether we are tired or not, and in this brutal fact lies the hope of endurance. A little sympathy would cause what is generally known as a 'swound' among the loaded fuses, or instant collapse into the bullet crate. It is amazing what we can do when there is no way of escape but desertion."[1] Moreover, during the First World War, women grew tired of the inconsequentiality of their lives. "We were sick of frivolling, we wanted to do something big and hard, because of our boys and of England," one woman said. "When the dreaded telegram came at last and everything was grey and bitter, we gave up talking and made our way to the lowest level — the gates of the nearest ammunition factory."[2]

When Canada entered the Second World War, women had a legacy of stoicism and martyrdom from which to draw: a war still fresh in their mothers' and grandmothers' minds and hearts. In some sense, it could be said, "it was in their blood" for patriotic Canadian women to give their all to war work.

Working in a Man's World

The Second World War brought women's employment in Canada to the forefront of industry. Seemingly overnight, women by the hundreds of thousands entered the workforce of industries that were previously male-dominated. In addition to a sense of patriotism, many factors drove women to seek work. For professional women, with men off to fight, the war provided an opportunity to progress in their career within patriarchal organizations. Other women found it a struggle to make ends meet on the small stipend their husbands fighting overseas sent home. Others worked because their menfolk were jobless from the economic effects of the Depression. For young, single women, war work offered the prospect of travelling away from home. City life looked romantic, exciting, and novel.

During peacetime, a company had the luxury of growing its workforce gradually, with new employees carefully selected to meet the requirements of the job. New hires could settle in, and slowly, but surely, become more productive as the days, weeks, and months passed. In times of war, when the company's purpose became one of maximum production that not only had to be attained, but maintained, this fundamental relationship — on which victory or defeat rested — became crucial. The relationship that existed between an employee and her employer was one of the most important within a wartime organization. Harmony and co-operation were at the heart of working well together.

War, Ammo, and Feminine Pads

GECO opened its Women's Division Employment Office on May 4, 1941.[3] Bob and Phil Hamilton made a strategic decision to hire a female personnel manager. In countless wartime factories across the nation, the mostly male-dominated management knew little about hiring and managing women. The traditional view that women belonged in domestic roles translated into a tendency to set low expectations for them in the factory. GECO's personnel director, Grace Hyndman, as a woman, recognized the huge potential within the girls she hired. She had three months to create an employment policy for hiring in an industry geared for battle. She interviewed and graded thousands of applicants, expecting to hire five thousand women.[4]

Grace, along with GECO management, including Dr. Jeffrey and Florence Ignatieff, recognized that while men saw no problem eating their lunch on a dirty bench on the shop floor, women would not flourish under such rudimentary conditions. Industry experts suggested women might tire more easily than men do, and not be able to lift and carry heavy loads.[5] They might be more sensitive to noise, dirt, odours, and fumes.[6] They would need easier access to washrooms, and perhaps being more fastidious than their male counterparts, need larger cloakrooms, storage lockers, and more pleasant lunchrooms.[7] Grace felt women thrived and worked more diligently under female supervision. Matrons in charge of change rooms, washrooms, and rest rooms, would set a standard for the women to follow.[8] There were health and safety issues, too. For example, it was decided that salt tablets and plenty of water should be provided to women since they might fatigue with loss of salt through perspiration.[9] Adequate lunch and rest periods were essential, along with reasonable hours of work.[10] Data had shown women found it harder to adjust to shift changes, and absenteeism might be greater than "normal" due to women calling in sick "to catch up on their sleep."[11] For women who worked on night shifts, adequate transportation and safety measures would be important. Outside activities to build morale, health, and a sense of community and belonging could help promote a happy team of women.[12] GECO strove to accommodate each of these unique considerations for their female employees, and met or exceeded most.

In addition to meeting workers' physical needs, Grace had to consider women's emotional well-being, too. Who would make the best GECO employee? How best to persuade her to work willingly with explosives? What could the company offer to keep her happy, motivated, and committed? A working woman, unlike a man, had not only her job responsibilities with which to contend, but also worried about feeding her family, keeping house, and providing care for her children.

GECO operators prepare bullets for tip lacquering. *Courtesy of Archives of Ontario.*

GECO issued booklets that sold the "perks" of working for a munitions plant to women.[13] The plant needed these pamphlets, especially during the plant's early days, due to widespread rumours that factory work was unfit for women, and that employers gave little regard to women's health and safety.[14] Jack Kennedy wrote in *History of the Department of*

Munitions and Supply: Canada in the Second World War that "welfare and women's organizations expressed considerable alarm about the adverse social effects of the employment of women in war industries."[15] The rumours became so pervasive, the government invited the media and women's welfare agencies to get involved to help quell the tales and educate the public.[16] In the end, the rumours were unfounded; in fact, some experts suggested the maddening stories were the work of seditious persons.[17]

GECO's hiring brochure read in part:

> The General Engineering Company at Scarboro offers an exceptional opportunity to women who want to do a vital war job. The ammunition filled in this Plant plays an important role in the defense of Britain and her allies, and makes our ships, guns, tanks and planes into effective weapons to invade and conquer the Axis' countries.
>
> Fortunately, this filling of fuses and other ammo is a job at which women excel. Their quick, skillful fingers are ideally suited to the fine operations which include most of the jobs in a filling plant.[18]

GECO's Bomb Girls

A large-scale employment campaign for female fuse-fillers commenced in September 1941.[19] GECO's hiring objective was to interview, hire, and train munitions workers in the shortest time possible. In addition to an employment office set up on Danforth Avenue, the company erected another employment booth at Yonge Street and Eglinton Avenue.[20] In a bit of fun, someone nailed a sign scribled in crayon to the booth: "If you can walk, talk, creep, or crawl, apply here!"[21]

During its initial hiring campaign, GECO received twelve thousand, predominantly Anglo-Saxon applicants;[22] the vast majority had no industrial experience and had relatives on active service.[23] Due to security requirements, war plants in Canada could hire only British subjects.[24] Grace looked for workers who were of average intelligence, in good health, patriotic, could manage home responsibilities, had the ability to get along with others, and perhaps most importantly, had agile fingers for the delicate and intricate task of packing fuses with high explosives.[25]

New hires were given a half-day's training and then put to work.[26] Their training outlined employee services and opportunities, the myriad rules and regulations of GECO, safety standards, firefighting techniques and anti-sabotage procedures, the nature of the work to be done, respect needed for the materials they would be handling, and the importance of quality and quantity of production.[27] They also met their foreman and workshop supervisor, who provided specific fuse-filling training, which they'd be involved in.[28]

"From offices, stores, factories, schools, and homes, from universities," wrote editor Ross Davis in the April 11, 1942, issue of GECO's employee newspaper, "have come the recruits for a swiftly expanding army of overalled women who by their amazing aptitude in mastering unfamiliar tasks have become a vital factor in our wartime industrial front, and have brought us in sight at least of the total production for total war towards which we are progressing."[29]

GECO's new recruits were reminded that men's lives — for many, their loved ones overseas — hung in the balance.

6

A Day in the Life of a Bomb Girl

By December 1941, GECO management had employed and trained more than three thousand operators, working on ten natures, six of which were already at their full monthly scheduled production.[1] At the height of its production, over 5,300 GECOites worked at Scarboro, of which over 3,400 were women, or about 67 percent of the plant's total population.[2] This percentage rose dramatically to between 85 to 94 percent as the war dragged on due to a severe shortage of available men.[3]

What was it like to work in a Second World War Canadian munitions factory? Did workers have to follow special rules? What did they wear? What were their working conditions like? Women who worked specifically in munitions factories answered to terms of endearment such as "Munitions Gal," "Munitionette," "Fusilier," and "Bomb Girl." GECO's workforce was referred to locally and fondly as "GECOnians" or "GECOites."

A day in the work life of a "GECOite" started the moment she boarded a designated bus at selected bus stops in Toronto's east end, and ended when the bus dropped her off at the same bus stop approximately eleven hours later.

All Aboard

Women who worked at the Scarboro plant congregated at selected stops in Toronto to board a specially marked bus to GECO. Four main routes served the east end of the city, with terminal points including Yonge Street and St. Clair Avenue, Bloor and Church Streets, and Victoria Park Avenue and Danforth Road.[4] Eglinton Avenue did not span Toronto's vast Don Valley in 1941. Buses had to meander their way through East York, along Millwood Road, over the Leaside bridge, down Donlands Avenue, and up O'Connor Drive, which then rejoined Eglinton Avenue east of Victoria Park Avenue. In March 1943, GECO introduced a new bus route to operate between Eglinton Avenue and Yonge Street and the plant.[5] This new route helped reduce the overcrowding of non-GECO streetcars and eliminated roundabout routes.

Munitions production at GECO ran twenty-four hours a day, six days a week — pausing only for rest on Sunday. At prime time, during shift changes, buses picked up or dropped off fifty employees per minute at the GECO facility.[6] Buses jostled for a place to unload and pick up passengers in the factory's jam-packed parking lot. Eventually, about a year after plant operations commenced, shifts were staggered over a two-hour period to manage the arrival and departure of thousands of women.[7]

"I Do Solemnly Declare …"

It is no surprise that security at a top-secret munitions plant was tight, and of paramount concern. Throughout the war, fear of a Nazi invasion upon the shores of North America weighed heavily on the minds and hearts of every Canadian.

Every GECOnian had to present identification in the form of a government-issued "pass" at Time Office wickets, and then clock in.[8] No one was exempt. Even the two most recognizable faces at the plant, Bob and Phil Hamilton, had to produce their passes to gain access to the compound.[9]

Clean-side employees who wore GECO's uniform left their passes in lockers.[10] All other employees in the Danger Zone and all employees on the dirty side of the plant carried their passes at all times to present if challenged.[11] Employee names and their respective employee numbers were sewn on GECO name tags prominently worn on their uniforms.[12]

All workers were photographed, fingerprinted, took an oath of secrecy upon securing employment, and underwent a background check from the Royal Canadian Mounted Police.[13] Due to the RCMP's diligence, approximately one hundred "undesirables" were discovered and kept from employment.[14] Employees of war-industry plants in Britain and Canada signed an oath of secrecy under the Official Secrets Act 1939, and, in particular, for GECO, under Chapter 49 of the Statutes of Canada, 1939.[15] It was an offence punishable by fine or imprisonment, or both, "to obtain or to communicate to any other person any information which might be, or is intended to be useful to a foreign power."[16]

Article 2 of GECO's Secrecy Oath read, in part:

> You are now an employee of the General Engineering Company (Canada) Limited, because we consider you a responsible, reliable and loyal person. As an employee of this plant you will possess certain information regarding the Company's activities. You have taken an Oath of Secrecy concerning all such information. Be sure that you do not break this Oath, either through carelessness or by thoughtlessness in conversation.[17]

First Things First: Ground Rules

Work life at GECO, as with any other wartime factory, had many rules and regulations that had to be obeyed, without exception. From the moment a GECOnian stepped off the bus in the plant's parking lot, to the time she left at the end of her shift, a workshop employee was subject to innumerable imperatives and instructions.

Management defended its seemingly endless rules, claiming the regulations had been reduced already to a bare minimum, leaving only those necessary to provide a healthy balance between GECO's obligation to protect its workers and the employee's obligation to fill and ship the highest quality munitions as quickly as possible.[18] These regulations had evolved through generations of experience in handling and manufacturing explosives in the United Kingdom.[19]

Each employee received several booklets, all colour-coded, when she was hired. One of these booklets, *Regulations of the Scarboro Plant*, began by outlining general "do's" and "don'ts" of a GECO worker. All persons had to enter and leave the GECO site through the main gate on Eglinton Avenue, be willing to be searched, remain in their respective workshops except when asked or "by demand of nature," be sober at all times, and deposit all contraband and all articles not required in the performance of their duty in lockers in the change houses.[20]

"The cordial co-operation of every worker is earnestly sought," wrote Bob and Phil Hamilton in *Regulations of the Scarboro Plant: Clean Workers*. "In fairness to those who wholeheartedly support the safety effort, any willful or deliberate infringements of these regulations will merit, and indeed, compel, drastic measures to deal with the offender.

"BE LOYAL to your family and your fellow worker. THEIR security and safety are in YOUR hands."[21]

Please Check Your Brassiere

After punching their time cards at the gatehouse, GECOites proceeded to their designated change houses — also called "shifting" houses — that bordered the clean side of the plant.[22] Employees entered and left the Danger Zone — the clean side — through seven change houses. Three large buildings were situated on the High Explosives side of the plant and three on the gunpowder side. On each side, two change houses were designated for female employees, the third for men. There was an additional change house for visitors located in Building No. 20.

General Engineering Company's roots were in mining before war broke out, and the Hamiltons designed Scarboro's change houses in a fashion similar to those servicing a mine.[23] When miners emerge from deep underground, they are sopping wet from humidity. Clothing needs to dry before the men's next shift, so wet clothes are hung on hooks in the change house and hoisted to the ceiling to dry. GECO's change houses were designed likewise; uniforms were hung up on hooks to air out between shifts.[24]

Even with staggered hours, shift changes were chaotic at the plant. Hundreds of women descended on the change houses at the end of their shift, donning their "civilian" clothes to leave the plant, while hundreds more arrived, rushing to prepare for work. During GECO's production heyday, each change room had the capacity to house 1,060 employees, and processed five hundred women every thirty minutes during a shift change.[25] At least one change room remained open at all times since the change rooms provided the only route to the fuse-filling workshops.[26]

Features of GECO Change Houses

GECO workers had to follow many rules in the plant's shift houses. Posters on the walls reminded employees of their responsibilities. One poster read: CIGARETTE BUTTS MUST NOT BE CARRIED INTO CHANGE HOUSES[27] This seemed sensible given the nature of the women's work. Employees removed their street clothing and footwear upon entering the change house and deposited all personal belongings in steel lockers outfitted with combination locks.[28]

GECO's promotional hiring material described the plant's change houses to be "splendid facilities for personal daintiness, with plenty of basins, showers and towels provided."[29]

Change houses were divided into two distinct sections, similar to the rest of the plant. The north end of the massive room was the dirty side. The clean side sat at the southern end of the house, near the entrance to the galleries leading to munitions workshops. Once a GECO employee entered a change house on the dirty side, she performed any ablutions needed at sinks large enough to accommodate 140 operators, stripped down to her cotton bra, panties, and socks, hopped over a low barrier to the clean side, and put on the plant's uniform.[30] The barrier was a long, short wooden bench, one to two feet high.[31] *Clean* was written on the side facing the dirty area and was painted red.[32] Similarly, the side facing the clean area was painted grey and bore the word *Dirty*.[33]

Two female guards stood at the barrier to inspect the women as they crossed over to the clean side, to ensure employees were clean, free of anything that might cause static electricity or ignite a spark. GECOite

Sylvia Nordstrand, who was eighteen years of age when she began working at the plant, said, "We stepped over [the barrier] after being scrutinized visually by two elderly women referred to as matrons"[34]

The women declared they were clean as they jumped over the low hurdle by calling out, "All Clear!"[35] Declaring "All Clear" was a verbal contract between the company and its employees, who were responsible for being clean of all prohibited items.[36] Any contraband found on an employee after an "All Clear" rendered the employee liable to severe penalties, since even a minor infringement could result in a serious explosion.[37] Employees were warned that ignorance was not bliss, and claims of unfamiliarity with the rules would not be accepted as an excuse.[38] Prohibited items included nail polish, hairpins, and jewellery of any kind.[39]

Keeping hair tucked up under cotton turbans without the help of hairpins posed a chronic challenge to female operators. "You put the bandana on your head," Sylvia said, "brought the two long ties or ends once or twice around your head and tuck each end under the bandana, with no hair showing."[40]

While GECO had no fatal production-related accidents, its employees had their share of minor work-related injuries when women whacked their feet stepping over the barrier.

Some confusion remains today as to whether metal clasps in brassieres were allowed. GECOite Elizabeth Ellis recalls that they wore special brassieres that laced up. Others do not recall having to remove their bras. Sylvia Nordstrand recalls removing the metal clasps from her brassiere and improvising with elastic.[41] Most probably, women bought cotton undergarments then removed the metal clasps from the bra to replace them with buttons secured by lace or elastic.

There is a story still fondly recalled after seventy years of a time when, as a "lark," to liven things up, GECOite Carol LeCappelain and her friend dyed their bras, socks, and underwear yellow. The act was a small, spirited rebellion against their otherwise pristine white uniformed existence, as well as making a tongue-in-cheek statement about the awful yellow staining of women's hands, face, and hair from working with tetryl powder. Carol and her friend were dubbed the "Two Canaries" by change house staff.

A "Harmless" Pack of Matches

General Engineering Company took uniform breaches very seriously, as did the Government of Canada. From the July 1942 issue of the employee newspaper came this warning:

> This week an employee of Scarboro appeared in police court, pleaded guilty to a charge of violation of Section 38A of the Defence of Canada regulations, and was fined the minimum of $50.00 and costs.
>
> The section under which he was charged states: "Every person who has in his possession a match or other fire producing device in or upon any premise in Canada used for producing, treating, handling or keeping explosives, or used for the manufacture of primers, detonators, or time fuses, shall be liable to a fine of not less than $50.00 and not more than $100.00, or to imprisonment not exceeding one month."
>
> The offender was found in the clean area with matches in his possession.
>
> In a regrettable incident such as this, there is a very natural tendency towards sympathy for the person involved. Such sympathy, however, should be tempered with a realization of the seriousness of the offence. When it is appreciated that many innocent people might have lost their lives because of one person's carelessness, it does not seem that the punishment meted out was unduly harsh, especially since ample warning had been previously given.[42]

In an ironic twist, GECO provided packs of matches with the company logo to their employees. The inside of the match cover read:

> Keep me on the "Dirty Side"
> Never on the "Clean"
> Feed the Guns with Shells and things
> But keep me off the scene.[43]

Keep me on the "Dirty Side," Never on the "Clean" Feed the Guns with Shells and things But keep me off the scene.

Despite the lethal hazard associated with a spark or fire around explosives, GECO provided matches to their employees for personal use. *Courtesy of Barbara Dickson.*

Non-Explosive Uniforms

While there was concern over what employees carried in their uniforms, management was also concerned about the outfits themselves, and the design of employee uniforms received special attention from GECO's medical team, who spent weeks designing the workers' clothing, considering the health, comfort, and safety of employees.[44] Management sought the advice of the medical officer, personnel director, safety officer, and employees in developing the uniforms. This consultation was an example of the use of "complementary talent," which formed a basic policy of the organization.[45]

The plant's team decided "factory" cotton would be used as opposed to the heavy wool used in Britain's arsenals.[46] Cotton seemed to be much more suitable to Canada's variable and sometimes harsh climate.[47] The material chosen for employee uniforms was one example in which the company's management adapted munitions plant design and operation from its British historical counterparts to improve safety, comfort, longevity, and efficiency.

Specifically, uniforms had to meet all safety requirements in the Danger Area. Company clothing could not contain metal or be made of silk, rayon, or wool, in order to minimize the chance of producing static electricity.[48] The material had to be slow burning in case of explosion; to ensure this, uniforms were treated with a boracic solution regularly.[49] Closely weaved, uniforms had to be tight-fitting, especially at the neck and wrist, to protect skin, and be free of cuffs, folds, or pleats, so as not to accumulate ammunition "dust."[50] Workers wore special nail-free shoes, made from soft, caramel-coloured leather that laced up the front, along with turbans that covered as much hair as possible, not only to minimize the transfer of explosive dust from workshops to employees, but to protect women from getting their hair caught in moving machinery.[51]

To add to the rigid specifications, operator uniforms had to be two-piece, side-fastening with wooden buttons, attractive to wear, economical, and comfortable.[52] Finally, employee attire had to last at least one hundred washes.[53]

Uniforms bore the employee's name or number, and were colour-coordinated with trim — red for H.E., black for G.P., and blue for I.G. workers.[54] A coloured armband worn on the sleeve indicated rank.[55] Higher-ranked clean-side officials and office staff wore smocks, and uniforms suited to the work undertaken were supplied to tradesmen such as carpenters, mechanics, medical and cafeteria staff, and messengers.[56]

It is hard to imagine GECO's medical team designing a uniform that would conform to the myriad demands and restrictions as outlined above. Incredibly, they did, meeting every single requirement.

A GECO worker models a munition worker's "clean-side" uniform, which could not contain metal or be made from silk, rayon, or wool — any fabric that could produce static electricity. Uniforms were tight-fitting and free of cuffs, folds, or pleats, so as not to accumulate ammo "dust." Workers wore turbans that covered as much hair as possible to minimize the transfer of explosive dust from workshops to employees. Inevitably, a wayward lock would take on a yellow hue from exposure to tetryl, to become a tell-tale sign to Toronto's public that its owner worked at GECO.
Courtesy of Archives of Ontario.

What did laundry staff do with discarded or stained uniforms when they no longer were suitable for factory wear? GECOnians could purchase them for 50 cents. Their suggested use? Pyjamas.[57]

An Ode to Ye Olde Shift House

GECO's employee newspaper published a humourous poem written by the "23 Gang" — the women who used Change House No. 23. It speaks to the tight security, restrictions, and impeccable standards expected of all GECOnians:

Our Barrier Lady

Into the change house
Strip off your clothes,
Up to the mirror
To powder your nose.

Back to the locker
Fasten it tight,
Or out to the guard house
You'll trot — to-night.

Over the barrier
Chanting "All Clear!"
Mrs. Hall answers
"Please check your brassier."

Look at your peg
No clean uniform!
Back to the barrier
Ready to storm.

No clean suit, girls?
Sweetly says Mrs. Hall;

I can't understand
That Laundry at all.

What size do you take, dear?
Only sixteen?
Then off to the cupboard
To get your eighteen.

And you lose your anger
As with twinkling eyes,
She says "bring me a slip please,
Mark on the right size."

Take off your net please —
No pins or rings?
Where's your towel dear?
She tirelessly sings.

But some day in heaven
She'll get her reward,
For the GECOites there (if any)
Will with one accord,

Say "Welcome, dear Lady
We hold you most dear.
Don't forget to give Peter
The famous "All Clear."[58]

Working on the "Clean Side"

When a GECO worker left her change house, having declared herself "All Clear!" she walked to her respective fuse-filling workshop through above-ground heated/air-conditioned galleries that connected all buildings on the clean side.[59] She travelled only through areas for which she had clearance — usually her workshop — and was not permitted to

Operators filled 13,426,587 No. 251 fuses over GECO's tenure in Building No. 67, the largest producer of any single fuse in Canada during the war. Simple, one-storey wood structures, these clean-side buildings could contain several fuse-filling workshops separated by fire walls. Escape doors to the outdoors were provided in case of explosion or emergency evacuation. *Courtesy of Archives of Ontario.*

wander. She needed a barrier pass to leave her workshop, even for calls of nature.[60] Most clean-side employees had a very restricted view of the entire complex, not knowing or seeing much outside the narrow scope of their individual jobs, especially since all fuse-filling workshops and the gallery system were windowless.[61] "Everything looked the same for miles and miles inside the buildings," Sylvia Nordstrand said.[62] "Cream coloured walls and caramel coloured flooring."[63] Employees informally identified themselves using a shortened form of the building and workshop they worked in, such as working in "Shop 67A" — representing Building No. 67, Workshop A.

Production at GECO ran twenty-four hours a day, and management expected women to work shifts, each running between eight and a half to nine hours, rotating weekly. Day shift ran between 7:00 a.m. and 3:00 p.m.; afternoon shift ran from 3:00 to 11:00 p.m.; and the overnight shift ran from 11:00 p.m. until 7:00 a.m.[64] Shifts were problematic for mothers who relied on daycare. The company did attempt to ease these childcare concerns by allowing employees to reduce their Saturday shift by half if they worked an additional thirty minutes each weekday.[65]

There was no flexibility, however, when it came to safety rules. Stringent rules and inflexible regulations, vital to the safety and security of work within the munitions plant, extended to workshops on the clean side. Management strove to make employees "safety-conscious" not "accident-conscious."[66] They worked to put a positive spin on what could be considered a plethora of negative "don'ts." Scare tactics were not used; no lectures or posters outlining the consequences of carelessness were used either.[67] On the contrary, GECO's employee newspaper regularly printed safety reminders, oftentimes using cartoons and humour. Well-known Canadian cartoonist Mr. Lou Skuce contributed several cartoons emphasizing safety. In one depiction, two GECOnians are observing a male employee filling a fuse. One comments to the other, "He's worked here ever since the plant opened and he's still so careful you'd think he'd just started." The other woman replies, "Maybe that's just why HE HAS BEEN here so long!"[68] Skuce's Goose — an iconic character appearing in many of his cartoons — has been listening to the women's conversation. "That's right," he thinks, "careful folks last longer on dangerous jobs!"[69] Some cartoons were printed as posters adorning cafeteria walls.[70]

The company laid out myriad clean-side rules in their "Regulations of the Scarboro Plant," given to every employee:

> It is <u>essential</u> that you:
>
> Obey all rules, regulations or instructions given verbally or displayed in print or writing.
>
> Conduct yourself quietly at all times and in all places.
>
> Do not indulge in argument, "horseplay" or "skylarking."
>
> Touch no article, apparatus or thing in any part of the factory EXCEPT as necessitated by your work or when instructed to do so.
>
> Report any case of infectious or communicable disease either in yourself or in your place of residence.
>
> Do not wear torn or frayed factory clothing.

> Do not wear factory clothing impregnated with explosive, without reporting to your supervisor.
>
> Proceed at a walk by the most direct route to your destination.
>
> Do not obstruct any other worker.
>
> Give way to explosive traffic.
>
> Place nothing on any part of the heating system.
>
> REPORT IMMEDIATELY ANY INFRINGEMENT OF THE REGULATIONS COMING TO YOUR NOTICE IN ANY WAY WHATSOEVER.[71]

GECO management recognized this last regulation was difficult to obey, knowing most people did not like to be a tattletale, especially where a friend was involved. There was, however, no other option in GECO's collective mind. Employees were expected to report an incident as impersonally as they would report a fire. To drive the point home, management described a fire in most cases to be "much less dangerous than the worker who will not respect the 'sane' regulations" designed for their safety.[72] This section containing clean-side rules wrapped up with an appeal to patriotism: "THIS IS YOUR FACTORY. THE WORK IS YOUR PART OF CANADA'S WAR EFFORT. IT IS YOUR RIGHT AND DUTY TO PROTECT BOTH."[73]

Work It Out

Controls, decrees, rules, and regulations did not end when an employee reached her fuse-filling workshop. In particular, her company handbook outlined many more demands she had to keep foremost in her mind while on the job. Most statutes were common sense, but some requirements were unique to a munitions plant, such as remembering to use both hands to carry a tray, and remembering to pass explosives to another worker by first placing the fuse on a bench or table, then waiting for the other worker to pick up the ammunition.[74] Adhering to imperative workshop directives was paramount to the safety of the workers inside as well as to Canada's national security. Shortcuts or workarounds were forbidden. Safety signs hung outside every door displaying the maximum quantities of explosives and number of operators permitted in each shop.[75]

GECO workers Agnes Brown and Sybil Irwin dry fuse covers after stencilling in Shop 43A. *Courtesy of Archives of Ontario.*

GECOnians heartily embraced the countless rules and regulations they were compelled to follow. With their lives and those of their work-mates at stake, there was no room for negotiation.

Fuse-Filling 101: No. 251

After touching the grounding rod at the entrance to her shop, a GECOite walked to her workstation, expecting to perform one of up to one hundred steps in the process to fill one unit of munitions.[76]

As an example, operators at GECO filled 13,426,587 No. 251 fuses in Building No. 67 over its tenure; the largest producer of any single fuse in Canada's history.[77] Fuse 251 was used in 40-mm anti-aircraft guns, such as those manufactured by the Swedish arms manufacturer Bofors, which were exploited heavily by the Allied forces during the Second World War.[78]

Building No. 67, where operators filled Fuse 251, consisted of three main shops — "A," "B," and "C" — with an annex attached to each shop.[79] The original set-up for each workshop in Building No. 67 followed traditional, tried-and-true English processes that kept each fuse and all its components together until final assembly.[80] While this system worked in the First World War, it involved many different actions performed by one operator, and in turn slowed the filling process considerably.[81]

During the summer of 1943, after extensive investigation, staff switched Shop "C" over from English production methods to a bulk assembly production line.[82] Each operator performed a single step in filling the fuse. The new assembly line consisted of worktables extending almost the entire length of the shop.[83] A grooved track or channel was set up on each side of the tables.[84] GECOites passed fuses down this track from one operator to another in small trays holding five fuses each.[85] As each operation was completed, the worker passed the fuse in its block to the next operator and the subsequent operation.[86]

Shop 67C's assembly line required seventy operators and twelve inspectors.[87] An additional nine workers and another inspector worked at a sub-assembly line set up in the annex, isolated from all other workers, where detonators and detonator plugs were assembled — by far one of the more dangerous elements involved in munitions production.[88] Stemming, the pressing of a specified quantity of high explosive powders into certain areas in a fuse without causing an explosion, which had been done in workshops, was moved to Building No. 60 in an effort to limit the potential for explosion from tetryl, and confine its troubling effects to the smallest number of women.[89]

In filling Fuse 251, empties had to be disassembled or broken down upon arrival for almost three years, until early 1944 when the manufacturer agreed to ship the fuses' many parts, such as the body, detonator lug, and fuse magazine, as separate components.[90] Once a worker had unscrewed the fuse's various components, an operator transferred its pieces to the workbench according to the filling function to be performed. Steps included inserting a detonator that had been filled to the correct density in the annex, "papering" in layers for added power, reassembling all components, stamping Scarboro's emblem, along with

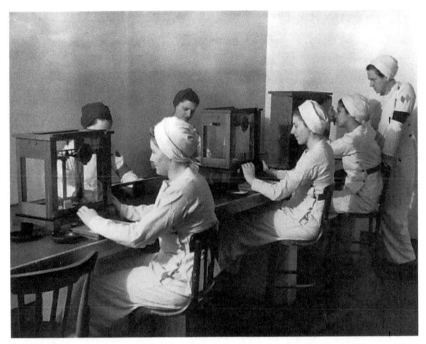

GECO workers check correct density of tetryl that has been packed in munitions components. *Courtesy of Archives of Ontario.*

the date and lot number on the fuse, and waterproofing its magazine with cement.[91] Each fuse lot — about two thousand fuses — was given a number, which tracked it throughout its life at the plant and thereafter, right into the hands of the Allied forces.[92] The fuse was inspected at ten separate times during filling to ensure explosives had attained a proper density within the fuse, as well as to certify all parts were appropriately tightened.[93] Filled lots were packed and trucked to X-ray, and then to a bond warehouse to await final inspection and proofing.[94] Before shipment, representative samples from the lot were test-fired in the Proof Yard to ensure accuracy, reliability, ease of use, and safety.[95]

GECOites worked diligently, with a sense of patriotic pride in producing top-notch ammunition. GECO's logo represented them on the world stage. They would not let the world down.

Where's the Beef?

Munitions workers at GECO were entitled to two ten-minute "rest pauses," or coffee breaks, and an hour for a meal during their shift.[96]

"Pelletiers" — employees who worked in pelleting at the south end of the complex — were thrilled when, in May 1942, cafeteria staff set up an afternoon clean-side coffee service in Building No. 148 in the south "cross-over" gallery, close to packing on the G.P. line.[97] Their elation was sincere; the dirty side of the sprawling plant was a twenty-minute walk north.

Eventually, four simple counter-style servers were constructed within the expansive gallery system (Building Nos. 148–151), supplying hot and cold drinks for five cents.[98] Since rules forbade any metal in the Danger Zone, workers purchased canteen tickets in the cafeteria.[99] GECOite Sylvia Nordstrand said of the clean-side canteens, "… it was standing

Four simple counter-style servers were constructed within GECO's expansive gallery system, supplying hot and cold drinks for five cents. Fuse-filling employees took their breaks on the clean side since ten minutes was not long enough to travel back to the change house (up to a mile away), change to civilian clothing, and take a break in the cafeteria. *Courtesy of Archives of Ontario.*

room only. No seats or tables were provided. It didn't matter as we sat nearly eight hours a day every shift."[100]

GECO's main, two thousand–seat cafeteria served approximately three thousand meals per day, or sixty-five thousand meals per month, more than all of Toronto's downtown hotels combined at that time.[101]

The cafeteria, run on a non-profit basis, offered a full menu, including "the nicest fruit salad" Carol LeCappelain had ever eaten, or a full hot meal, both costing twenty-five cents.[102] For ten cents more, employees could buy more expensive cuts of meat if, as Dorothy Cheesman recalled, "… you were really posh."[103] Despite steep price increases nationwide on several foodstuffs, such as beef, potatoes, and onions, Florence Ignatieff managed to keep prices in check.[104]

Typically, a GECOite could expect her quarter to buy a choice of daily soup such as split pea or corn chowder, a selection of two daily meat options such as roast pork or poached salmon, and a choice of two vegetable options including potatoes, carrots, or a crisp salad.[105] She finished her full-course meal with an option of desserts such as deep-dish rhubarb pie or chocolate pudding, and a choice of beverage such as tea, coffee, or whole milk.[106]

Employees arriving for work or finishing up a night shift could enjoy a full breakfast served from 6:30 to 9:00 each morning for a quarter.[107] During non-peak times, when the full menu was not available, a snack bar in the cafeteria offered light refreshments such as baked goods, ice cream, sandwiches, fruit, and coffee, tea, milk, and cigarettes.[108] One of GECOite Betty Ellis's best memories of her days at GECO was the food served. "They had really good food in the cafeteria," she said. "They had great butter tarts. I can remember them even to this day."[109]

"We're completely spoiled," one employee conceded in an interview for the *Toronto Daily Star*.[110] "When we go downtown nothing is good enough for us, and often we stay after work and have dinner here rather than go home and cook for ourselves."[111]

In fact, the only real complaint about the food came from those who worked the night shift, and then the complaint was not about the quality of the food — rather it was about the strangeness of eating in the middle of the night. GECOite Molly Danniels found it odd, while on night shift, to take her lunch break in the wee hours of the morning.[112]

At Day's End

When a GECO operator finished her shift, she returned to her change room, hung up her uniform, hopped over the barrier back to the dirty side, donned her civilian clothes, and clocked out at the guardhouse. Bus drivers welcomed tired employees as they boarded to make the long commute home. A typical shift at the plant, including time spent in the change room and commuting, was approximately eleven hours in length. For the two-thirds of GECO's women who were married, domestic demands waited for them at home. These strong, dedicated women had to juggle home, work, children, rationing, and the general pervading unease that came with living in a country at war.

They were truly unsung heroes.

Paying Tribute to the Girls

In the March 27, 1943 edition of *GECO Fusilier*, a group of white-collar workers — stenographers to be exact — took a tour of the GECO plant. Their observations, in a small way, pay tribute to Scarboro's bomb girls:

> … not only the usual things impressed us — the length of the Cleanways, the bright and busy atmosphere of the Shops, the cheerfulness of the operators — but smaller things too — like the monotony of turning a handle nine hours a day, and the fine skill of the women fuse-painters, and the identification marking of every fuse. Figures stuck in our head: the four-and-a-half ton press, the turning out of forty-eight thousand slugs a day for igniters.
>
> We were struck by the great cordiality of the Supervisors who showed us over; they spared no pains to explain things to us, and gave us a graphic description of work in their Shop. And as for the operators, we realize now, if we didn't before, that keeping cheery and looking bright and intelligent while you do some small monotonous job all day or all night, is a real war effort.
>
> In one Shop a gang of women had the Spring fever and was giving out with a full-throated chorus of "Apple Blossom Time"

— which made one reflect that by apple blossom time, maybe some of those igniters they were so swiftly assembling would have found their mark, in far-away skies — every one a shot for Victory.[113]

7

It All Depends on Me

There is no argument GECO had a lethal product line, but the munitions plant's real vim and vigour did not come from explosives. GECO's true strength came from its employees, who faithfully showed up for their shifts, six days each week, with only a day's pause for the Sabbath. With surnames ranging from Aneson to Zuber,[1] patriotic men and women put their personal and family needs aside to produce ammunition, jeopardizing their own lives, and those of everyone working alongside. As the war progressed, the ratio of women to men in the plant rose to a staggering nine women for every man.[2] These women — before the battle cry came — were content in their domestic duties, tending to husbands, house, and children, or they were single young women living out their carefree years as far away as Alberta and British Columbia in western Canada. These same women, who patriotically heeded the call, were thrust into wartime work by the hundreds of thousands throughout Canada and the United States.[3] Many men and women who worked at GECO had loved ones in active service overseas. Some had not only husbands, but multiple brothers and sons, grandsons and granddaughters engaged in war work both on the front line and on the home front.[4]

Every wartime worker had a unique experience and story to tell. The stories contained here chronicle the lives of GECO fusiliers collected from several sources, including first-hand accounts, surviving family members, and stories shared in the plant newspaper. Children of mothers who worked for GECO are particularly proud, and rightly so.

This chapter is dedicated to those whose stories are told below, and to the countless others who lived out their lives in peacetime after the need for their services ended, and died with no recognition, no fanfare, without any medals to recognize their unique sacrifice and contribution in claiming victory over Nazi oppression.

GECO Gals
On the Dirty Side
Mum's the Word: Dorothy Cheesman

Dorothy Cheesman, born in 1924, was hired in March 1941, very early in Project No. 24's story. At just sixteen years of age, Dorothy was a high-school student at Eastern Commerce when the Hamilton brothers hired her as GECO's first secretary. Her first assignment was to type up top-secret engineering notes at 1218 Danforth Avenue. She remembers getting fingerprinted, taking an oath of secrecy, and receiving wages of $15 to $17.50 per week.

Dorothy transferred to 1350 Danforth Avenue, then to the newly completed administration building at the GECO plant in Scarboro in May 1941. Dorothy worked for Mr. Duff, GECO's production manager, and moved with him to the clean-side office housed in Building No. 153 after a stint in administration on the dirty side. Dorothy stayed with GECO until the end of the war.

The Operations (Time and Motion) Study Office was just across the way from Dorothy, and one of her very good chums, Molly Danniels, worked there. A twenty-eight-year-old gentleman, William McRae, worked in that office as well. Unable to serve his country overseas due to vision problems, Bill did his part at GECO. In 1945, when the war was won, Molly, Dorothy, and Bill moved on. Bill almost immediately saw an opportunity to woo the pretty lady in the clean-side office. Dorothy and

GECO hired Dorothy Cheesman at only sixteen years of age to type up top-secret engineering notes when construction for the munitions factory was just getting underway. GECO staff entrusted Dorothy to lock their safe each evening with classified engineering notes safely tucked inside. Dorothy, a steadfast employee, stayed with GECO until the end of the war. *Courtesy of Dorothy McRae.*

Bill began dating and married two years later. They raised a happy, large family of seven. Dorothy continues to live in Scarborough today.

Too Young to Fill: Elizabeth Ellis

Elizabeth Ellis was born on May 23, 1927, in her grandmother's home on Broadview Avenue at Pottery Road in Toronto. She was the oldest of four daughters born within four years to Harry and Isobel Ellis. The Depression hit the family hard and her dad, a bricklayer, could find little work. He turned to government relief to feed and clothe his young family during the 1930s.

Betty grew up overlooking the gorgeous Don River, and enjoyed swimming in its clear, fresh water with friends. During the war, a German POW camp was built in the Don Valley below her house. The men lived in wooden huts, hung their laundry out on clotheslines just like their Canadian neighbours, and were picked up each morning by bus to go to work on wartime projects. The simple, down-to-earth everydayness of their routine amazed Betty. The camp was not fenced in. The prisoners did not attempt an escape. Perhaps the fate that awaited them back in Germany was a lot worse than life as a POW in the Great White North.

Elizabeth struggled with math in high school, and after failing and being kept back, she left at the age of sixteen. Needing a job to help support her family, she discovered a wartime munitions plant's employ-ment office on "the Danforth." She applied and started the commute via the Hollinger bus out to GECO in Scarboro at the end of May 1943. She remembers the bus would meander its way up Victoria Park Avenue to Eglinton Avenue. Scarboro seemed so far from where she lived on Broadview Avenue.

Because Betty was only sixteen, she was not old enough to fill muni-tions.[5] This restriction did not bother her. "Office work would be more what I was used to," she said. Elizabeth performed basic office duties such as filing and typing. Within her office was a large laboratory where a handful of men worked. Windows allowed the office staff to watch the men, but they were not allowed to enter the room. She remembers feel-ing out of place. "I was so young," she said. "Everyone was older, they were married, had children."

In fact, with the naiveté of youth, it never dawned on Betty that women were filling munitions. "I had no idea what they did in the workshops," she said. She saw women who had yellow hair and hands from working with tetryl, but she did not know that that was the cause at the time. She was also completely unaware of GECO's tunnel system.

As a healthy, athletic young woman, Betty took advantage of the extra-curricular activities offered at GECO. She played first base on one of GECO's softball teams, and still remembers going to play an exhibition game for the troops at an army camp located at Niagara-on-the-Lake. "I leapt up to catch a ball," she said, "and fell into a hole, spraining my ankle." A military doctor taped up her injury onsite, but she was out of the game, and missed three days of work. When she returned, she visited GECO's Medical Department, where the nurses were aghast at the state of the army doctor's "quick fix." On another occasion, Betty, wanting to do her part for the men fighting overseas, attended one of GECO's blood donor clinics. Unfortunately, the nurses discovered she was anemic and instead of taking her blood, instructed her to take iron pills and eat lots of lettuce and liver.

By March 1945, talk of the war ending was already on the lips of hopeful Canadians. Betty knew she would soon be looking for work. She left GECO that spring to work at Queen's Park, performing clerical duties.

Early in 1945, Elizabeth rekindled a fledgling romance with a young, handsome sailor, Victor Warner, who, while serving in the Royal Canadian Navy as part of D.E.M.S. (Defensively Equipped Merchant Ships), had come home on a ten-day leave. When he shipped out, they promised to write to each other. Today, almost seven decades later, two of Victor's dear letters can be found tucked in Betty's wallet.

Victor was discharged in November 1945, returning to work at Canada Wire, where he had worked before he enlisted. Elizabeth left her job at Queen's Park and moved to Canada Wire to be closer to Victor.

Elizabeth and Victor were married in the summer of 1948. The next morning, Victor slipped the receipt from their first breakfast as a married couple into his wallet. A treasured memento, he carried it with him until he died in his sleep in 2004.

Victor and Elizabeth had two children. Today, Elizabeth lives in south Scarborough, near the Golden Mile.

A Star Is Born: Helen Fraser

By the time Helen Fraser joined GECO, she had lived most every girl's dream. Just a few years earlier, as a single young woman, Helen Gray lived in Medicine Hat enjoying a recent Alberta Beauty Contest win. Scouts from Paramount Studios in Hollywood arrived, searching for beauty as part of a North American contest. Unbeknownst to Helen, the town's local theatre manager gave them a picture of the attractive young lady. Not long after, she received a wire, requesting she travel to California.

Suddenly, Helen, along with twenty-nine other starry-eyed young ladies, was a Hollywood hopeful. She signed a six-month contract with the film studio, earning $50 a week. She first appeared in *Hollywood on Parade*, a film starring a group of beauty contest winners who visited several Hollywood nightspots. The film featured big names, including

Mae West, Gloria Swanson, Cecil B. DeMille, the Marx Brothers, Gary Cooper, Cary Grant, and Canada's Mary Pickford. Helen also starred in *Search for Beauty*, which came out a year later, but her contract ended and Hollywood did not ask her back. "I was there six months," she said, and while "it was lots of fun," she returned home, humility intact. She married, and soon after, the war broke out.

With seven brothers — all but the youngest fighting overseas, with one missing in action flying over Germany — she needed little urging to help the war effort. Even her husband was serving in the RCAF, as a flight sergeant. Helen moved east specifically to join the ranks at GECO. She was given a unique job — driving employees and special guests around the plant in a company taxi. She loved her job, but admits with a wistful smile she left a small bit of her heart in Hollywood and hoped to pursue her acting career when the war ended.

Of the thirty young women selected in Paramount's Search for Beauty contest, Helen's colleague, actress Ann Sheridan, was the only one to really make it in film.[6]

A Run-In with the Boss: Barbara Holmes

Barbara Mary Jarman grew up with a love for sports. Born in August 1915 in Edmonton, Alberta, Barbara was the daughter of international rugby star John Wallace Jarman, who played for Bristol, and who immigrated to Canada around the turn of the century. Barbara had an idyllic childhood, and after completing high school, attended the University of Alberta, where she earned a bachelor of science degree.

As a young, single woman, she moved to Toronto, hoping to find work as a dietician. She secured a job in Eaton's iconic College Street store. A newcomer to the city, Barbara joined the Badminton and Racket Club, where she developed a life-long love for tennis. A dear friend, Ruby, played matchmaker, introducing Barbara to a handsome young man named Hartley Holmes. Hartley, a chartered accountant, lived with health issues, including diabetes, and was not able to enlist when Canada entered the Second World War. Barbara and Hartley were married in June 1940. Barbara quit her job for a brief time, but went back to work when GECO opened in Scarboro.

Barbara remembers the plant's buildings "were in a U-shape where women were filling shells for the war." Along with cafeteria manager Florence Ignatieff, Barbara helped set the meal plan for the massive munitions plant. "We did a lot of cooking," she says proudly. "We had to have fruits and desserts all ready to go. It was the cleanest place to work at that time."

Barbara recalls fondly a serendipitous "run-in" with GECO's president, Bob Hamilton. Late one Saturday afternoon as Mr. Hamilton was leaving the plant, he spotted Barbara waiting for a bus. He stopped and offered her a ride home. To Barbara, this would have been quite extraordinary — getting a ride home from the president of the company. When Bob discovered through casual conversation that Hartley was away on business, he invited her home for dinner. Barbara balked — she couldn't possibly impose on Mrs. Hamilton without proper invitation. Bob put her at ease when he simply replied, "Never mind, you'll like her; besides, we're having roast beef." Barbara and Betty Hamilton became fast friends that Saturday evening. The spur-of-the-moment ride home and subsequent shared meal around the dinner table brought two families together who enjoyed a close life-long friendship. Barbara and her family spent many happy times at the Hamilton cottage on Bass Island. "It was the happiest part of my life," Barbara, now ninety-seven, says. "It was a wonderful part of my life, knowing Betty and Bob Hamilton. Bob and Betty were very generous, remarkable people."

Barbara left GECO when she became pregnant with her daughter and namesake, Barbara, born in 1944. As testament to the close friendships Barbara built while at GECO, Grace Hyndman, GECO's personnel director, and Florence Ignatieff became her daughter's godmothers. Betty Hamilton became godmother to Barbara's son, who was born two years later.

Sadly, Hartley died from a heart attack in 1967. Barbara remarried in 1970. Her second husband, Basil Langfeldt, passed away in 1986. She smiles when she remembers them. "I was very happy with my two husbands."

Barbara played tennis most of her life, proud to say she played in the "over ninety" category in tennis tournaments in Florida. She now lives in Toronto in the same retirement home where her treasured friend Betty Hamilton once resided.

Barbara Holmes Langfeldt with John McLean Parsons Hamilton, Toronto, 2013. Barbara, while at GECO, worked closely with Florence Ignatieff, the cafeteria manager. GECO's main two-thousand-seat cafeteria served approximately three thousand meals per day, or sixty-five thousand meals per month, more than all of Toronto's downtown hotels combined at that time. *Courtesy Barbara Dickson.*

Chief Dietitian and "Guiding Genius": Florence Ignatieff

Florence Ignatieff, director of GECO's massive cafeteria services, managed a staff of 120 employees. She brought an armload of impressive credentials to her new job, including an extensive academic background and successful record of managing food operations at the Georgian Room of the T. Eaton Company.

Born in 1902, Florence Hargreaves was the youngest of five. Mika, Florence's daughter, said, "[my mother was raised] in a fairly Victorian family that seemed to be trying to keep her doing the 'correct' thing, and she wasn't going to let them stop her."[7]

As a determined young woman, Florence wanted to study science at university. Her father refused to enrol her, calling the pursuit not "lady-like enough."[8] Florence put a plan together. "She always found a way," Mika said, "to do what she wanted to."[9] Not particularly fond of cooking,

Florence discovered she could meet the undergraduate course requirements needed for biochemistry by taking a bachelor of arts in household economics, which her father liked. She then went on to earn her masters in biochemistry from the University of Toronto.

"She had an extraordinary group of friends at university," her son Paul says from his home in France.[10] "They were a very strong group of ladies; very moral, very principled, very influential."[11]

"Her group of friends at university didn't ask if they could or could not do something," Mika adds, "they just went ahead and did whatever they wanted to. That pretty much sums up my mother's approach to life."[12]

After earning her master's degree, Florence enrolled at the University of Toronto and completed her program, but before she defended her dissertation, her professor, Dr. Wasteneys, asked her to supervise a new biochemistry Ph.D. student, Count Vladimir "Jim" Ignatieff.

Vladimir Ignatieff was a man of renown in his own right. His father, Count Pavel Nikolayevich Ignatiev, was minister of education, as well as former governor of Kiev in Russia — at that time a part of the Russian Empire. Count Ignatiev was imprisoned by the Bolsheviks during the Great War. The count presumed he would be executed as the Romanov family had been. "However, his wife, Princess Natalya Meshcherskaya, alerted the local educational establishment," Mika said, "who regarded Ignatiev as a positive reformer, and mounted a public demonstration, and negotiated his release."[13] Count Pavel and his family fled, first to France, then to England in 1919, and finally immigrated to Upper Melbourne, Quebec, in 1925, where Paul and Natasha built a home.

While Jim Ignatieff acknowledged Florence as his Ph.D. supervisor, it wasn't until he asked her to attend the annual Russian ball in Toronto — resplendent with Russian nobility such as Grand Duchess Olga Alexandrovna of Russia, Nickolas II's younger sister — and watched Florence walk into the room in a midnight-blue, low-cut velvet dress, that she captured his undivided attention. They were married a year later.

Jim completed his Ph.D. and the young couple moved to Edmonton, Alberta, where he took up a teaching position at the University of Alberta in 1935. Their children, Paul and Mika, were born in 1936 and 1939 respectively. Within days of Canada entering the Second World War, Jim enlisted, wanting to fight for his adopted country. He headed overseas that September with the Calgary Highlanders in their infantry division as a chemical war specialist. At six-feet six-inches tall, he was an imposing figure in his military-issued kilt.

With no family in Alberta, Florence moved back to Toronto early on in the war, with her little ones, to live near her brothers, sisters, and friends. While working at the Eaton store on College Street, she was approached to help plan and manage the cafeteria at a new fuse-filling plant in Scarboro.

"We hired people who knew their job, expertise," Bob Hamilton explained.[14] "We went seeking them; we didn't wait for them to appear on the doorstep. Through inquiry of several restaurants [we learned Florence] had run the Eaton's food service, so she knew her job and she got good staff."[15]

The little family moved into one of six bungalows situated at the GECO site, where they lived for the duration of the war. As a working mother with long, demanding hours, Florence hired a live-in housekeeper, an older woman with whom she worked while at Eaton's. "Lizzie" became "a second mother" to the children, Paul and Mika recall, and she stayed with the family for the rest of her life.[16]

Joyce Hibbert, in her book *Fragments of War: Stories of Survival of World War II*, offers a glimpse into the magnitude of Florence's responsibility: "From 1941 until the war's end, [Florence] worked as head dietician in a war supplies plant in Scarborough. During the most intensive production period at the fuse-filling plant, shifts worked around the clock seven days a week and Mrs. Ignatieff was responsible for 8,000 meals every twenty-four hours."[17] In a *Toronto Daily Star* newspaper article about GECO's food quality, Florence was referred to as "Mrs. V.P. Ignatieff, Chief Dietitian, and 'Guiding Genius.'"[18]

"Mom was very happy at GECO," Paul remembers.[19] "It was quite an amazing atmosphere at work, lots of effective, dedicated people. The leadership was very strong. The Hamiltons were very patriotic people. They didn't make a lot of money on war business. They were very, very good employers, pioneers in engineering and feeding operations."[20]

Paul recalls visiting the cafeteria with his mom and seeing the feeding stations where food was passed out. "I went into the kitchen to see large vats of soup," he recalls.[21] As a young boy, he was especially impressed watching butchers cut up large sides of beef. He did not get the opportunity to visit the clean side of the plant, or to learn about the tunnel system. A fond memory Paul has of his mom's days at GECO is of the aftermath of the 1944 snowstorm. "GECO's parking lots had to be plowed" he reminisces, "and there were snowbanks as tall as houses to toboggan down."[22]

"She planned, developed nutritional menus," Mika said, "and organized the preparation and serving of meals."[23]

Toward the end of the war, automobile maker Henry Ford heard about the Hamiltons, who were managing an amazing war plant in Toronto. "He came up to see them," Paul said.[24] "The Hamilton brothers took him over to see food operations at GECO. He was quite impressed."[25] Henry offered Florence $40,000 to manage food operations for the Ford Empire worldwide. She didn't take the job. "She deferred to Father," Paul said, "out of respect. Socially, women didn't excel above their husbands."[26]

Major Ignatieff, like most of the men in Canada's fighting forces, could not return home during the war to see Florence, Paul, and Mika. Florence and Lizzie nurtured the children during their formative years. Even when Jim demobilized late in 1945, he saw his family for only a short time before he got a call from a friend. "Mike Pearson called him after the war," Paul said, "and he said, 'you're going to fly to Quebec City tomorrow in the belly of a Lancaster bomber for a conference on food and agriculture.'"[27] The Food and Agriculture Organization — the FAO — for the United Nations was founded at the conference, and Jim, armed with his background in agriculture, was one of the first to be hired. He moved the family to Washington, D.C., to work for the fledgling organization.

A year later, Jim felt Paul and Mika were missing the benefits of living in Canada. He bought a four-hundred-acre farm with two hundred head of purebred Holstein and Guernsey cattle in Richmond, a small English/French town in Quebec, and although he continued his work in Washington, he moved his family north of the border. Florence managed the farm for about five years. Always an academic, Florence became interested in genetics, particularly in upgrading the quality of cattle through breeding.

She saw some success, but when the FAO moved its headquarters from Washington to Rome in the mid-1950s, Jim and Florence relocated to Italy, where they stayed until he retired. "I adored living in Rome," Paul says.[28] "[Mother] was very fond of music and ballet and taught us to appreciate the arts, galleries, museums. It was a real treat to be taken around Rome by her. She could have been a leading guide of Rome."[29]

She no longer worked. "The Food and Agricultural Organization had a policy," Mika explained, "as most large organizations [did, and] including universities frowned [upon] hiring wives of their professional staff."[30]

"Mother suggested I should learn some French," Paul said of his days in Rome.[31] He attended the University of Lausanne, where he not only learned French, but also met his future wife, Katharine. They married in 1960.

Jim and Florence returned to Canada to live out their retirement in Quebec. Florence died in 1990, with Vladimir following four years later. They are buried in a family plot in Melbourne, Quebec, alongside Vladimir's parents.

Paul Ignatieff enjoyed a long career in Canada and internationally with UNICEF, a children's relief agency that brought food, clothing, and healthcare to children who faced famine and disease after the Second World War. Paul attributes his big break in securing his job at UNICEF to his mother's university friends.

In 1975 he and Katharine were captured by Pol Pot's Khmer Rouge in Phnom Pen, the capital of Cambodia. "We were providing food and medical supplies to member organizations," Paul said.[32] They, along with members of other relief agencies, fled to the French embassy, where they hid as the city was besieged. Paul remained calm. "I was not afraid of losing my life.... In a stressful situation you made a decision whether you were going to survive or not; and you did it."[33] Thankfully, they survived and were evacuated to Bangkok.

Today, Professor Paul Ignatieff, having been endowed with the title of

Professor of Social Science by the University of Glasgow, lives in the south of France with his son and grandchildren. Mika married an American attorney who became a human rights professor and university administrator, and the first American to be president of the Inter-American Commission on Human Rights. Mika focused her career on community development, helping economically challenged neighbourhoods to regenerate. She and her husband live in Colorado.

Paul says, "I'm immensely proud of my mother and full of admiration for her. She was a very stimulating woman."[34]

Mika adds, "My mother never was a follower — she was an initiator and organizer. She had a good sense of humour and told us many funny tales about various people who had worked with her."[35]

On the Clean Side
Don't Drop That Det!: Molly Danniels

Molly Danniels joined GECO in 1942, at the age of twenty, after hearing about a job opportunity there through a friend. Her first memory of GECO dates from when she was hired. Security had trouble fingerprinting her because she had a wart on one of her fingers.

Molly's duties included packing detonators the size of her small fingernail with explosives. Her supervisors cautioned her and her shop mates that if they punctured one it would blow up, causing severe injury, if not death. Molly admitted, in hindsight, and with the wisdom that comes with age, that her work was quite dangerous, and that she "wouldn't do [it] today." While she and the rest of the team were encouraged to be efficient in their work, safety always came first. The management worked tirelessly to meet production quotas to supply the armed forces, but the Hamiltons did not pass along those quotas to their workers for their own safety.

Even with adherence to myriad safety regulations, accidents did occur. Molly remembered one mishap that happened in her workshop. A tracer shell accidentally ignited, filling the entire shop with a large flare. Twenty-five women quit immediately. "There were other small incidents," she said, but they were "hush-hush, like nursing home deaths."[36]

Despite the dangerous nature of her work, Molly collected many fond memories of her time at GECO. She remembered men getting "fresh" with the women operators. The girls used to say light-heartedly, "Watch that fellow — he's getting tricky." She recalled the famous snowstorm of December 1944. Only three people made it to the bus stop with Molly to catch the GECO bus to work. They made it to the plant to find just six women in Molly's shop.

Molly took advantage of the "Victory Gardens" at the plant and eagerly planted carrots in her vegetable plot. Unfortunately, "the Scarboro clay wouldn't give anything up," she said, not even with the use of a pick ax.[37]

Toward the end of the war, GECO management asked if any of the girls in her workshop knew how to type. Molly, having previous typing experience, offered her services and transferred from the Danger Zone to administration, where she worked as a teletypist for the remainder of the war. She completed her days at GECO late in the summer of 1945, after most employees had moved on.

After the war, Molly married her love, Fred, and raised a family in Scarborough, near Warden and Lawrence, not far from where she did her part for the war effort. Molly and Fred moved to the Bluffs area of Scarborough in 1990. Fred took ill in 2009 and they moved into a retirement home, where he passed away in February 2010. Molly was reunited with him in March 2014 at ninety-two years of age.

"Truckerette": Hilda Keast

Hilda Eileen June Keast was born in 1927 in Toronto. Tragically, and all too often for the time, three of Hilda siblings died before they reached adulthood. Her sister Mary died as an infant, in what might be called "crib death" today; her brother Tommy, at six months, kicked away a blanket that had been wrapped around a hot water bottle, and was scalded to death; and Pearl, a twin to another sibling, died at six months due to an ear infection.

Hilda decided at a young age that gaining real world experience was what she wanted, more so than formal education. She left school armed with a Grade 7 education and entered the workforce as a house cleaner.

Hilda's mom and dad received regular dairy deliveries from their local milkman, like most families in Toronto during the 1940s. Few girls, however, fell in love with their milkman. Hilda, at fifteen years of age, grew fond of Walter Harris, their Silverwoods dairy man, even though Walter was fourteen years older. "Dad would have killed me if he found out," Hilda admitted when re-telling the story to her children.

When Canada went to war, Walter left Silverwoods to join the Royal Canadian Army Service Corps with the 86th Bridge Company. He fought as a despatch motorcycle rider and was wounded by mortar fire when, while under attack, he rescued a Polish soldier. He pulled the soldier to safety under a truck and Walter was hit. He spent six days in hospital then went right back to his unit to fight. Walter received a citation and was promoted to lance corporal.

Meanwhile, Hilda did her part for the war effort by joining GECO. Hilda lived on North Bonnington in the Birchmount and St. Clair area of Scarboro at the time, so she enjoyed the unique privilege of walking to work. At GECO, she worked as a "truckerette." She was responsible for the delicate, precarious transportation of empties and filled munitions through the plant. It was strenuous work but Hilda and her workmates were more than ready for the challenge.

Hilda talked about her days at GECO long after the war ended. "She had a lot of fun at GECO," her son John says.[38] "'There were all these girls,' she said, 'all around the same age. They built bombs and there were tunnels under there on Civic Road.'"[39]

After the war, Walter returned to Silverwoods. They were married in 1949 and had three children. Hilda died in 1990 from complications of Hodgkin's disease. Walter predeceased Hilda, dying in 1977.

On the back of a faded photograph from her GECO days, Hilda carefully documented the names of all her "truck mates." She wrote, "Taken at G.E.C.O. — General Engineering Company — sometime in 1944. We trucked skids of ammunition from X-ray Dept. to shop to be finished or from shop to shop."[40] Hilda noted four women accompanied each truck. She also documented her shifts: "7–3, 3–11, and 11–7."[41] A short note accompanied a shop photo that appeared in the company's newspaper: "In the early days of Scarboro trucking on the 'clean side' was done by men, then the manpower shortage intervened and like so many other war jobs, the women stepped into the breach and took over."[42] The family also has a picture of Hilda with her "Ping Pones," perhaps a

Hilda Keast (back row, second from left) poses happily with her fellow "Truckerettes." *Courtesy of John Alan Harris.*

Ping-Pong team to which she belonged. Hilda memorialized each team member by name on the reverse,[43] including her sister who also worked at GECO.

Hilda's written words carry her sentiment across the decades: "What fun we had."[44]

Yellow Canary: Carol LeCappelain

Carol LeCappelain, born in November 1921, first learned about GECO from a newspaper advertisement in her local paper, the *North Bay Nugget*. She was earning $12 a month at that time. After reading GECO would pay her $22 per week, it did not take much to convince this nineteen-year-old to move to Toronto.

Carol's first day at GECO was on October 27, 1941, and she completed her service on June 23, 1945. She earned three diamond badges, sewn on her uniform sleeve, to commemorate her dedicated service. Although proud of those, she was disappointed that she did not receive her fourth diamond because the war ended. She never missed a day of work.

Carol was hired by the Inspection Board of the United Kingdom and Canada. She was responsible for inspecting filled munitions in her workshop before they left the plant. She was part of quality assurance at GECO, specifically involved in the inspection of No. 33G fuses: fuses filled in Building No. 33, Shop G. She wore a navy turban to identify herself as a government employee, a "G.I." — Government Inspector — and a red armband to identify her as an inspector of No. 33G fuses.

As a bench leader, her duties included ensuring the time fuses could be set easily, something that involved calibrating a series of numbered grooves etched into the base, including two rings that could be set to take a certain amount of time to go off so that a shell would explode at a certain distance from a gun. The bottom ring could be rotated to lengthen

Carol LeCappelain was a government inspector who inspected fuses at GECO through all stages of filling them. She took her job to heart, once rejecting an entire skid of filled ammunition (approximately two thousand fuses) because their timing rings didn't turn easily enough. She completed almost four years of faithful service at GECO, with perfect attendance. *Courtesy of Barbara Dickson.*

or reduce the time lapse before detonation. She also had to ensure that the layer of gunpowder was applied safely and correctly, and that the waterproof seal had been affixed properly. Carol would then escort the skid of ready fuses through the underground tunnel system to the Proof Yards at the south end of the plant, where they would be tested.[45]

Carol took her job very seriously. The fuses had to be perfect, without the slightest defect. "I didn't want any soldiers killed due to a faulty fuse," she said.[46] She could sleep at night only if she knew that each fuse would do what the soldiers expected it to do — ignite and burn long enough to reach its target.

Carol recalled that women preferred to work on the "gunpowder" line of the plant, as opposed to the "high explosives" area, due to yellowing of their hands from working with tetryl.

While she did not receive a paycheque from GECO because she was a Canadian government employee, Carol viewed herself as part of GECO's family.

Carol passed away on New Year's Day, 2014.

For the Love of Her Country: Helen Leslie

Helen Gertrude Browes was born on the nineteenth of May, 1909, in West Hill, Ontario, a small community nestled on the eastern edge of Scarboro. In 1925, at sixteen years of age, Helen married Howard Leslie, a First World War veteran who had been only fifteen years old when he enlisted and fought for freedom. Helen and Howard started their family, bringing five little ones, including a daughter, Jacqueline, into the fold over the next decade. Life was good.

However, tragedy struck when their third child contracted polio at the age of six during the autumn of 1937. Her mom and dad took her to the Hospital for Sick Children in Toronto, where doctors put her in an iron lung, an early type of respirator, because she could not breathe on her own. To add to their angst, the entire family went into quarantine for six months; as a result, Helen and Howard were unable to see their little girl. Howard lost his job, too. Because Canada's health care system was still evolving, free doctor and hospital care were not available, and their daughter's illness took a steep toll on Helen and Howard's finances.

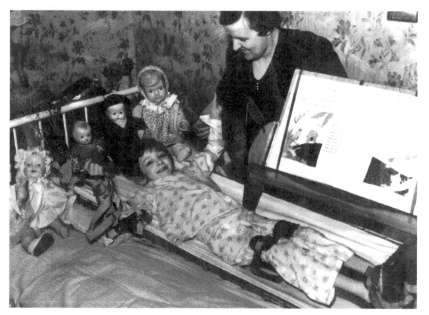

In addition to working full-time at GECO, Helen Leslie, along with her husband, raised five children, including caring for their daughter who, diagnosed with polio at the age of six, spent many months in the Hospital for Sick Children in Toronto. *Courtesy of Jackie Eden.*

It would take two years, and a war, before Howard found another job. Helen needed to find a job too, to help pay for their little girl's staggering medical bills. GECO offered a wonderful solution.

Life was busy. Howard and Helen worked full-time. Helen took the GECO bus to the plant and worked shifts, even overnight. Howard's mom, Maggie, helped care for the little ones at home on Newmarket Avenue. Their daughter continued to convalesce in hospital.

"Mom was a very busy woman," Jackie recalls. "She worked, cared for our sister when she could come home for a visit, and cared for us other kids. She was very thankful for our grandmother's help."[47]

Jackie remembers her mom speaking about her work at GECO. Helen recounted the story of a woman being injured by an explosion in the workshop next to hers. It made Helen skittish around explosives, yet she filled munitions out of economic necessity and for her love of her country. Jackie remembers with pride, "Mom always did say she did her part to support the war effort."[48]

Helen Leslie's connection to GECO did not stop with the war's end. Harold and Helen and their younger children would become the first residents to live at GECO in its newly renovated postwar emergency housing.

A Woman of Sorrow: Peggy MacKay

Mrs. Peggy MacKay of Shop 35B filled primers. While being interviewed for an article in the plant newspaper, she was focused so intensely on filling fuses that she did not pause from her work during the questions.[49] The article revealed a life of sadness and sorrow: her son, Sergeant William MacKay, had been reported missing;[50] her husband, Private Peter MacKay, had been transferred recently to "parts unknown," not knowing his son was missing;[51] and her two little boys had drowned eight years earlier, at the tender ages of five and seven, back in Dundee, Scotland, her homeland.[52] Only two little girls remained — Stella, nine, and Barbara, aged six.[53] Peggy's sister was killed in the London Blitz, and three uncles and ten cousins were lost aboard the ill-fated ship *Benato*.[54]

"I often think that every primer I help fill may be helping some other mother's son," she said in the newspaper interview. Although, "all I do seems so small beside what the folks over across there are going through."[55]

Mrs. MacKay was such an exemplary employee that GECO hired fellow employee and prominent Canadian sculptor Howard Pfeiffer to construct a beautiful head-and-shoulders brass statuette of her in the spring of 1943 as "a tangible symbol ... of the vital part that women are playing in the furnishing of 'tools' of war to fighting men of the United Nations."[56] Peggy spent more than three months sitting in her kitchen perfectly still, every weekend, with a piece of ammunition tucked in the crook of her arm, as Hal moulded and chiselled his masterpiece, titled *War Worker*.[57]

"To us at 'Scarboro,'" the author of the employee newspaper story stated, "it has particular significance for it will form a permanent record of the patriotic devotion of the women of this Plant and will keep their memory green long after the peace bells have rung."[58]

Management proudly displayed the attractive, heart-stirring sculpture in GECO's cafeteria. Peggy dedicated every waking moment to the war effort. She helped raise funds to purchase a Salvation Army mobile canteen used overseas to serve tired troops.[59] In addition, she gave blood regularly.

Sadly, not all was what it seemed. Peggy's true-life story barely resembled the tragic version inked for newspaper stories, yet was still just as heartbreaking. Decades later, Peggy's daughter Stella, one of the wee lasses mentioned in the *GECO Fusilier*'s initial account, shared her own recollections.

Stella's mother, Margaret "Peggy" Ferguson Wallace was born in 1908 in Dundee, Scotland, to an impoverished family. Life was tough. At thirteen years of age, she worked in a jute mill to help feed her family. In 1923, at the age of fifteen, Peggy met her future husband, ten years her senior. He offered to take her away from her meagre existence, promising a more comfortable life. They married quickly. Their first son was born three years later in 1926. Perhaps Peggy felt secure for the first time in her life.

Any sense of stability was short-lived. Her husband left her and their infant son, and sailed for Canada in April 1927. His hope was to build a better life for his family and send for them when he got settled. Peggy, possibly feeling abandoned and needing security for both her and her little boy, immediately met another man who fathered two sons with her, and a daughter, Stella, born in 1933.

Eight years after leaving his homeland and his family, Peggy's husband wired money to Peggy to join him in Canada. Inexplicably, Peggy sailed for Canada, leaving her two little boys behind with their father, with no note or explanation. She took her firstborn and little Stella, then three. "[He] fell to pieces when Peggy left with his little girl," Stella said, then reasoned, "She must have been so poor in Scotland, so desperate for a new life, a new start."[60]

The boys' dad, unable to provide ongoing care, relinquished custody and moved them to an orphanage. Peggy reunited with her husband in Canada, who must have had quite a shock to see a little girl disembark from the ship *Letitia* with his wife and son.

New immigrant Peggy, who was more than likely pregnant with Stella's sister, had her story ready. If anyone should ask of the boys' whereabouts

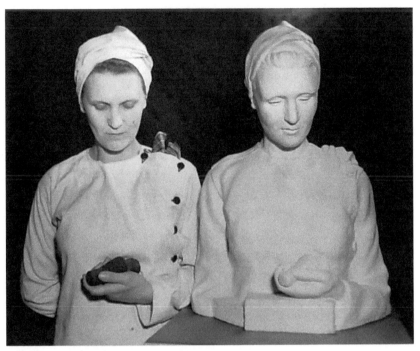

GECOite Peggy MacKay, an exemplary employee, sat for fellow munitions worker and renowned sculptor Harold Pfeiffer while he moulded and chiselled his masterpiece, titled *War Worker*. Management proudly displayed the attractive sculpture in GECO's cafeteria for the duration of the war. *Courtesy of Archives of Ontario.*

— not that anyone in Canada would know of their existence — she would tell them the boys had drowned. About seven months after landing on Canadian soil, Peggy gave birth to her fifth child.

Life in Canada was not any better for Peggy or her children. The writer in GECO's newspaper account reported that Peggy and the girls spent cozy "evenings making quilts in aid of the British War Victims Fund." Stella doesn't remember anything "cozy." There were many nights Peggy didn't come home at all. "My mother was like a chameleon," Stella said, "changing her story to suit the situation she found herself in."[61]

While Peggy worked at a fever pitch at GECO, her children back in Scotland enlisted and served their country heroically during the war. One joined the RAF and the other the Royal Navy.

After the war ended and GECO closed its doors, Peggy, with her husband no longer in her life, moved on, securing a position as a cook aboard the cruise ship the S.S. *Noronic*. During Peggy's time in service, in the early morning hours of September 17, 1949, the *Noronic* caught fire while docked in Toronto.[62] Of 524 passengers, close to 120 people lost their lives.[63] While the cause of the fire remains a mystery, some say it started in a linen closet.[64]

When Stella was fourteen, she learned she had two older brothers when her mom inadvertently blurted out that she had left two sons in Dundee. Stella, shocked, sought out her newfound siblings and located them. In 1956, almost twenty years after deserting her children, Peggy returned to Scotland to reunite with her boys.

Peggy died in 1964, at fifty-six years of age, from pancreatic cancer.

Some may challenge this second account of Peggy MacKay's life — it's almost as extraordinary as her own tale told seventy years ago, so convincingly, to a wartime journalist. In the end, neither story's merit matters. What matters is that Peggy MacKay, truly a "woman of sorrow," and despite perhaps serious mental health issues, worked her fingers to the bone for the Allied forces. What matters is that her children, despite their mother's alleged abuse and abandonment, were able to rally, marry, and have children of their own. "Peggy gave birth to five children, and we all suffered from the decisions she made," Stella said, "but I'm so proud of my mother for the work she did for the war."[65]

Today, Stella lives in Pefferlaw, Ontario, with her daughter and family.

A Breath of Fresh Ayr: Mary Plain

Mary "Maimie" Plain brings a distinctive perspective to women's war work in Canada. Before she emigrated, she worked at the Stamping and Engineering Company in Ayr, Scotland.

Maimie was born in Ayr, a quaint fishing village about thirty miles south of Glasgow. Because Britain had instituted mandatory war service requirements for both men and women, she was called up in 1942 at twenty years of age. "If you volunteered, you got to choose what [war work] you did," Mary recalls.[66] "If not, you were conscripted and you did what they told you to."[67] Maimie was given three choices: work at

"Naffi," a canteen service for the military; work for the Land Army, which entailed working on a farm; or work at the stamping and engineering factory. Convinced she "would get ringworm and eaten alive by midges" doing farm work, Maimie opted to help manufacture tanks.[68]

Maimie worked on a Keller Die Sinking Machine cutting patterns out of a large piece of steel about the size of a dining room table, to be used for plane or tank parts. She cut two patterns, identical in size, and then placed them together to form a mould. The mould was transported to the forge, where one pattern was put into the top hammer, and the other into the bottom hammer. Workers poured molten steel into the hammers and pressed the steel into the mould. Men helped set up the steel. Cranes — operated by women — were used to move big pieces of steel. Girls sharpened the cutters and they also made rockers, a small piece needed for planes. "It took thirty-two hours to cut rockers," Maimie recollects.[69] "Sometimes a whole week to cut a mould."[70]

Like her Canadian counterparts, she worked shifts, but the similarities end there. Her workweek totalled fifty-four hours over six days, either on days or nights. As the war progressed, labour laws slackened and the factory "could make you work any hours they wanted."[71] While she was used to hard work, she found it "miserable to work the night shift especially from midnight to six a.m."[72] Maimie earned about three pounds a week. However, "the faster you worked," she says, "they paid bonuses."[73]

She wore overalls, as GECO workers did, but there were few other stipulations since she did not work with explosives. She wore her brother's two-piece coveralls. "Easier to use the washroom!" she quips.[74] She donned a cap as well, with no hair showing. "If you leaned forward your hair could get caught."[75] At some point, she recalls upgrading to wooden-soled shoes to protect her feet from sharp steel shavings. There was no protection for her eyes or from the "deafening noise in the forge."[76]

Men badgered the women — they did not think women could do the work. Instead of saying, "Give us the tools, and we'll finish the job," men would call out, "Give us the job and we'll finish the tools."[77] She recalls a particularly bad accident when the top hammer in the forge dropped too fast, dislodging a support pole and impaling a man. Emergency personnel had a hard time getting the injured man into the ambulance.

Remarkably, the pole did not puncture any organs and he survived.

As a young woman, Maimie appreciated the more subtle benefits to being at war in Scotland. Ayr was awash in troops, and Maimie loved to dance. "Loads of eager partners!" she says, smiling.[78] She danced with Englishmen, Irishmen, Australians, New Zealanders, and Americans. She loved the Canadian boys, calling them "lovely boys with lovely manners."[79] John Shearer, in the Signal Corps during the war, attended a dance after demobilizing in 1946, where he met Maimie. They were married two years later, and welcomed their only child, a little girl, in 1949.

While Britain had returned to a time of peace, the debt to its allies kept the nation poor. "Housing was so bad you couldn't find a place to live," Maimie explains.[80] "You put your name in for housing but there was close to a twenty-year wait. In fact, you couldn't even put your name on the waiting list."[81] So, like countless others before them, John and Maimie left their homeland in 1954, looking for a better life in Canada. Today, Maimie, now ninety-two, lives in Toronto, enjoying her time with her family, especially her three grandsons.

"Fireball": Edith Reay-Laidler

Eliza Head was a survivor. She entered the world December 30, 1896, born into the socio-economically depressed eastside of London, England. Two little brothers came along quickly, and tragically, after Eliza's little sister was born when Eliza was four, her mother abandoned the family, leaving her dad to care for his four children on his own. Unable to provide for his family, and knowing the wretched future the girls faced if they stayed in London with him, he gave up Eliza and her sister to live in Dr. Barnardo's Home for Orphans when Eliza was seven and her little sister was just three years old.

Thomas John Barnardo, while training to be a doctor in London, witnessed the abject poverty of homeless children sleeping in the streets and begging for food.[82] Barnardo believed every child, regardless of their social or economic upbringing, was valued, and deserved a chance to reach their potential. In an effort to give these waifs a better life, he started his first "Home" in 1870, at the age of twenty-five.[83] At the time of his death in 1905, Barnardo had affected the lives of more than a

Victims of circumstance, Eliza and her sister lived in a home for orphans, run by Dr. Barnardo in England at the turn of the twentieth century. Dr. Barnardo shipped them to Canada when Eliza was fourteen, where she lived and toiled on three farms over four years. When Eliza turned eighteen she left the farm, changed her name to Edith, and headed to Toronto to work toward a better life. *Courtesy Ronald Reay-Laidler.*

quarter of a million destitute children.[84] About thirty thousand children immigrated to Canada between 1869 and 1939.[85] Sadly, while some were able to better their lives, many suffered abuse at the hands of their "adoptive" families.

Eliza was fourteen when she was sent across the ocean to Canada to live with "foster parents." She, along with the more than four hundred other children aboard the ship, had to earn their way working on farms once they arrived. Eliza lived and toiled for four years on three different farms in Southern Ontario. When she turned eighteen, she turned her back on her sad life, changed her name to Edith, and headed for Toronto.

Edith thought that, as one of Canada's biggest cities, Toronto offered the best chance for a bright future. The Toronto Carpet Company hired her as a weaver. At first, they told her she was too small, but she insisted she could do anything, despite her tiny frame. True to her word, she worked hard and became their head weaver. Each year during Canada's National Exhibition, held at the end of August, Edith would demonstrate weaving to hundreds of thousands of passersby.

Edith met Hector Reay-Laidler while working at the carpet company and they were married in 1921. They raised two girls and a boy, their youngest, Roland, who was born in 1929. When war broke out, Edith, wanting to do her part for the war, started at GECO as it got underway in 1941. At about forty-four years of age, she sneaked in under GECO's upper age limit by one year.

Roland, at the age of twelve, remembers that his mom worked shifts at GECO. She spoke about the tunnels, referring to them as the "underground," but loyal to her oath of secrecy, she did not mention much more.

Times were tough during the war. Roland remembers his mom giving him a quarter to go stand in line at Woodgreen, a social agency nearby, to buy used clothes. Although there was much rationing, they never did without. Roland, even today, marvels at how well his mom managed food and material shortages. He jokingly suggests his mom, a "fireball," probably traded ration coupons amongst her neighbours and GECO friends to take care of her children.

From their home on Main Street, Edith walked to Danforth Avenue, then over to Dawes Road to catch the GECO bus. Roland fondly recalls walking his mom to the bus stop sometimes. In 1942, the family moved to Wheeler Avenue, "down the beach," close to Kew Beach off Queen Street. Committed to her job at GECO, the extra-long commute did little to deter Edith.

Edith's petite stature was a source of fond stories. She was so small she wore a blue one-piece children's snowsuit to work in the frosty winter months.

Edith and her husband Hector, both from England, were proud of their British heritage and instilled that pride in their family. Roland had a shirt he wore during the war that read, "There will always be an England."

Edith's sister had returned to England to settle down when she was still a young woman. Edith visited England as an adult, but Canada had become her home. The sisters shared a cordial but distant friendship. Hector passed away in October 1983; Edith died three days short of her ninety-sixth birthday, on December 27, 1992.

Widow with Five Children: Winifred Stewart

Winifred Dady never shied away from hard work or adventure. Born in 1901 in East Suffolk, England, she joined Britain's Land Army during the Great War. When the war ended, the Women's Branch of the Board of Agriculture and Fisheries awarded Winifred a "Certificate for Farm Work Efficiency," having earned a grade of 95 percent for thatching.

Winifred, then eighteen, along with her sister, sailed to Canada looking for fun. They had a grand plan: see the sights, cross the country to see the Pacific Ocean, and then head home. Winifred got as far as Toronto, where she met a handsome Scottish immigrant, Lockhart Stewart, at a dance, and fell in love. Her sister continued the journey, travelling as far as Vancouver, where she met her future husband.

A milkman with Silverwoods Dairy, Lockhart made Winifred his blushing bride in 1923. They settled in the west end of the city and welcomed five children to their family, but the Depression years hit the family hard and they moved around a lot trying to make rent. Tragically, Lock developed stomach cancer and died in 1940, leaving Winifred a widow with five children to raise, their youngest only a toddler. With Lock's life insurance, she bought a home, but she needed to find a job. Thankfully, there were many wartime positions available. Winifred worked at several wartime factories — Massey Harris, GECO, and D.I.L. in Ajax. Commuting to work was difficult; Winifred rode the Bloor streetcar across the city before meeting up with a bus to travel to GECO, and to D.I.L. in later war years.

Home life was a struggle. Lock's mother moved in to help. Their daughter, Audrey, at fifteen, helped babysit her younger siblings so mom could do shiftwork at GECO. Winifred took in two boarders, Ellen and Zella, from Calgary. They too worked at GECO. Winifred packed powder into fuses at the plant. She was very proud of the work she did to help the war effort. "Mom was proper English," Audrey remembers, "with a stiff upper lip. She did what she had to do."[86]

Winifred's oldest, Roy, joined the RCAF and flew as a mid-upper gunner during the war. He did two tours over Germany, surviving a narrow escape when enemy shrapnel narrowly missed his head. Roy returned home to his mother after the war, but in a tragic twist of fate, died from cancer six years later at the age of thirty-one.

With Canada now at peace, Winifred lost her job. As a single parent, she still needed a steady income; she found a job at Steadman's, a department store. Tragically, cancer would enter Winifred's life a third time, touching her personally when she developed cancer of the breast. While she lived another twelve years, the cancer returned and Winifred died in 1959.

D.I.L. Gal: Rena Sweetman

Rena Sweetman answered an advertisement for war work in 1941 at the age of nineteen, keen to earn money to help support her widowed mother and eleven siblings. Rena applied for work at the brand new shell-filling plant in Ajax, operated by D.I.L, a "sister" plant to GECO.

There were many similarities between work at GECO and D.I.L. Like GECO, D.I.L. used special buses to transport employees. A bus picked Rena up at Danforth and Coxwell Avenues — one of GECO's bus stops — and transported her, along with her co-workers, out to Ajax. However, the buses dropped them off directly at their workshop. The building housed everything the women needed for their shift, from change rooms to a café. Rena remembers being warned not to tell anyone where she worked or what she did.

D.I.L. employees wore a uniform similar to the clothing supplied at GECO, but theirs were grey and one-piece with navy blue turbans. However, unlike GECO, Rena recalls women not being allowed to keep on their brassieres or underwear. She had to strip down to the nude and walk naked a fair distance before she could don her jumpsuit. This practice was particularly awkward and uncomfortable for Rena and her workmates.

Rena worked at long tables set up as an assembly line. As small shells passed by, she put a marking on them. In another position she held at the plant, she worked with white powder under a glass while sitting at an enclosed cubicle, very similar to work done at GECO. However, unlike GECO, she had to wear a mask that covered her nose and mouth completely. In her naïveté, she did not realize the powder she handled had the potential to blow up her and her shop mates.

D.I.L. supervisors were strict but nice, and came from England since there was no one with munitions expertise in Canada at the time. Women were not permitted to talk while they worked — no singing either. She remembers being paid well. "It was wonderful," she said "I could go out and buy a new dress."[87]

Rena married Ross O'Hagan on November 28, 1941, shortly after starting at the plant. Ross was in the service but he got sick with pneumonia and pleurisy, lost most of one lung, and was discharged. Shortly after they were married, Rena and Ross moved into the barracks at the Malton Airfield. Rena received a wonderful Christmas present that first year: within a month of her wedding day, Rena learned she was pregnant. Fortunately, babies and high explosives did not mix. When she informed her supervisor at D.I.L., she was dismissed the same day. Her firstborn, a son, Barry, was born September 27, 1942. Three more little ones would arrive in the ensuing years, two within two years of the war ending. Her youngest, "the only planned one," Rena explains with a twinkle in her eye, was born almost a decade later in 1956.[88] Barry recalls their days living at the Malton Airfield. "We ran around every day getting dirty like little street urchins," he says with a wistful smile.[89] Rena and Ross lived at Malton until after the birth of their third child, and then they bought a house in the Avenue Road and Lawrence Avenue area of Toronto in 1949.

Ross had a long career working with Rogers Radio, in his nursery/florist business, and in real estate brokerage businesses. He died in 1983 at the age of sixty-four.

Rena, loving grandmother to eighteen and great-grandmother to eight, passed away in June 2013 at the age of ninety-one. While Rena's days at D.I.L. were short, she did her part in helping to get ammunition into the hands of fighting men overseas.

Bench Leader: Norma Turner

Norma McGregor was born in Belfast, Northern Ireland, in 1918, but immigrated to Canada in 1924 with her mom and dad after the Irish Rebellion. Despite the Great Depression setting in, her dad, George, was fiercely proud that as a relief streetcar driver, he could support his family without asking for a handout. Norma grew up around Danforth Avenue and Dawes Road. During her final year of high school, she found a retail job for the Christmas season, earning seven to eight dollars a week. Coming from humble roots, and enjoying the pleasure of a little money in her pocket, she did not return to school in the New Year.

Norma worked for a few years before Canada went to war. She met her first husband, getting married in 1940. In the fall of 1941, as a young, married woman, she learned of a wartime plant opening in Scarboro. The starting salary of thirty-two and a half cents an hour was double her current salary. Like so many others, she was eager to take the lucrative job at GECO, where starting pay was $16 per week.

Norma's daughter, Victoria, remembers her mom telling her family she had to replace the metal clasps in her brassieres with buttons while at GECO to lessen the chance of causing a spark, and she had to touch a metal plate at the entrance to her filling workshop to remove all static electricity before going in.

During Norma's tenure at GECO she was promoted to bench leader. She supervised six other women who packed tetryl powder into detonators — highly dangerous work. The operators filled the detonators through protective glass to shield them from tetryl dust wafting up into their nostrils and faces and to provide some protection should an explosion occur.

On a humorous note, Victoria recalls her mom complaining mildly to her family about a small but significant detail regarding the plant site. The sprawling factory was built on slightly rolling farmland gently rising from the shores of Lake Ontario. Every time she made the long walk to and from her shop, she felt as if she "was always walking uphill."[90]

Norma also spoke about the adventures she had with her workmates catching the "rattling old bus" at Dawes Road and Danforth Avenue. It seems it broke down a lot. One night the women had to get out and help push the bus up the hill on Dawes Road, where the Walter Massey Farm was situated. In another more lucrative adventure, Norma was able to save enough money at GECO to buy her first car, a 1935 Ford, even though she did not have a driver's licence. The car stayed up on blocks during the war years due to rationing of gas and rubber. In addition to a new car, Norma saved $500 to help her parents buy a house that would stay in the family to present day.

Norma worked at GECO from 1941 to 1943. Her family speculates she left after learning she was pregnant. Sadly, her firstborn, a baby boy, died at birth. A beautiful little girl came along a year later, but regrettably, Norma's marriage failed. She moved back home to raise her little girl with her parents' help.

Her brother, who served in the Royal Canadian Navy and was a bachelor about town, brought home a friend a few years later who had served in the North Africa British Army Royal Engineers during the war. Richard Drake had drilled drinking wells to provide water for troops as they made their way through North Africa. He immigrated to Canada after the war as part of the "Drew Plan" — devised by Ontario premier George Drew, this plan brought ten thousand British immigrants to Canada. Richard met Norma at her parents' cottage on Wagner's Lake north of Uxbridge, Ontario, which they fondly called "Glocca Morra." Norma was on the dock when she was introduced to Richard, who promptly tossed her into the lake. She couldn't swim. She was not pleased but her mom told her to "give the poor boy a chance." Richard and Norma married in November 1953, settled in Port Credit, Ontario, and Richard went to work as a plumber. Life was good. They added two more lovely girls to the family.

Tragically, heartache would strike the family again, when, in 1960, at the age of forty-three, Richard suffered a brain aneurism. He survived risky surgery but became disabled and had to move into long-term care at Sunnybrook Hospital's new Veterans' unit. Norma returned to work and moved back home with her mom and dad to raise her three girls.

Maria, Norma's mom, died in 1966. She left the home her daughter helped buy, located just north of Danforth Avenue, to Norma. Norma lived a long life and died in 2009. Victoria, her daughter, resides in the family home today.

In an interesting GECO connection, Norma's brother, a pilot officer during the war, trained, before heading overseas, at both Malton and Fingal, two of GECO's former wartime endeavours.

"I Want to Work with Munitions": Anne Wilmot

Anne Wilmot was born in 1915 in Montreal, Quebec, shortly after her parents and two siblings moved from their homeland, Jamaica. As a pre-schooler, Anne and her family moved again, this time to Toronto, and settled in the Parkdale area, just west of the Dufferin Gates of the Canadian National Exhibition. She attended Queen Victoria School as a child and then took a four-year high-school course in secretarial studies at Western Technical and Commercial School near High Park, specializing in legal practices. When war broke out many of her friends and colleagues signed up for war work, either close to home at John Inglis, where guns were made, or in the far reaches of Scarboro, where a munitions plant was being built.

Anne had heard about people who worked at GECO, that they had been sworn to secrecy. "No one knew anything about GECO," Anne said.[91] "GECO was really looking for people, and out of curiosity, I applied as a war worker, not a secretary."[92] Given Anne's excellent secretarial skills, management wanted Anne to work in administration. "They didn't think I would want to work on the line," she said, "but I wanted to work in war work, with the munitions."[93]

A sense of pride still resonates when Anne, now ninety-seven, speaks about her time at GECO. "I worked for General Engineering, a well-known firm not just created for the war. I had to swear my allegiance," she said.[94] "You were sworn to silence because of secrecy during the war."[95]

She remembers riding the GECO buses, being dropped off at the front door, showing her pass at the guardhouse, heading to the change house where they donned 100 percent white cotton two-piece uniforms with buttons along the shoulder and down one side. She recalls the turbans they wore, and the special shoes. "You couldn't have any metal on you at all. They were smart uniforms," she said.[96] "We had to strip down to our underwear, which had to be cotton."[97] Thin cotton undergarments did not offer much warmth against Canada's harsh winters. "But we stuck it out," Anne said.[98] "I remember the Timothy Eaton Company was the only place the girls could buy cotton brassieres."[99] She also recalls her wages: "I made forty-nine cents an hour," she claimed proudly.[100]

Anne worked on the H.E. side of the plant, filling No. 119 fuses. She was aware of the strategy of the spacing between buildings. "There was enough space that if one shop blew up it wouldn't affect other shops."[101] It was a sombre admission for a new employee. In fact, just two days after she started, during her one-week introduction period, there was an explosion in one of the shops. "No one was hurt," Anne said, thankfully.[102] Undeterred, Anne worked at GECO, faithfully filling 119s until the war ended, and only a skeleton staff remained at GECO.

Anne worked with tetryl powder. As a young black woman, the explosive powder turned her skin orange, not yellow, like those with fairer skin. "My fingernails turned orange," she said, "and the bottoms of my

Anne Parkin (née Wilmot) with nephew Brian Roberts in 2009. Although Anne had excellent secretarial skills and would have been an asset to GECO's administration, she wanted to do her part for the Allied war effort and asked to work with munitions. She worked with tetryl, a dangerous high explosive that turned her skin orange. *Courtesy of Brian Roberts.*

feet and the palms of my hands. You had to be careful or you'd get a rash."[103] Anne did get tetryl rash once, but it cleared before long. Some women suffered more. "You could get a horrific rash."[104]

To Anne, GECO was a big place, filled with dedicated people wanting to do their bit for the war. "There were nationalities of all kinds at GECO," she said.[105] She said she was accepted readily and felt no discrimination.

When asked, "Where do you work?" Anne answered simply, "I'm doing war work."[106]

After the war, Anne moved to Vancouver and worked for a family friend in his burgeoning law practice. Anne met and married Al Parkin, and while she had no children of her own, she became stepmother to Al's daughter. Today, Anne continues to reside in British Columbia.

Anne's nephew Brian says of his aunt, "Anne is a selfless person caring more for another person instead of herself. If there is a place last in line Anne would be glad to take it. That is her nature. She is my favourite aunt."[107]

"Shamed Be He Who Thinks Evil of It": Roxaline Wood

When Canada went to war in 1939, Walter and Roxaline Wood and family lived in the back of the blacksmith's shop situated on the northwest corner of Pharmacy and Lawrence Avenues in Scarboro. The Canadian government mandated that war workers take the bus to work. Since local bus service ended at Danforth Avenue in the early 1940s, the government apportioned gas tickets to Roxaline's neighbour so he, another GECO employee, could drive her to and from the plant.

Roxaline, like GECOite Carol LeCappelain, worked as a government inspector at the munitions plant, ensuring top quality ammunition for the Allied forces. Her son, Bruce, "Bob" to family and friends, joined the Royal Canadian Air Force when he came of age, and flew over one hundred missions in the fight to end the war in Europe.

Roxaline's son Ron remembers the big snowstorm in December 1944. When they woke the morning after the storm, he had to help dig out their '42 Ford, which had been buried completely in huge snowdrifts, so that his dad, Walter, could get to work.

When the war ended, the Inspection Board of the United Kingdom and Canada issued a card recognizing Roxaline's dedicated service. The card displayed a crest with the phrase, "HONI - SOIT - QUI - MAL - Y - PENSE" or "Shamed be he who thinks evil of it." Controller General, Major General G.D. Howe, signed it.

The card read:

> This is to Certify that Mrs. Roxiline [*sic*] Wood served as an employee of this Board from 11-7-42 to 8-6-45 and was engaged in duties directly connected with the Inspection of War Materials for the Armed Forces.[108]

Ron was too young to work at GECO filling munitions; however, as a firefighter for the Scarborough Fire Department in his adult years, he did "work" at GECO, battling a blaze that broke out in one of the old buildings off Sinnott Road. Ron also spent the latter half of his firefighting career in the Training Division. He enjoyed taking rookie firefighters down into the old GECO tunnels to teach them how to manage a fire "if ever one broke out."[109] Ron enjoyed a thirty-one-year career with Scarborough's fire department, retiring prior to their amalgamation with Toronto.

Walter Wood, the youngest of twelve children, passed away in 1986 at the age of ninety-two. Roxaline, a sister to eleven siblings, lived to ninety-two years of age as well, and passed away in 2000.

Bomb Boys
On the Dirty Side
Someone's Got to Pay the Bills: William Howe

Classified as "C1" due to vision problems, William "Bill" Howe thought he would not be recruited into active service. His father had fought in the trenches at Passchendaele during the Great War. Bill understood all too well the horrors of war. Nevertheless, as luck would have it, he received a call-up notice in 1942, at the age of nineteen, with his classification jumping from C1 to A3. He had a choice: enlist in the armed forces or work in a war plant. Not wanting to relive his father's First World War experience, he chose GECO, joining Accounts Payable for nine dollars a week in the administration building.

Because Bill worked in administration, he did not see the clean side. "I saw nothing to do with the actual filling of fuses. I never got down to the bottom end of the plant," he says.[110] "It was a city unto itself."[111] He knew about the tunnel system but did not see it. He did see women with yellowed hands and "towels (turbans) around their heads."[112]

Running a top-secret government-owned munitions plant came with its own set of headaches. Bill remembers the year he spent at GECO as "a real rat race. I sat down at a desk," he recalls, "with bills to pay with a whole bunch of invoices. I had to sort through them. It was hit and miss with no real bookkeeping. We sometimes paid bills twice. There were boxes and boxes of material and receipts."[113] Around a half-dozen employees worked with Bill in A/P. "We couldn't pay a bill unless you had an MRR (Material Received Report) attached to it. Then it was okayed for payment and went to Checks to be paid."[114] On the weekends, Bill, along with a colleague, worked on improving the A/P system at GECO.

Bill enjoyed GECO's extra-curricular activities, playing softball with the "Operating Stores" team. "We had a really good time there. It was a picnic."[115] In fact, his interest in the finer things at GECO almost got the young accountant fired. He dated a fellow GECOite a few times, and when she needed a drive to the airport, Bill left work to help. "I got in trouble," he says.[116] "It got around that I might be fired."[117] So he hastily looked for another job, and found one at R.E.L. — Research Enterprises Limited — starting at $18 a week — double his GECO wages. "I quit before they could fire me."[118] Did his dedication to the young lady pay off? Apparently, Bill never heard from her again.

In March 1944, Bill was called up again, the need for fighting men now desperate. "No bloody way I'm going into the army," Bill said at the time.[119] The Canadian Army had other plans. He had no choice but to enlist and do basic training. He was sent to Halifax, Nova Scotia, to prepare to ship out. Getting out of fighting did not look good, but Bill had a friend who worked on the Draft Board and told him he "could go anywhere." So Bill was assigned to HMCS *Niobe* in Greenock, Scotland, then to Portsmouth, and then to Northern Ireland. The most action Bill saw occurred when he and a pal were caught wearing their military uniforms — a treasonable offence — in Ireland, a neutral country during the war. The police swiftly shipped them back to Northern Ireland.

Bill was on leave in Canada when the war ended. In 1954, he married Marie, a family friend, and raised a family of four. He enjoyed a long, successful career with Canada Customs. Bill passed away in May 2013, in his ninetieth year, and is survived by his wife, Marie, children, and grandchildren.

"Piston Packin' Moma": Donald John "D.J." MacDonald

Some personal stories of GECO employees tug at the heartstrings more than others. Donald John MacDonald's story will tug a little harder than most.

"D.J." was born April 7, 1911, in Hillside, Cape Breton, Nova Scotia. At the tender age of just three, he was given up by his parents. Unable to care for him, they gave him to his grandparents, who took him in and raised him. Sadly, he never returned home. "His own brothers and sisters didn't even know him," D.J.'s son Phillip says.[120]

Despite dealing with a profound sense of loss and abandonment as a small child, D.J. managed to grow up, marry, and have a large family of his own. Tragically, his namesake, little Donald Francis, died from muscular dystrophy when he was just a toddler.

D.J. established himself in the construction industry on the East Coast in the 1930s. When Canada went to war, he heard about work in Ontario and moved west to help build a wartime munitions plant, situated in Scarboro. He asked his close friend, native Ontarian Joe Sullivan, to join him. After construction was completed, D.J. stayed on at GECO as manager for mechanical services and as master mechanic. "He was in charge," his son Stanley writes in a letter about his dad, "of what might be referred to as 'rolling stock.'"[121] D.J. was also manager for transportation services. This once-rejected little boy had been given the honour of overseeing GECO's massive fleet of vehicles. His friend Joe would become foreman for the Trucking Department.[122]

D.J. helped design and build GECO's famous "Blue Goose," a big blue twelve-passenger station wagon "He had the capacity to cut down cars that were no good," Phillip recalls, "weld them together and put them on a frame, like a stretch limo."[123]

GECO's "Blue Goose." *Courtesy of Stanley MacDonald.*

Stanley agrees. "It was lengthened by cutting it in two, and inserting the two rear-passenger car sections, between the two pieces, thus making it a twelve-passenger car."[124]

In addition to the Blue Goose, D.J. and his team built munitions trucks, ambulances, fire trucks, and taxis at GECO, including Station Wagon No. 28, affectionately dubbed "Piston Packin' Moma" by the mechanics. Decades later Phillip wonders aloud what became of his father's fleet.

After the war ended, D.J. went to work for Standard Paving, taking "a bunch of GECOites with him," Phillip says.[125] Later on, he and some of his friends worked at his own company, MacDonald Construction, on Kennedy Road in Scarborough. His company constructed roads and

Pictured here with his department staff, Donald John MacDonald (front row, middle), manager of Mechanical Services and master mechanic, oversaw GECO's massive fleet of vehicles. *Courtesy of Phillip MacDonald.*

other structures in Ontario, including most of Highway No. 7, north of the city.

"He asked a lot from his guys, but if you put in a day's work, you got paid for it. If the sun was shining, they were out working. They worked long hours in the summer time."[126] Was he a good father? "He was fair and patient," Phillip says.[127] "'No' meant 'no' but I don't remember getting punished." He recalls fondly, "Our backyard was a construction playground."[128]

Donald John MacDonald passed away at the age of eighty-one on Remembrance Day 1992 while undergoing heart surgery.

Keep on Truckin': Joe Sullivan

James Joseph Sullivan, familiarly known as Joe, entered the world on October 6, 1910, at the family's two-hundred-acre farm in Dornoch, Ontario, a small town south of Owen Sound. Joe originally envisioned a career in ministry as a young adult, but after the early death of his father, he left the seminary and moved to Nova Scotia to try his hand at construction. He helped build Sydney Airport during the 1930s. His sweetheart, Grace Irene, followed him to Nova Scotia, where they were married in 1934. Kerry, their firstborn, arrived the next year. Two more children would follow in close succession. Family history suggests that during this time in Joe's career, he met and established a close lifelong friendship with Nova Scotian Donald John (D.J.) MacDonald, who worked for the same construction company.

When Canada declared war on Germany, Joe was too old to go overseas. His friend D.J. headed to Ontario to help build a munitions plant in Scarboro. Joe soon followed, packing up his young family in their '37 Chevrolet and moving back to his home province. "Dad's way of helping [in the war] was working in the munitions plant," Kerry, Joe's eldest son, said.[129] "Dad went from driving a field truck at Standard Paving to being in management at GECO," Jim, Joe's youngest son, added.[130] "It was quite a change going from equipment operator to running a staff."[131]

Joe Sullivan managed GECO's large fleet of more than thirty vehicles.[132] As foreman and chief despatcher for the Trucking Department, he reported directly to his friend D.J. MacDonald. Joe's responsibilities included managing his driving staff and keeping the fleet in good working order, not an easy task given the material shortages and rationing in place at the time. By 1944, G.E.C.O.'s trucks' odomoters had registered 620,000 miles in total; the fleet had hauled more than seventeen hundred tons of product every month. Chief Dispatcher Joe Sullivan and his truckers brought a whole new meaning to the phrase pass the ammunition.

Joe and D.J.'s professional relationship extended after the war, and included management of an Imperial Oil gas station together. However, "Dad got out of the gas station business," Kerry recalled, "because the lease went up each time they made a little money."[133] Joe and Grace expanded their family after the war, bringing James — "Jim" — into the fold in 1949.

Eventually both Joe and D.J. set out on their own, going back into construction. Joe started his own construction company, MacDonald-Sullivan Construction, with a colleague, coincidentally named MacDonald. "He did very well," Jim said, "but then he took sick."[134] Joe Sullivan developed a heart condition and passed away tragically in 1956 at the age of forty-five. "The night before he died," Jim recalled, "he said he'd play ball with me the next day." He paused. "He was dead in the morning."[135]

"We had a 'Father Knows Best' family," Jim says.[136] "We were four kids together; a happy, stable family."[137]

A Name Couldn't Sound Any Sweeter: Alex Licorice Waddell

Born in 1886 in Scotland, Alexander Licorice Waddell became a carpenter's apprentice as a lad of twelve. After the tragic death of his older brother, Alex left Scotland and sailed to New York. He found work at Coney Island, and helped build John D. Rockefeller's residence near New York City. He then moved to Schenectady, New York, to join a large population of Scottish kinfolk who had settled there during the First World War. Alex attended a baseball game where an errant baseball hit a spectator. He rushed to see if the woman was injured. Remarkably, the woman was Bessie, his dead brother's girlfriend who had left Scotland years earlier.

A quick romance ensued and Alex and Bessie married. They immigrated to Canada and started their family, bringing three children into the world. Alex made his livelihood as a joiner carpenter, helping to build several prominent buildings in Toronto, including Maple Leaf Gardens, which opened in 1931. Unfortunately, construction of Maple Leaf Gardens was the last steady work Alex had during the Depression era, and he had to take odd jobs to support his family. At Christmas, he built homemade toys in his basement workshop. "He was just like Santa's elves," John, Alex's son, recalls.[138] "We always had a Christmas. We never went hungry."[139]

Alex heard about a munitions plant under construction in the spring of 1941 and eagerly joined GECO's ranks as a construction worker, always dressed in a crisp white shirt and bow tie. "My dad went to work each day with his lunch pail," John remembers.[140] "He always looked like he was going to the office even though he was just a carpenter."[141]

Once construction of GECO was completed, seventy-five older men who boasted 2,300 years of combined construction experience, stayed on in GECO's carpentry shops housed in Building Nos. 8 and 142.[142] Under the direction of Mr. Bob Blair, these talented men built everything from wooden crates, in which ammunition would be stored, to fine desk furniture for GECO administration personnel.[143]

Mr. Waddell stayed on as a member of the sawdust brigade. His mandate was to ensure GECO ran smoothly. He did everything from installing and repairing complicated assembly line parts to assembling crude crates that would house filled fuses for shipment. Alex respected the oath of secrecy he took and did not talk about his work, although John remembers his dad commenting about building the wooden munitions boxes — perhaps a trivial, tedious task to the casual observer, but every job at GECO was critical to ultimate victory. Fuse crates, poorly constructed, had the potential to fall apart, destabilizing the filled fuses housed within, and triggering deadly explosions. Alex was so dedicated to war work that on weekends he and other men helped out at the D.I.L. plant in Ajax. "As far as I can remember," John says, "Dad never took a day off."[144]

Alex was among the first round of layoffs that occurred at the end of May 1945 after Germany capitulated. He received a personal letter of recommendation from GECO president Robert Hamilton. After Alex left GECO, he went on to help build Sunnybrook Hospital and the T. Eaton warehouse north of the city. He became a construction foreman and was never out of work again.

"He laid down his tools at seventy-six," John says, over sixty-five years after his dad first became a young apprentice in Scotland. Six years later,[145] Alex died at the age of eighty-two. His beloved Bessie died ten days later.

On the Clean Side
It's a Bust: Harold Pfeiffer

Harold Pfeiffer, born in Quebec City in 1908, joined GECO late in 1941 to work in the I.G. X-ray Department.[146] By the time "Hal" passed through GECO's gates, he had made a name for himself as a sculptor in clay, metal ware, and in weaving; very different from his first carvings made in blackboard chalk in school.[147] Harold had had a few public exhibitions of his work, including a large portrait bust of the late Canadian Arctic explorer Captain Bernier.[148] When the war broke out, Harold enlisted but failed the medical exam.[149] Wanting to do his bit, he worked at the munitions plant in Valcartier, Quebec, and then moved to Toronto to offer his services at GECO.[150] "As our work was very dangerous," wrote Harold in his autobiography, "handling amatol and tetryl and other extremely volatile explosives, everyone had to wear jump-suits with buttons down the sides to minimize the risk of friction and sparks. A spark could end it for all of us."[151]

A retiring sort of fellow, Hal tried to keep his artistic accomplishments to himself, but an anonymous letter arrived at the editorial desk of Ross Davis, and when challenged, Hal was left with little choice but to admit modestly that he had done some modelling in clay.[152] Management was so impressed with his talent, they asked Hal to sculpt a bust, capturing the epitome of "Woman War Worker." He chose as his subject Mrs. Peggy MacKay of Shop 35B.[153] "Among the employees, there were many terribly sad stories, but this was almost inconceivably tragic."[154]

Harold started to exhibit troubling respiratory symptoms due to an allergic reaction to ragweed that grew in the countryside of Scarboro,

and from exposure to tetryl.[155] With GECO medical staff's encouragement, he left his position. Harold went on to teach arts and crafts and
interior design at several schools.[156] In 1956, he became a cataloguer in
Canada's National Museum of Man.[157] He made trips to the Arctic and
sculpted portraits of prominent Aboriginal and Inuit people.[158] He also
travelled around the world, sculpting many famous subjects, including
the Bishop Desmond Tutu.[159] Harold's memoir was published six months
after his death in 1997, entitled *The Man Who Makes Heads With His
Hands: The Art and Life of Harold Pfeiffer, Sculptor.*[160]

A Long Road to Peace: Ernest Herbert Pickles

Ernest Pickles, born in 1925, was thirteen when Canada entered the
Second World War. His childhood was typical, he attended Eastern
Commerce high school and kept two paper routes to earn some pocket
money. All that changed in 1943, when, at the age of seventeen, Ernie
spotted a GECO employment ad in the paper and discovered he could
earn a lot more money handling explosives.

The trek to GECO was arduous. Living at Greenwood Avenue and
Gerrard Street at the time, Ernie took the Gerrard streetcar to Coxwell
Avenue where he boarded the streetcar to Danforth Avenue. From there,
he got on the Danforth car to Dawes Road where he boarded the GECO
bus. "I didn't have the slightest idea where this plant was," he recalls.[161] "I
got on a bus at Dawes Road and it took us out to the country and then
the plant appeared. Anything north of Danforth was like farmland."[162]

Ernie worked at GECO on the high explosives side of the plant during
the summer that year. He wore soft shoes with leather soles. "They were
more like a slipper than a shoe," he says.[163] Men "had to strip down to
nothing in the change room."[164] Then they donned work overalls and
moved to the clean side. Ernie worked at the end of the line in a workshop where women filled fuses used in anti-aircraft military hardware,
such as fuse 251 used in 40-mm Bofors guns. "In the workshop were two
production lines," Ernie recalls, "consisting of eight stations. The first
person on the line started the process by doing the initial work and placing the fuse in a slot in a tray of about fifty slots. Whe[n] the tray was
filled she passed it to the next person in line. With the work tray on the

right she would add her piece to the fuse and then transfer it to a[n] empty tray on her left until all slots were filled and she transferred it to the next station."[165]

Ernie placed a fuse in a large iron box where he tightened its parts with a clamp to ensure they would not come loose. He then transferred the fuse to a second iron box specially designed with an etching device inside. Ernie scored three marks on each fuse to prevent loosening.[166] He took his work seriously. "I didn't want the guy on the front having his fuse falling apart."[167] Workers then placed the fuses in trays. Finished fuses were put on a dolly. "Older men would take them away."[168] Ernie's workshop filled ten thousand fuses in an eight-hour shift. Dangerous working condition didn't bother Ernie, although he was cognizant of the three-foot-high firewalls separating the building's workshops for protection should an explosion occur.

During his two ten-minute breaks on shift, Ernie and his shop mates sat on the floor outside the workshop. "The women told the dirtiest stories to try to embarrass the boys," he recalls, smiling.[169] "My mother would never tell those stories."[170]

"I had a good time there," he says.[171]

In August 1944, Ernie enlisted. The air force and the navy were not accepting applications. Infantry was his only option. He trained and was prepared to ship out on December 13, but the infamous snowstorm hit Toronto and he left the next day, his nineteenth birthday. Ernie fought in Germany and Holland during the last desperate, brutal days of war. The mission was to reach Wilhelmshaven, a German naval port. "Towards the end we walked twenty or thirty miles a day," Ernie recalls.[172] The war ended while they were still outside Oldenburg, before they achieved their objective.

When the war ended, Ernie came home and enjoyed a thirty-five-year career with Gulf Oil. He met his wife, Gwyn, at a YMCA dance in 1952. They married in 1954, bought their first home a year later in the Brimley and Lawrence area of Scarborough, and raised two children.

All in the Family

Mother- and Daughter-in-Law: Hilda and Dorothy Clements

As the war progressed, management relaxed its age restrictions. Mrs. Hilda Clements, at fifty-one years of age, signed up to work at GECO. A mother to five children, Hilda's four sons enlisted in the Royal Canadian Navy during the war, her youngest signing up when he was just sixteen years of age. With four boys in active service, Hilda worked tirelessly at GECO, doing everything she could to help bring her boys safely home.

Hilda's third son, Harold, born in 1918, married Dorothy Horler in May 1942, just before he went off to serve his country. Newlywed Dorothy Clements, twenty-one, went to work at GECO shortly after, joining her mother-in-law. Dorothy worked at GECO until she found out she was pregnant late in 1943. A pregnant woman could not work with high explosives, if for no other reason than for endangering the mother and her workmates to accommodate her growing girth.

Harold trained with the Naval Shore Patrol. Stationed at HMCS *Shelburne* on the eastern shore of Shelburne Harbour in Nova Scotia, he patrolled the Canadian coastline. His and Dorothy's first child, a little girl, Sharon, arrived in May 1944. Dorothy had a difficult time finding a baby carriage due to a shortage of steel.

Hilda worked faithfully at GECO until the war ended. Thankfully, her four sons all returned home safely. Harold and Dorothy added a son to their family in 1946. In peacetime, Harold had a varied career, working for National Cash Register (NCR), as well as for a real estate firm, and as a personal chauffeur for a wealthy gentleman. Hilda passed away in 1979; Dorothy followed her mother-in-law ten years later. Harold died in 1999.

The Darnbrough Way: Walter and His Girls

Corporal Walter Darnbrough epitomized bravery, survival, and a true war hero. Born in 1894 in Leeds, England, Walter, the second youngest of seven children, was a victim of circumstance. Walter lost his father to consumption when he was only four. His mom died of dropsy (edema) and a tumour when he was twelve. His older sister was the only family member who earned an income — a meagre livelihood working as a domestic servant. Within a year of his mom's death, Walter's grandmother begged Dr. Barnardo's Home for Orphans to take in Walter and his brothers. Like GECOite Edith Reay-Laidler, Walter became a Barnardo Child.

A year after entering the orphanage, he was shipped to Canada and made to earn his keep on a Saskatchewan farm. His brothers joined him the following year. The boys' sponsoring family treated them like hired hands and made them live in a shack attached to the house. Harsh, bitter Canadian winters on the prairie were especially hard to bear. The boys, familiar with suffering, stayed only until they could get a plan together to run away. By 1914, Walter had found his way to Jones Avenue in Toronto.

War broke out and Walter joined Canada in the fight. Lance Corporal Walter Darnbrough was a Royal Canadian Dragoon and shipped overseas in October 1914. He was with the 7th Calvary Field Ambulance and was assigned as an outrider, someone who escorted ambulances carrying the wounded away from battle. During a brutal battle at Le Cateau, France, cannon fire hit an ambulance Walter was accompanying and the driver and horse were killed instantly. Walter, with shells bursting around him, unhooked the dead horse from the ambulance, fastened his own horse, collected the wounded, and led them safely off the battlefield. Walter received a Medal of Bravery for his heroism.

Walter met and married a young lady named Florence — ironically, with a very similar last name, Darnborough — while stationed in England during the war. Their firstborn, Mary, arrived in 1918. Walter stayed in England with his family until the spring of 1921, when with two little ones now part of their clan, and another on the way, they sailed for Canada under much happier circumstances from Walter's first voyage to the New World. Florence Irene, nicknamed Rene, arrived in August 1921, shortly after their arrival in Toronto. Finally, Walter looked to his future with hope.

Tragically, his hope would be short-lived. While Florence eventually would give birth to thirteen children, five would be stillborn. On May 13, 1931, their eldest, Mary, at the age of thirteen, died from a ruptured appendix. The Depression years were unkind to the Darnbrough family.

As a result of being gassed by the Germans during the First World War, Walter spent time at a sanatorium. His family, left to survive on government relief, struggled.

When Canada declared war for the second time, Walter enlisted again, but he was discharged only three months later in December 1939 due to fragile health sustained in the First World War. His granddaughter Sue said her grandfather believed in "King and Country and would have continued to fight had he not been medically discharged."

The Allied forces lost a good man; GECO reaped the benefit of that loss. Walter joined the ranks of GECO and did various jobs there, including filling detonators. He quickly realized his co-workers were nervous because, should anyone accidentally drop a detonator onto the floor, they might, as Walter would say, "blow their legs off."[173] Walter recommended, through the plant's suggestion program, that management supply the workshops with straw mats so that if a detonator should fall, it would bounce safely instead of potentially exploding. Walter received

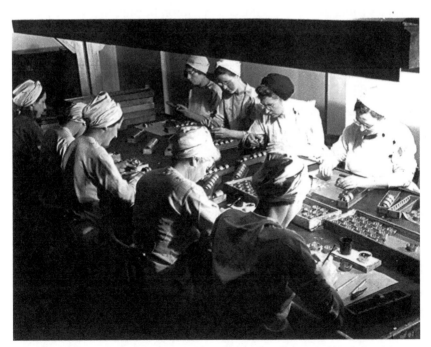

Irene Darnbrough and her shop mates filling detonators. *Courtesy of Linda Petsinis.*

a $40 Victory Bond for his suggestion — more than two weeks' wages. More importantly, workshops were outfitted with mats.

For the Darnbrough family, GECO was a family affair. Two of Walter's children, Rene and another daughter, also worked at GECO. Rene packed explosive powder into detonators. She likely was very happy when the straw mats were installed in her workshop thanks to her dad's suggestion. Rene earned thirty-five cents an hour like her dad, and rode a bus to work, but as a twenty-year-old woman, Rene would meet up with her girlfriends regularly for a beer at the Danforth Hotel before they headed to work. Money was tight. "Mom and her friends often would walk through Pine Hills Cemetery on their way home from work," her daughter Sue said.[174] "Because no one had any money to buy extra things at that time, they would check the area where the caretakers would throw out the old flowers from the graves, and they would gather the ribbons from them for their hair."[175]

After the war, Rene, like many women her age, got married and settled down to raise a family.

Walter ended his time at GECO as a janitor, helping to give the plant a reputation for being meticulously clean. After the war, he worked for the Scarboro Township as a sewer inspector. "He was a strict inspector who insisted that the work be done properly," Sue said.[176] "The workers used to say, 'Better do it the Darnbrough way.'"[177] After Walter retired, a street was named in his honour. Darnborough Way can be found off Birchmount Road, north of Finch Avenue, in Scarborough's north end — a long-lasting tribute to a valiant man who was fiercely devoted to his country.

General Delivery: John Everest and Family

John Everest's family emigrated from England in 1863, settling in the quaint farming village of Scarboro, Ontario. In 1896, prominent resident Bob Bell purchased a store on St. Clair Avenue, east of Kennedy Road, which would become Everest & Sons General Store. The Everest family's store served the surrounding farms, and grew into a bustling business that made deliveries with three horses and wagons.

In 1939 Canada went to war, and eighteen months later excavation started on expropriated farmland located just northwest of their store for a sprawling munitions plant. The Everest family was given the unique opportunity to do their part for the war effort by delivering supplies and provisions to GECO. John remembers delivering sacks of potatoes to the military site. He still recalls one time when they arrived at GECO's main gated entrance on Eglinton Avenue and he hopped out of the truck, expecting to unload the potatoes. "I would have been around twelve to fourteen at the time," he said.[178] "Security was very effective — I was ordered back to the truck."[179] John, no matter how curious, was prohibited from stepping through the barbed-wire gates.

By the time John joined the family business in 1948, his family owned four trucks and delivered everything from milk and bread to seed and basic hardware, making several hundred deliveries per week. Everest Grocers evolved post war, eventually turning into a Pro Hardware store, with John at the helm. John married and had two children, and his son helped in the store until John retired and closed the business in 2002. "I couldn't keep up with the big box stores," he said.[180] Ironically, these big box stores were built next to the old GECO plant where he'd delivered potatoes sixty years earlier.

Today, John lives with his wife in south Scarborough and maintains a local archive in St. Paul's United Church, commemorating the Scarboro Junction of which GECO was a part. As a lasting tribute, in September 2014 muralist Mitchell Lanecki painted a mural on St. Clair Ave. east of Warden Ave., to commemorate the Everest family store and the Junction.

Truck 'Em and Fill 'Em: Sidney Ledson and Family
Sidney Ledson worked at GECO for about nine months in 1942, before he was old enough to enlist. He joined as a "trucker," responsible for the delicate transportation of skids of munitions around the plant, including empty and filled primers, timers, fuses, bomb components, and tracers. Sometimes his job included the precarious and potentially perilous undertaking of stacking trays of explosives one on top of another on a skid. Even the smallest misstep could have meant a deadly detonation. Sidney worked exclusively on the gunpowder side of the plant. "I got around quite a bit on the clean side," he said.[181]

Sidney has many memories of his short time at GECO. He recalls taking the bus from Dawes Road and Danforth Avenue for the approximately fifteen-minute ride out to "the wilds of GECO out in the country."[182] To a seventeen-year-old like Sidney, GECO "felt like a huge place."[183]

Sidney remembers the lockers and showers in the change house, and how they stripped down to their briefs and socks, leaving "smokes" and matches in their lockers, along with rings and watches. They were not allowed to chew gum. The men stepped over the barrier onto the clean side and donned their white GECO uniforms. Once on the clean side, Sidney took the main north/south gallery on the west or gunpowder side of the plant to the trucker's office to check in and prepare for his shift. He recalls the galleries as being wide, windowless, and quiet, with little traffic except during shift changes. As all munitions and components were transported through the gallery system, he never saw GECO's elaborate tunnel system.

Sidney recalls fondly impromptu wrestling matches breaking out among the young truckers when work was slow. Sidney also had a stint working in a fuse-filling workshop, made up predominantly of women, with only a few men working who were either unfit for service, too young, or too old to go to war. Women poured gunpowder into the metal ring of a fuse, secured within a framework, and placed a brass ring on top. They then handed the unit to Sidney. He placed the frame into a press and pumped a lever until the desired pressure — to, as Sidney says, "squash the gunpowder" down into the ring — was achieved.[184] When he relieved the pressure, the gunpowder was evenly compressed within the ring, ready for the next operation in filling.

Like many other GECOites, working at GECO was a family affair for the Ledson family. Sidney's mother, Lillian, and his sister also worked there, though they did not work the same shifts as Sidney and he does not recall what they did.

Sidney fondly remembers how on hot evenings during the summer months, the doors to the workshops would be opened and they would watch the dewfall.[185]

When Sidney reached the age of eighteen, he left GECO and joined the RCAF. His training took him to Moose Jaw, Montreal, and then to

As the war dragged on, more and more men were called up, especially once conscription started, leaving more jobs for women to fill. Female "truckerettes" stepped into the
breach and took over the transportation of munitions around the plant. This shipment
was headed to D.I.L. in Pickering, Ontario, in 1943. *Courtesy of Archives of Ontario.*

Yarmouth, where he stayed for the duration of war. As the war dragged on,
more and more men were called up, especially once conscription started,
leaving more jobs for women to fill. Female "truckerettes" stepped into the
breach and took over the transportation of munitions around the plant.

After the war, Sidney, always with a zest for life, attended the Ontario
College of Art, becoming an accomplished artist. He has written nine books,
and founded the Sidney Ledson Institute for Intellectual Advancement,
where children as young as two years of age, are taught to read.

Modern Misses: The Neufeld Gals

Margaret Neufeld was born in 1921 at home on her family's farm in
Aberdeen, Saskatchewan. Her Mennonite father, Abraham, fell in love
with her mother, Helen, a Hudderite, and married against their families'

wishes. Their families, church, and community shunned the young couple for their "scandalous union."[186] Abraham and Helen had fourteen children; only nine survived. Tragically, Helen died giving birth to Margaret's little sister, leaving Abraham to raise nine children, one a newborn, alone. Margaret was only seven years old when her mom died. The family heartache did not end there. Abraham and the children lost everything when their farmhouse burned down.

Abraham raised his family with sheer grit and determination. Margaret and eight siblings grew up, Canada declared war, her five brothers went off to fight, and in 1943, at the age of twenty-two, Margaret saw an ad in the local paper offering employment at a wartime plant in Scarboro, Ontario, thousands of miles away. She was tired of the Saskatchewan wind and rural life. This was the perfect opportunity to leave the Prairies and head for the big city. Her sister, at sixteen, accompanied her to Toronto. GECO paid their expenses up front and then deducted a small portion each paycheque to repay the debt.

Margaret was glad to be off the Prairies. She embraced life at GECO, loving the food, the camaraderie, and the work. She filled bullets on the gunpowder side of the plant. She bowled in GECO's league.

As an attractive young woman, she turned the heads of more than one GECO fellow. One would-be suitor made a maple leaf broach for her out of hammered steel. Another admirer made her a broach from a bullet casing. She was invited to enter the Miss War Worker Beauty Contest, but she politely declined. Margaret met the handsome William Hermann at a YWCA dance in Toronto in April 1945, just before the war ended. He was in the RCAF, stationed to Mountainview A.F.B. in Belleville, Ontario, during the war, repairing aircraft. William had brought another girl to the dance but took one look at Margaret and dumped his date. After William took Margaret home, he realized he only knew her name and that she worked for a place called "Gee-Ko."[187] He wrote GECO's personnel manager asking about the lovely girl from the dance. The manager wrote back, "I have found your Margaret and your inquiry was met with a warm response."[188] A whirlwind romance ensued, with the couple marrying two months later.

Margaret's sister headed home after the war and eventually settled in Alberta. All the Neufeld men made it home from the war safely.

GECOite and modern-miss Margaret Neufeld (on far right in a plaid skirt) enjoying an evening of bowling with her shop mates. *Courtesy of Archives of Ontario.*

Margaret's husband, William, worked for a company called Columbia Products, and in his later years for the Scarborough Board of Education where Margaret worked as well. William and Margaret raised four children.

Margaret's adventurous spirit sustained her throughout her life. Family and friends considered her a Suffragette. She had her own bank account, independent from her husband, in the 1960s. Tamara, Margaret's daughter, summed up her mom nicely: "Mom was a modern miss."[189]

Zaida's GECO Becomes Son's Wonderland

When the Simerson family moved to Scarboro in 1939, they settled in an old farmhouse located on Rosemount Drive, which they bought from a gentleman named John Hough. At the time, Mr. Hough owned a good-sized tract of land, including a large farm and a carriage shop located at Birchmount Road and Eglinton Avenue. Neither the Hough nor Simerson family could have predicted that, two years later, King George VI of Britain would expropriate Hough's land, as well as other landowner's holdings, to build GECO.[190]

The Simersons lived so close to the future site of the munitions plant, it was an easy decision for Mary "Zaida" Simerson, thirty-five, to apply for work at GECO when it started its massive hiring campaign in the fall of 1941. A dedicated employee, Zaida was the embodiment of the early working mother. She worked rotating shifts full-time, kept house, and raised seven children. In fact, GECO was a family affair in the Simerson household. Two of Zaida's daughters also worked at GECO.

Greg Jr. remembers his mom and sisters' days at GECO. He recalls the women talking about the uniform, how workers could not wear their hair down. They talked about the dirty and clean sides of the plant, and how they called, "All Clear!" when they stepped over the barrier to the clean side.

Although Greg was too young to work at GECO — not yet a teenager — he was a typical boy and always up for adventure. There are a couple of special GECO memories that remain fresh in his mind seventy years later. During the winter months, Greg chased a puck around a hockey rink set up on GECO's premises. What made this time extra sweet was sharing the ice with men from the Royal Navy, and in particular, one fellow named Gaye Stewart, who, barely out of high school, had played with the National Hockey League's Toronto Maple Leafs.[191] Greg was too small to play offence — or defence for that matter — so he played goal. During one game, a flying puck hit him in the nose. "Kid, you'd better go home," Gaye Stewart told him, but Greg was so thrilled to be part of the game he refused and kept playing, bloody nose and all.[192]

Greg's brush with celebrity did not end with the war. When GECO was adapted into post war emergency housing, a sports field was set up across from Sinnott Road. Greg played touch football with GECO resident Don Getty, who not only went on to be a quarterback with the Edmonton Eskimos, winning two Grey Cup championships, but became the Honourable Donald R. Getty, eleventh premier of the province of Alberta, holding that office from 1985 until 1992.[193]

After the war, various businesses moved into the area, establishing the Golden Mile along Eglinton Avenue. Greg still recalls one plant erected on Warden Avenue where aerosol cans would explode from time to time. "They were like bombs landing," Greg says, "coming all the way to Rosemount. We had to put out these lit missiles."[194]

The Simerson family eventually built two new homes on Rosemount Drive. When Greg married in 1956, he and his bride, Fran, moved into his parents' old house. Greg worked with the Scarborough Fire Department for thirty-two years.

"Hefty Work": Peter Cranston

In 1944, Peter Cranston was a seventeen-year-old high-school student looking for a summer job. He headed to National Selective Service's office on Spadina Avenue in downtown Toronto to be placed where most needed. GECO was at the top of the list. The thought of filling munitions did not bother Peter. He felt, along with his fellow Canadians, that at the time it was a just and necessary war, and that meant doing whatever it took to stop Hitler.

Peter recalls the strict rules associated with working for a munitions plant. In the men's change house, he stripped down to his underclothes, stored his street clothes in a locker, then stepped over a barrier to the clean side and declared himself all clear; all under the watchful eye of a guard. "After donning a white coverall including shoes with no metal in them," Peter recalls, "and a cap covering your hair, you walked to your work station."[195]

Peter was trained with a team of several young men as a trucker, calling it "hefty work."[196] He trundled boxes of parts from the receiving area to fuse-filling workshops, or "assembly sheds" as Peter calls them.[197] He remembers hauling trucks full of boxes along long corridors.

When Peter wasn't trucking around the plant, he helped fill fuses. He doesn't remember the women being young, like depicted in the Miss War Worker Contest. As a healthy seventeen-year-old, he definitely would have had potential young female friends on his mind.

By 1944, GECO had introduced assembly line production.[198] Peter recalled working at a long table with a small trough in front of him. "Each component was in a special box," he says.[199] "The person at the front took a wooden box the size of a brick with a hole cut to hold a fuse and pushed it along the trough to the next person, who put in the first part and passed it to the next. The explosive parts were in special boxes allowing only one to be removed at a time."[200] He remembers the slight odour emitted by the fuses and explosive powders. He also remembers how these powders reacted with hair products that women used. "If the caps they wore allowed a few locks to show, they turned (the hair) orange. You recognized GECO employees anywhere in Toronto."[201]

Peter enjoyed his time at GECO. He found the lack of loud noise from heavy machinery pleasant, and the work was undemanding. Everyone chatted on the assembly lines. He enjoyed working with people from other countries, his first real exposure to the international community. "Four of my new friends were from British Guyana. One was Chinese, one English, one black and one East Indian."[202]

Peter worked at GECO during the summer of 1944, and then continued to work there on weekends during the school year. In April 1945 he enlisted and trained with the Sixth Division to fight against Japan. "It all ended with the sudden capitulation after the first atomic bomb," he says.[203]

Positively Electrifying: Hartley "Tony" French

Hartley French, a university student, joined GECO's construction team in May 1941 as an electrician's apprentice. He spent his summer helping lay GECO's electrical foundation, primarily housed underground in the rapidly evolving tunnel system. He recalls the summer of 1941 was very hot and he relished the time he spent in the emerging cool underground tunnel system.

Hartley worked six days every week and some Sundays as well. Although he cannot remember how much his wages were, he recalled they were very good — good enough that he had no student debt that fall. He received time and a half for Sundays and double time for holiday work. He was one of about twenty apprentices to work at GECO during its construction, and the only university student. Other apprentices originated from Danforth Technical School, a local vocational school that offered trade training.

Hartley lived near Yonge Street in Toronto, between Lawrence Avenue and York Mills Road. When he started at GECO he took the Yonge streetcar south to Danforth Avenue, where he picked up a streetcar heading eastbound. He then transferred to a GECO bus, most likely at Dawes Road, to the plant. As the spring and summer progressed, he shared a ride with a mentor as far as Danforth Avenue.

Hartley headed back to school in September, earned his degree, and went on to have a successful career. He married his love, Irene, and raised a family. Today, at ninety-three, Hartley and Irene enjoy life in Don Mills, Ontario.

Without a Name

The *Fusilier* shared poignant stories of GECOites, sometimes failing to mention the name of the worker. This by no means detracted from the employee's distinctive contribution.

Man Lays Down His Life on the Home Front

A veteran of the First World War with a serious heart condition was living in Montreal when Canada called for skilled toolmakers and master artisans. The First World War had left its mark on the now elderly gentleman, but he stepped out of retirement to help out. Bob and Phil Hamilton needed him to train three bright young men in toolmaking, especially in creating intricate gauges. His doctor warned him the work might kill him. However, this extraordinary fellow felt the risk of defeat by Hitler was greater and more dangerous than the risk to his health. He would rather die than see Canada fall to the Germans. To stay alive, this dedicated man saw his doctor every night for an injection. When the doctor reprimanded him, he replied: "Doc, it's up to you. You simply must keep my old heart going until these boys are ready to carry on."[204] His physician did his very best, and so did the man. He trained the engineers well — they were pall-bearers at his funeral a short time later.[205]

With Our Deepest Gratitude

While large families were more common during the 1940s, having seven siblings go off to war was not. Bill, Norman, Phil, Angus, Jack, Sandy, and Murray headed overseas, despite, or perhaps in spite of, hearing their dad's war stories from the Great War. Bill, the oldest at thirty-two, volunteered and shipped out even before a uniform was ready for him. Bill, Phil, Jack, and Sandy fought the terrible battle at Dieppe; Bill and Phil never made it off the beach. Jack and Sandy were captured and became prisoners of war.

Their dear sister, grieving her brothers' deaths, tried to join the women's army, but with her husband also fighting overseas, she had to consider the well-being of her two babies. She joined GECO instead, to wage her own kind of war, ensuring her husband and surviving brothers, and other women's brothers had all the ammunition they needed to get the job done.[206]

I Wish to Remain Anonymous

Born in 1914 in Nova Scotia, one young girl grew up in a traditional home, expecting to fulfill the traditional role of wife and mother as an adult. Newly married, she moved to Toronto in 1936. Her first baby, a son, was born two years later. She lived a settled life.

When Canada declared war, her husband, who was not eligible to fight, instead served his country by working in a converted plant building warplanes. Life as a mother and homemaker did not satisfy his young wife. "I got nothing to do," she said to her neighbour.

"You should get a part-time job," her neighbour offered. "Why not go to work in a war plant?"

The young woman applied and worked for GECO from 1942 through 1943. She remembers the uniform and the strictness of the change room supervisor. "A girl at the door was checking you for pins," she remembers. "We couldn't have nothing."

The work was easy — dangerous, but easy. "Ten of us were at a table with chairs," she recalls. "A tray held discs that the powder went in. Then a machine came down and put the powder in. The powder was put in by pressing a lever with your foot on the floor," she continues. "I was good at it. Many girls had a problem to get the powder in the hole of the disc. One girl was the leader," the GECOite further explains. "She had a red armband on her arm."

This young woman had a great time working at GECO. "We sang war songs all the time," she says, recalling one popular war tune sang by Vera Lynn "(There'll Be Bluebirds) Over the White Cliffs of Dover." "The boss came in all the time and we didn't even notice," she recounts. "We just sang away. Then he'd count the tray to see what we'd done, then he'd take the filled trays and take them away. We had a lot of fun sitting at the table."

She remembers the hazards of working with tetryl powder. "The powder made your skin yellow. One girl got pregnant and she had to go to the doctor. The doctor asked where she worked when he saw (her) yellow hands. She told him 'GECO.' He told her get out of there right away."

As the war progressed, working shiftwork six days a week wore the young mother down. She missed her baby. "My son was being cared for by a baby-sitter." Worse, when her shift at work ended, her work at home began. "When you were done, you had to go home." Housework, laundry, and childcare, had to be managed. She left GECO and settled into her domestic duties once again. In November 1943, her daughter was born.

In retrospect, the long-retired GECOite is quite clear about her war work and its ultimate purpose. "We used gunpowder to kill the Germans." Now a centenarian, she lives in Scarborough, Ontario.[207]

The Dynamic Duo
Philip Dawson Prior and Robert McLean Prior Hamilton's Story

The Hamilton brothers' story is steeped in strong Scot-Irish roots and Canadian pride. Their grandfather, Robert Hamilton, born in 1825 in Ireland, immigrated to Canada in 1853. He settled in Montreal, Québec, where he met and married Margaret McLean. They had twelve children; ten who survived to adulthood. Robert secured a job as groundskeeper at the prestigious McGill University, where he worked for thirty-nine years.[208]

Robert's eldest, Edward Henry Hamilton, or "Harry," was born in 1861. Years later, at the age of twenty-three, he graduated with an applied science, chemical option degree from McGill.[209] Harry moved to New Jersey to work as a metallurgical chemist, where he met his future wife, Maud Prior.[210] They married and moved to Pueblo, Colorado, where Philip Dawson Prior Hamilton — "Phil" to family and friends — was born in 1898.[211] Tragically, Maud, suffering from tuberculosis, died from

infection thirteen days after giving birth.[212] Four years later, Harry and
his little boy, Phil, moved to Anaconda, Montana, where he married
Maud's sister, Ethel.[213] A year later, in 1903, their son Robert McLean
Prior Hamilton — "Bob" to those close to him — was born.[214] Phil and
Bob as young tykes couldn't imagine the many adventures that lay ahead.

The Bloody Red Baron

Years passed, the boys grew up, and with the First World War underway, the family returned to Canada. In a budding family tradition, Phil
enrolled at McGill University. With his first year complete, and wanting
to do his part for Canada, Phil abandoned school to enlist in the Royal
Flying Corps.[215] At nineteen he was two years too young to be a pilot … so
he lied.[216] He trained at Downsview AFB in Toronto, soloed after twelve
hours, got his wings, and was shipped overseas.[217] Phil successfully flew
several sorties over France before he, along with Allied squadrons, took
on the infamous Red Baron, notorious for ditching his German flying
formation to pick off any plane that dared cross the German lines to
hunt him down. A dogfight ensued, resulting not only in Phil's aircraft
getting torn up in a hail of machine gun fire, but also in Phil receiving a
serious gunshot wound to his elbow.[218] Miraculously, he was able to coax
the crippled plane across German lines into No-Man's Land close to the
English defence, where the plane hit land and ground looped, leaving
Phil hanging upside-down in the cockpit. British troops, who emerged
from their trenches to rescue Phil, did so at their own peril.[219]

Phil's flying days were over. He was taken to a mobile hospital behind
British lines where doctors intended to amputate his arm … without
anesthetic. Phil refused. Doctors removed the bullet, set his arm, and
sent him back to England as a casualty of war. He was discharged in 1918
as a member of the newly formed RAF.[220] Upon his return to Canada, he
headed back to McGill with his arm still in a sling. His arm recovered
well; all but for the hole left by the bullet.

The Roaring Twenties

Bob, when he finished high school, moved to Montreal to join his older
brother and pursue a degree at McGill. Phil graduated with a bachelor of

science degree in 1922; Bob graduated with a bachelor of science degree in geology two years later.[221]

The early 1920s were good to the Hamilton brothers. Phil met his future wife Evelyn Banfill while at McGill. In August of 1923 they married and moved to Tacoma, Washington, where Phil worked with the American Smelting and Refinery Company as a chemist.[222] Bob was hired as a field engineer in Ontario and Quebec by the General Engineering Company.[223] In 1927, Bob moved to GECO's headquarters situated in Salt Lake City, Utah.[224]

Phil and Evelyn started their family, bringing Mary and Philip into the fold. Unfortunately, when the Great Depression hit the United States at the end of the 1920s, Phil lost his job. Bob found him a position with GECO in Salt Lake City.[225] Needing to move, Phil tried to sell his house. He tried to find tenants to rent. He even invited tenants to live there rent-free. All attempts failed. Defeated, he packed up, and, leaving the house and most of their possessions, moved to Salt Lake City with his young family.

The Thirties: A Prelude to War

By 1932, the Pre-Cambrian Shield in Canada presented an exciting new mining opportunity. Bob suggested to GECO executives that an office should open in Toronto, the mining centre of Canada. GECO founder, Mr. Gayford, long-time mentor to Bob and Phil, agreed and named Bob as president and Phil vice president of GECO's new Canadian office set up at 100 Adelaide Street West.[226]

Bob Hamilton, still a single young man in 1933, easily made the move to Toronto, establishing GECO's Canadian operations. But his life was about to change. He met native Torontonian Betty Parsons at a party and was utterly besotted. Meanwhile, Phil, Evelyn, and their little ones packed up and headed for Canada to start a new life in Toronto, where two more children were eventually born.

Bob and Betty were married in 1935.[227] They built their first home in the Lawrence Avenue and Avenue Road area of Toronto. Their first child, John, arrived in 1937, followed by their daughter Susan in 1940.[228]

Although North America struggled to recover from the Great Depression, Bob and Phil were able to get the Canadian arm of GECO on its feet. However, when Canada went to war, the need for wartime facilities took centre stage. The Canadian government, recognizing GECO's expertise in building temporary buildings, hired Bob and Phil to build several wartime projects, including the munitions plant at Scarboro.

Thus began the story of Scarboro, and with it the opportunity, not only to plan and construct the massive wartime facility, but to oversee its day-to-day operations as well.

Like many of his employees, Phil Hamilton took the Second World War personally, especially because of his own war experience. His dear wife Evelyn's brother was captured in the fall of Hong Kong on Christmas Day 1941.[229] For many, many months he was presumed dead, but miraculously he survived and was repatriated in 1945.[230] Despite a world at war, Bob and Phil enjoyed their days at Scarboro. They were approachable, compassionate, passionate, firm, and fair. They participated in employee events and grew their own "Victory Garden." In an article, "A Ton of Books," J.J. Carrick wrote, "R.M.P. Hamilton, President of GECO, seldom hears himself addressed as Mister. This demonstrates the friendly association existing in the great organization built by 'Bob' and his brother 'Phil.'"[231]

Bob and Phil's wives, Betty and Evelyn, did not engage in war work. As homemakers, they raised their little ones and supported their husbands by tending to domestic duties and fostering a nurturing home environment.

When the war ended, Scarboro closed. The Hamilton brothers invited their younger brother Edward to join GECO's team and pursued what they knew best — mining. After investing their own money, and investigating a possible prospect in northern Ontario, Bob and Phil Hamilton backed three "weekend prospectors" living in Geraldton, Ontario, who discovered a massive mineral deposit of copper, silver, zinc, lead, and gold.[232] They opened a profitable GECO mine in Manitouwadge, with a plan to mine 3,300 tons of ore per day.[233] Ore reserves at the end of 1954 were estimated at almost fifteen million tons, with each ton containing 1.72 percent copper, 3.55 percent zinc, and 1.73 ounces of silver.[234] In his book, *Noranda*, Leslie Roberts called GECO's operation a first-rate mining undertaking.[235] He suggested the burgeoning mine's success was the product of Bob and Phil's investment of exploration capital, mining giant Noranda's investment, the rapid construction of Canadian National and Canadian Pacific rail lines, and the installation of hydro-electric power. "A new and great mine had been born," wrote Roberts.[236]

The mine operated from 1957 to 1995, but unlike GECO's other many endeavours, success didn't come easily.[237] Another gold mine company launched a lawsuit claiming they were entitled to a share in the success of the mine.[238] Bob and Phil Hamilton eventually prevailed and won their case in October 1956.[239]

GECO's mining and engineering success spread around the globe under Bob and Phil's leadership. In 1955, they bought the rights to the U.S.-based counterpart, and expanded its scope into Ireland, Morocco, Scandinavia, Peru, and Chile.[240] When the boys were ready to retire, GECO was sold to SNC (Surveyer Nenniger Chenevert), a Montreal engineering firm, later to join with Lavalin Inc. to become one of the world's leading engineering and construction companies.[241]

In retirement, Bob Hamilton kept busy, taking up positions on several boards of directors, and, of course, enjoying cottage life.[242]

Philip Dawson Prior Hamilton died in 1982.[243] Robert McLean Prior Hamilton died in 1996.[244] In his eulogy to his father, John Hamilton said: "Can you remember being a high-school student in the early grades, wondering how the school would run after the exemplary leaders in sports and other activities graduated? I think that Dad is like one of those leaders, graduating from this school of life with us."[245]

A Son's Reflection
Philip Henry Banfill Hamilton

Philip Henry Banfill Hamilton, son to Philip Dawson Prior Hamilton, was born in Tacoma, Washington.[246] He remembered the Depression and its devastating effects on his parents and their fledgling family. "We only took a fraction of our belongings," Philip recalled, on having to leave the security and comfort of his home.[247] "Our toys, furniture were abandoned. We truly were children of the Depression."[248] He moved with his family to Salt Lake City, Utah, where his Uncle Bob had been able to secure a job for his dad with General Engineering Company.[249]

Judy Patton Hamilton and Philip Henry Banfill Hamilton with Barbara Dickson, Lac des Seize Iles, Quebec, 2012. *Courtesy of Barbara Dickson.*

GECO served Phil well. By the mid-1930s, he was able to move his family back to Canada after GECO's Canadian office opened.[250]

Philip joined his father and uncle at GECO in Scarboro while its operations wound down during the summer of 1945. He helped desensitize the shops by spraying a special solution on shop walls and floors, killing any explosive residue in the wood. He was paid fifty cents an hour and worked six days a week.

In keeping with a well-established family tradition, Philip pursued a degree in engineering from McGill University, graduating in 1954. On a skiing trip in the Canadian Laurentian Mountains north of Montreal, Philip met fellow McGill student Judy Patton, who graduated with a B.A. the same year as he did. They later married. After graduating, Philip found a job at Dominion Engineering Works in Lachine, Quebec, and went on to have a successful career.

Philip passed away on Remembrance Day 2013 at the age of eighty-five.[251]

John McLean Parsons Hamilton

Bob and Betty made two significant additions to their family in 1937: a brand new home and the safe arrival of their first child, John.[252] Life was idyllic for the recently married couple, with John's little sister Susan joining the Hamilton clan three years later. His mom, Betty, managed the home while his dad, president of GECO's fledging Canadian office, worked tirelessly to establish GECO's reputation as a paramount mining enterprise north of the border. John was only a toddler when Canada entered the Second World War and his father shifted his company's focus to war work.

"I had mixed feelings about (my dad) growing up," John says, reminiscing. "The job kept him away from home."[253] When the Second World War started, Bob was away more than usual. "I resented the war," he says.[254] "He was working at a fever pitch while at GECO. He worked long hours and brought work home."[255] Although Bob Hamilton provided well for his family, there wasn't much time for parental bonding. John recognizes the unique challenges a world at war brought to business. "Women were suddenly in a man's world; men suddenly were having to care for women in the workplace."[256] His dad and the team made the adjustment well. John fondly recalls accompanying his father to work. "I used to go with Dad to a lot of offices," he says.[257]

Betty, doing her part for the war effort, took pride in her victory garden located in a vacant lot beside their home.[258] There were three vacant lots, actually; lots of room, John says, to play hockey in wintertime. He enjoyed a privileged childhood, attending John Ross Robertson Public School, followed by UTS — a preparatory school leading to post-secondary education at the University of Toronto.

After high school, John earned an engineering degree from the University of Toronto. He did "the engineering thing" for his father, he says, then "went to England to study industrial psychology to try to get into the people side."[259] He obtained a master's degree in guidance and counselling and an Ed.D. (Doctor of Education) in adult education from the Ontario Institute for Studies in Education (OISE). John explains his doctorate as "examining the careers of teachers who had lost their jobs due to declining enrollment; the psychology of teachers' resilience to job loss."[260]

He speaks of the close friendship between his mom, Betty, and Florence Ignatieff and Barbara Holmes. "They were great pals. Florence and her children, Paul and Mika, would come for a visit often."[261] So close were the trio that Betty became godmother to Barbara's son, and the Ignatieff family often stayed in a cottage alongside the Hamiltons' rental cottage at Lumina Resort in Muskoka, creating happy summer memories that the family still recall fondly decades later.

John married, had children of his own, and went on to have a successful teaching and counselling career at several academic institutions at the secondary and post-secondary level.

"My father and his devotion to his work," John says, "whether it was GECO at Scarboro in those days, or the work he did in the mining industry — he was devoted to his standards he set for himself, and GECO was the medium in which he expressed those standards. I'm proud of the work my father did there."[262]

John grew closer to his dad as the years passed. In the early 1980s, he asked his father to accompany him "to the office" — a nostalgic trip to Manitouwadge in northern Ontario.[263] In his eulogy for his father, John said, "(Dad's) going to be hard to replace. He was a model to learn from for many of us among his family and friends."[264]

Today John lives with his wife Barbara in Elora, Ontario.

8

Safety First
Because Safety Lasts

From GECO's outset, their mandate was clear: "Scarboro was conceived, constructed, organized and operated for but one purpose — PRODUCTION — and to that end every department of The General Engineering Company (Canada) Limited made direct or indirect contribution."[1] Even the safety of its employees did not take precedence over production at a time when countless lives might be sacrificed for lack of dependable ammunition.[2]

Despite the Hamiltons' declaration that production reigned supreme, Bob, Phil, and their cohorts consciously, or perhaps even more so unconsciously, made safety one of their highest priorities. The protection of GECO's assets was an ever-present and solemn concern for GECO management.

Monday morning quarterbacks — critics who lament their game could have been won had someone made a different play — may have coined the expression "hindsight is 20/20." While bulldozers and 2,500 strong Canadian men worked around the clock to build GECO, no one could predict the duration or outcome of a world at war, just as they had no way to foretell what ultimate cost Scarboro might pay through the loss of life or limb due to explosion. They did have control, however, over the decisions they made. From the earliest whispers of bringing a top-secret munitions plant to Scarboro, to the last fuse filled, from plant design to safe working practices, from minimizing static electricity to strongly reminding wayward or negligent employees, every decision made, not only during construction but throughout the life of the plant, was first and foremost tested against a consummate safety standard. There could be no room for regret.

Scarboro's employee safety record was rare and perhaps without equal in global munitions handling.[3] GECO management attributed this success primarily to attentive care spent on eliminating the chance of fire and explosion and to minimizing the damage of such incidents if they did happen.[4] Experts in munitions would likely attribute Scarboro's stellar safety record — and they would face little if any opposition — to GECO's dynamic duo, Bob and Phil, and their safety officer, George M. Thomson, for not only their exemplary vision but also their conscientious and fastidious operating procedures.

The Hamiltons ultimately were responsible for the plant's safety; Safety Officer Thomson reported directly to them.[5] He managed all aspects of safety at the plant. His mandate included managing inspectors, maintaining safe limits in storing explosives, overseeing the entire Security Department, and ensuring proper ventilation, lighting, and humidity.[6]

Safety, of course, was a dominant consideration in ammunition filling in general in the United Kingdom, and in fuse filling in particular. The finished "product" was only as perfect as the many steps to prepare and fill the fuse. It had to be free from filings, grit, or other superfluous material that might disturb the delicate mechanism or agitate the explosives in the weapon.[7] Dirt could cause friction; static electricity might cause a spark. Both had the potential for catastrophic explosions that might not only disrupt production of critically needed war supplies, but could endanger the lives of thousands of employees. GECO did not want to repeat the tragic accidents experienced at other munitions plants during the Great War, where five fatal accidents occurred at Hayes, the plant from which GECO was patterned.[8] In addition, there had been four deaths from toxic jaundice at that munitions plant, bringing the total death count to nine.[9]

W.H. Pitcher wrote of Scarboro, "In designing this plant, safety has been the primary consideration — safety not only for its four to five thousand employees working on 8-hour shifts, but safety combined with efficiency to turn out the greatest number of completed fuses in the shortest possible time."[10]

From protecting the physical plant to building and workshops, from galleries and tunnels to the hazards of working with tetryl, safety and efficiency was foremost on everyone's mind.

Friend or Foe?

All interested parties agreed — buildings at GECO were to have a low profile, built mostly as single-storey workshops.[11] The plant was to remain as inconspicuous as possible from the ground and air. Of course, this mandate was not as easy to carry out when thousands of yards of eight-foot-high barbed-wire fence surrounded the complex, but for the most part, even from neighbouring farms, GECO could not be seen other than perhaps for its smokestack.

In addition to the barbed-wire fencing, the site was heavily guarded, with access restricted to a handful of entry points.[12] If, by some chance, a lost motorist came upon GECO unaware of what went on inside the intimidating military installation, he more than likely would have been quickly approached, challenged, and then escorted away by GECO's armed security personnel.

Older army men comprised 80 percent of the plant's security force, and their mandate was simple: keep undesirables out.[13] Successful applicants to the force had a background in police or military service, and had to clear an extensive background check.[14] The Commissioner of Provincial Police swore in each guard as a Special Constable.[15]

Armed guards patrolled the property continually, one guard responsible for between 350–500 yards of property.[16] Special Fence Patrols traversed the entire perimeter of the plant, consisting of over 347 acres, one lap of which took about an hour to complete.[17] The guards patrolled the plant, rain or shine, fair or foul weather, even during blizzards and bitterly cold blustery days.

Each shift included a parade for duty, roll call, and uniform and area inspections.[18] In addition to patrolling the site and keeping "a vigilant watch for possible sabotage,"[19] guards were also responsible for finger-printing, photographing, and checking letters of reference for all new employees, supervising loading and unloading of buses, being on hand at the bank on payday, and maintaining a "lost and found" area.[20] Special Security Observers, both male and female, were present in change rooms to ensure no prohibited material was transported onto the clean side of the plant.[21]

GECO commenced keeping guard statistics early, while still under construction. By July 1, 1941, twenty-three men walked the site twenty-four hours a day.[22] When construction wound down and production ramped up, so did the number of men hired to protect the plant's assets, interests, and employees. Eighty guards secured the site by the end of 1942, with a healthy aggregate of more than seventy men protecting GECO until the end of the war.[23]

As for employees, guards demanded they present valid ID pass cards before entering the compound.[24] All employees were subject to a physical search of their belongings and person.[25]

In addition, all employees understood anti-sabotage procedures and participated in air-raid drills,[26] and air-raid alarms were installed on all buildings.[27]

In Case of Explosion …

Running a top secret munitions plant with thousands of workers who handled high explosives meant incorporating extraordinary fire and explosion prevention strategies and emergency processes into its design, construction, and operation. A considerable water supply was impera-tive, including a regular supply from Scarboro Township's water main, two domestic water storage tanks of 250,000 gallons each, and an open water reservoir with a capacity of 2.5 million gallons.[28] More than five hundred fire extinguishers were placed strategically throughout the compound, including the extensive gallery and tunnel systems.[29] Indoor hoses — totalling more than two-and-a-half miles — were installed in all buildings and galleries.[30] Fifty-five outdoor hydrants were installed at regular intervals around the plant, including four-and-a-half miles of hose.[31] Twenty-six guards' stations were set up within the tunnel system.[32] Fire safety guidelines were taught to and enforced by all employees, and fire drills were held weekly at first, then bi-monthly throughout the duration of the war.[33] Smoking was allowed only on the dirty side of the plant because of the inherent fire hazard associated with matches and smouldering cigarette butts.

"Scarboro" possessed two fully functioning fire halls.[34] The larger hall in Building No. 90 was located on the dirty side of the plant close to the medical building, situated in the northwest area of the complex.[35] An auxiliary hall was housed in Building No. 145 at the southern end near the Proof Yard.[36] Fire Chief T. Benson was in charge of all auxiliary fire areas.[37] Before the Second World War there was only one fire hall in Scarboro Township, located on Birchmount Avenue north of Kingston Road.[38] The plant boasted the largest industrial fire department in the country, and the largest of any kind in Ontario, yet the only fires the brigade handled were doused with a bucket of sand before firefighters could arrive.[39]

Unique to its civilian counterparts, GECO sported blue fire trucks with flowers, perhaps as a salute to its predominantly female workforce, stencilled on the fenders.[40] One, a converted Chevrolet, included a pump with a capacity of almost two cubic yards per minute, 460 yards of hose, six chemical extinguishers, and a ladder.[41] The other, built onsite on a converted Ford chassis, contained a water pump that could pump two and one half cubic yards per minute, 351 yards of hose, six chemical extinguishers, and a twelve-yard extension ladder.[42] Of almost thirty firemen on site — mostly retired Toronto firefighters — any man without thirty years of experience was considered a rookie.[43] GECO's fire detachment also comprised about one hundred volunteer firefighters who had other regular occupations in the plant.[44]

Neither hoses nor water were allowed in GECO's expansive service tunnel system since the plant's electrical infrastructure was located within its confines.[45] Instead, Pyrene or carbon dioxide extinguishers were placed within the underground labyrinth.[46] Should a fire occur in a branch off the main tunnels running north/south, in an underground switch room, or in a transformer vault, fire doors were closed to keep the fire contained belowground.[47]

In addition to keeping GECO structures to one storey, buildings were staggered and arranged with the hope that in case of explosion, damage and injury would be contained to one building.[48] Structures, especially those that stored explosives, were constructed in a more scattered fashion toward the southern end of the plant.[49] Vestibules running directly above the tunnel system and spanning the length of most buildings on the clean side alternated between the north and south sides of workshops.[50] As for safe distancing between munitions buildings, the United States recommended a distance of six hundred feet.[51] This was quite different from Britain's recommendation of 100 feet between buildings.[52] The plant's First World War British counterpart, Hayes, built buildings only seventy-five feet apart.[53] GECO management decided two hundred feet was reasonable to leave between factory buildings.[54] A minimum of six hundred feet was maintained between plant buildings and main roads outside the plant.[55]

Ever fire-conscious, GECO engineers recommended weatherproof, fire-resistant "weatherboard" plywood to cover the outside of all buildings.[56] It was available, cheap, and could be applied quickly.[57]

Buildings in the Danger Zone, where workers handled explosives, were divided into "shops" and separated by reinforced concrete or masonry firewalls three feet tall.[58] Side walls were constructed from "flimsy wallboard," as GECOnian Ernie Pickles recalls.[59] "If an explosion occured [sic] it would not affect the next room down the hall," he states, "but the explosion would knock down the side walls and dissipate to the outdoors."[60] In addition, heavy explosion/fire doors, operated via a robust pulley system, separated all buildings from "cleanways."[61] Escape doors in each fuse-filling shop to the outside offered a way out in an emergency.[62] In total, over four hundred fire doors were installed throughout GECO's buildings on the clean side.[63]

For easy manoeuvrability of munitions, machinery, and operators alike, fuse-filling shops enjoyed an almost forty-six-foot-wide free-span frame with no internal support beams.[64] Buildings with no internal support could withstand an explosion that took out a large part of a wall or the roof without complete collapse.[65] GECO's ingenious solution to a scant or practically non-existent steel supply was to use their newly invented "super structure" or "timber beam."[66]

Life Expectancy

GECO's buildings were built with an estimated five years of useful life.[67] It was felt that a global conflict of the Second World War's magnitude could not possibly last more than a few years. Ironically, because GECO was a munitions factory, building construction and materials were often of a superior, stronger quality than normally would be expected in a temporary endeavour. In a short-term industrial undertaking, a rough and simple interior finish to inside walls typically would have been adequate. However, in GECO's case, interior finishes had to be clean and smooth with no crevices that could collect dust.[68] As well, maintaining a precise degree of heat and humidity in clean-side buildings was an absolute necessity and demanded extra care in construction.[69] With a scarcity of steel during the war, GECO employed their "super structure" technology in shops, which expanded to tunnel ceilings, providing superior workmanship and longevity.[70] As a testament to quality workmanship, almost seventy years past their end-of-use date several original GECO buildings remain today.

Special buildings called "magazines," where a substantial quantity of explosives were stored, such as Building Nos. 48–55 or Building Nos. 81–85, were isolated from other structures.[71] In some cases these magazines, nicknamed "igloos," were partially or completely buried by dirt conveniently made available from excavating the tunnel system. This provided some additional protection to surrounding buildings should an explosion occur.[72] Igloos were reinforced with concrete and steel as they were constructed.[73] Later, when steel became scarce as construction continued, igloos were supported with "super structures."[74] Berms built from excavated tunnel dirt surrounded some clean-side buildings, to minimize potential damage of surrounding structures in case of explosion.[75]

In Spotless Air-Conditioned Shops

GECO engineers had to consider many things when building fuse-filling workshops in the Danger Zone, from heating and cooling to controlling humidity, from preventing dust accumulation to avoiding static electricity, as well as anticipating the potential devastation of worker error, carelessness, and neglect. GECO, as an arsenal, was expected to incorporate many safety fuse-filling procedures based on British experience that never before had been used in Canadian industrial practice.[76] Conditions in Canada were quite different from those found in England, especially in coping with Canada's northern climate.

Each fuse-filling building was separated into several "workshops," each approximately 55 by 105 feet, and with each workshop having an "annex" measuring about 16.5 by 55 feet.[77] Walls were painted ivory and the floors were covered with resilient and easily cleaned brown linoleum.[78] Cleaners wiped down floors in some workshops every four hours. Walls, ceilings, and light fixtures in workshops were cleaned weekly.[79]

Static electricity was a munitions factory's worst nightmare. In a closed environment where high explosives were in use, a buildup of accumulated electrons within a person's body or metal-containing object could suddenly release and cause a "spark." A single spark could ignite highly explosive or inflammable materials, causing a catastrophic chain reaction.[80] GECO took extraordinary measures to prevent static electricity. Every piece of machinery on the clean side was grounded, and ground plates were placed at the door of each filling shop.[81] "You had to touch it every time you went through," GECOite Peter Cranston recalled. "It was a firing offence to forget."[82] The use of "super structures" in ceilings allowed for "tight" construction, minimizing dust.[83] All cracks and joints in walls were filled and taped before applying an interior finish.[84] Small dust-proof, explosion-proof push-button electric lighting was installed.[85] Bronze and brass were used in place of other metals.[86] Lightning rods were installed in all buildings.[87] Electrical fixtures in GECO workshops were not to exceed a surface temperature greater than 60 degrees Celsius to eliminate the chance of explosion.[88] Lighting in GECO's workshops provided fifteen foot-candles intensity.[89] Workshops were inspected at least once every shift.[90]

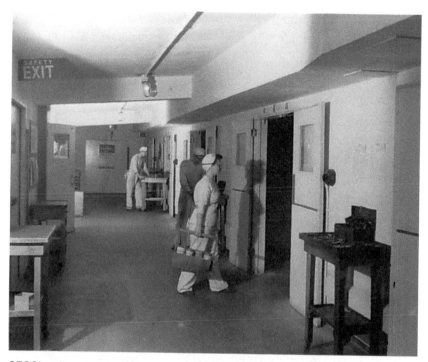

GECO's gallery system was connected to corridors that ran alongside filling shops on the clean side. These vestibules conveyed both workers and ammunition and were kept rigorously clean. Ground plates, situated outside the doors to each workshop, were touched by every employee before they entered to minimize the risk of static electricity. A small tool crib sat in various vestibules to ensure quick repairs when appropriate. *Courtesy of Archives of Ontario.*

To minimize the chance of static electricity and sparks, work could only be carried out in filling shops where air humidity was kept within certain limits.[91] GECO engineers and management mandated that humidity in workshops should be maintained at a constant 55 percent using an air conditioning system.[92] Uniform humidity in workshops resulted in a higher quality final product — fuses that would execute perfectly when it mattered most.

"Early in the plant's construction, the decision was made to erect buildings on the clean side without windows. This decision extended to the extensive gallery system. Windowless workshops sped up construction time; workers didn't have to fuss over preparing walls for the installation of windows and sills, and there would be no interruption in construction should glass or materials be delayed or not be available.[93] Fortuitously, windowless shops helped control humidity in hot, muggy weather and minimize condensation in damp winter months."[94]

Keeping thousands of operators, predominately female, comfortable was a huge challenge. A central heating/cooling unit in each workshop maintained a comfortable twenty-two degrees Celsius.[97] Fresh air was filtered in to each workshop every twelve minutes during summer months.[98]

W.H. Pitcher had this to say about GECO's cleanliness: "Of perhaps equal importance in maintaining safe working conditions about the plant is good housekeeping. Every bench, every workshop, all the corridors and the working personnel are scrupulously clean."[99]

Jack Be Nimble

GECO management used every opportunity to instill safety awareness in their employees, including communicating via their employee newspaper. Humour, poetry, and cartoons were often used to teach and remind employees of their responsibilities and the potentially deadly consequences should they lack diligence. One poem with its accompanying cartoon read:

> Jack be nimble, Jack be quick,
> Jack made eyes at a passing chick,
> He teetered and tottered and finally fell,
> Now we're all waiting for Jack to get well.[100]

Transporting detonators, the most unpredictable of all munitions, required specially marked red boxes, carried by hand by a seasoned GECOite, his red cap a warning to all to give him lots of room to pass. The July 4, 1942 issue of the plant's paper offered this reminder: "All the men wearing the dark red caps need the right of way — especially those with the scarlet wooden satchels. These satchels aren't filled with cough drops ..."[101]

Galleries, Tunnels, and More Tunnels, Oh My!

The expansive Scarboro site included an elaborate aboveground gallery network spanning more than three miles, and an extensive labyrinth of tunnels connecting most of the munitions facility's buildings on the clean side.[102]

The First World War's Hayes munitions plant in England, upon which GECO's design was patterned, linked clean-side buildings with board-walks — wood planks — laid out along the ground.[103] Both walkways and workers were exposed to all weather conditions. Depending on the daily weather, women brought dirt, mud, soggy hair, and damp clothing into their workshops. The Hamilton brothers knew they needed a safer, cleaner way for GECO's workers to travel to and from their shops. They decided to cover the plant's "cleanways," heat and air-condition them depending on the weather, keep them fastidiously clean, and attach them to the shift houses so workers would always be in an "All Clear!" state of mind.[104]

The expansive Scarboro site included an elaborate aboveground gallery network spanning more than three miles. Employees travelled to their respective fuse-filling workshops through these temperature-controlled, windowless, enclosed walkways. Berms surrounded some clean-side buildings to minimize potential damage to surrounding structures in case of explosion. *Courtesy of Archives of Ontario.*

At critical points in the covered corridors, workmen installed steel safety doors to prevent a potential fire from spreading through the complex via the hallways.[105] To minimize the spread of fire or explosion, the points at which lateral galleries entered the main cleanways running north/south were offset.[106] The engineering sketch of GECO depicts these offset cleanways and tunnels very well. For example, the entrances to the gallery system and tunnel system from Building No. 56 and No. 59 are staggered, not directly across from each other. If an explosion or fire occurred in one building, the hope was that it would be harder to spread to the building on the other side of the cleanway.

Canada's governor general, the Earl of Athlone, husband to Her Royal Highness Princess Alice, remarked on a visit to the plant that the galleries were "long, spotless, wooden-floored halls, where employees marched smartly, avoiding such dangerous static-producers as dragging their feet or rubbing their hands along the walls."[107]

Even more extraordinary than GECO's unique aboveground gallery system was the extensive tunnel system that ran under the complex.[108] The tunnels housed essential services like lines for water, electrical power, steam, and compressed air for the entire plant.[109] Installing services below ground allowed maintenance and repairs to be carried out without disruption to workers in the workshops above or risking explosion by carrying out maintenance in sensitive fuse-filling shops.[110] GECO's tunnel system was byzantine, and even during construction workers were warned of the potential danger of losing their bearings while underground.[111] All work was kept to short sections of tunnel. The tunnel walls were built from reinforced masonry blocks, tall and wide enough to easily accommodate skids of munitions.[112] This type of construction could withstand shock and collapse should an explosion occur, and survive a potential cave-in due to seismic activity, similar to precautions taken in earthquake zones.[113] The ceilings of the tunnels were made from two-by-eight-inch planks of local hardwood, turned on their thin sides, then nailed and glued, offering the same strength as "super structures" found in workshop ceilings.[114] The honeycomb tunnel system, in desperate circumstances, could have been used to protect GECO's employees from possible air raids, enemy invasion, and explosions, or provide an evacuation route. There is no oral or written record to ascertain if the tunnels were ever used for these purposes.

There is ongoing debate as to whether GECO situated washrooms in its tunnel system. According to Sidney Ledson and Philip Hamilton, two GECO employees, the tunnels were not accessible to workers.[115] Furthermore, through interviews, several surviving female workers confirmed they had no knowledge of tunnels running under their feet. However, in GECO's written account, it states: "… washrooms were situated inside, above, or adjacent to the service tunnels."[116] According to the 1956 Fire Insurance Plan of Toronto, there is a washroom seemingly underground, housed in Building No. 74.[117] Logically, and despite the debate, while the tunnel system ran underground on the clean side, they were not "clean." Accessing washrooms below ground would have rendered workers "dirty" and not fit to return to their shops. If there were washrooms located underground, they were used by maintenance workers only.

GECO's extensive gallery and tunnel system were remarkable accomplishments. Even more extraordinary, a *second* tunnel system stretched out directly beneath the upper tunnels to house GECO's plumbing infrastructure.[118]

Guns and Gum

In addition to the specific safety precautions taken in the design and wearing of her uniform, operators were trained in first aid, the use of fire extinguishers, expected to follow strict workshop regulations, and prohibited from carrying contraband onto the clean side of the plant.[119] The list of prohibited items was extensive and demanded a good memory. "I forgot" was not an acceptable excuse.[120] In fact, there was a zero tolerance policy for contraband found on any GECO employee. Contraband included food; drink; chewing gum; matches, or any other means of lighting a fire; any type of tobacco or snuff; any metal object such as keys, knives, scissors, watches, or loose change; any article made from silk or artificial silk in any form; and live animals.[121]

Dorothy Cheesman recalled that the list of banned items was much lengthier; they were not even allowed a deck of playing cards.[122] Molly Danniels remembered they had to keep their fingernails short.[123]

Death and Disfigurement

While GECO suffered no fatal occupational accidents during its operation, inevitably, by the very nature of the work carried out at the plant, mishaps and explosions did occur.[124] "We had a lot of small explosions," Bob Hamilton recounted in a media interview.[125] "The unit which gave us the most trouble was the tracer; a four-inch-long steel tube which fit in the bottom of a shell. When the shell is ejected, the heat ignites the tracer and you can see where it goes. Specs call for compressing the ignitable material almost to its breaking point. Occasionally there would be slag in the shell, and the compression would ignite it in the shell and there'd be a large flare in the shop; twenty-five women quit."[126] Molly Danniels confirmed Bob's account; she was in the workshop when a blast occurred, and witnessed more than two dozen women walking out. Molly stayed.[127]

Another mishap, more serious, occurred when Assistant Forman P.W. Meaham "suffered severe injuries to his arms" while "proofing" filled munitions for quality assurance in the Proof Yard.[128] After recovering, Mr. Meaham, perhaps appropriately, joined the Safety Department.[129] Bob Hamilton recalls one big accident toward the end of the war after a night shift. "The head of the Proof Department was obviously tired and wanted to go home," Bob said, "and he hurried up proofing a shell, a fuse it was, and it went off in his hands and practically blinded him."[130] Bob continues, "That was due to fatigue and a Saturday night wanting to get home. He broke three safety regulations in doing that. You do those things when you're tired."[131] A cartoon ran in the newspaper warning clean-side employees: "Fingers do not grow on trees — watch what yours are doing, please."[132]

An internal review of industrial relations at the plant took place mid-1943, with the following comment made in regards to GECO's accident history: "The record of this Company in accident occurrence is low to an outstanding degree in comparison with other (including non-explosives) companies, throughout Ontario."[133]

The Tetryl Dilemma

Munitions filling at GECO included using a yellow crystal-like concoction called tetryl, a highly sensitive explosive used in Britain and the United States during the First and Second World Wars. In its solid state, tetryl didn't pose much of a hazard to GECO's personnel — other than it being highly explosive — but when it was ground into a fine dust it became airborne, likely to settle on employee uniforms, caking their hands, and getting into their eyes and lungs. Tetryl had the potential to be highly toxic to some operators, and was a potent source of occupational illness.[134] Severity of symptoms varied depending on the degree of exposure to the tetryl and how sensitive the operator was to its components.[135] Symptoms included eye and skin irritation, including discolouration, or "yellow-staining," of hands, neck, and hair, stomach upsets including nausea and diarrhea, cough, sore throat, upper respiratory wheezing and congestion, headache and fatigue, and nose bleeds.[136] While it was not known if tetryl affected reproduction, a rumour circulated around the plant that women who worked with tetryl could not bear children.[137]

Bob and Phil Hamilton and their entire management team, including Dr. Jeffrey, GECO's chief physician, recognized the potential hazard in working with tetryl. The First World War English munitions plant at Hayes (which GECO mirrored) recorded four deaths due to toxic jaundice.[138] To minimize the hazards associated with tetryl, GECO management considered its effects in every decision made, even during the early days of construction. The toxic nature of airborne tetryl dust made it necessary to keep H.E. filling operations entirely separate from other areas in the plant. Only women who worked directly with tetryl were exposed to its potential toxins, not every employee.

During GECO's initial hiring campaign, Dr. Jeffrey wrote that, "special attention was given to skin conditions and chronic respiratory ailments which might incapacitate operators working with tetryl."[139] Some women were hired to work solely on the G.P. line due to pre-existing conditions such as eczema or asthma, which, with repeated contact with tetryl, could endanger their health.[140] Dr. Jeffrey noted later on that skin conditions were not as important as certain chronic respiratory ailments in choosing workers for tetryl filling shops.[141]

To further segregate operators who worked with tetryl, GECO set up a separate area in change houses where specific attention was given to uniforms needing more rigorous laundering and skin protection, including the application of special creams.[142] Nursing staff were in attendance during shift changes to offer tetryl-related advice.[143] Sue Szydlik, GECOite Irene Darnbrough's daughter, remembers her mother using a cola soft-drink to wash off the yellow stains. "They would wash in it before leaving the plant."[144] Sylvia Nordstrand's sister filled tracers. "She became all yellow, clothes and skin, and she never seemed to get rid of it until she left for any length of time, holidays, etc."[145] The methods used in GECO's change rooms to manage tetryl rash became a standard for other munitions plants across Canada.[146]

The art of stemming — pressing a specified quantity of high explosives powders into certain areas within a fuse — caused a fine dust of tetryl to spread, and in spite of standard precautions taken, an inordinate number of women were exposed to its potential ill effects.[149] Management decided that only specially selected operators who tolerated the effects of tetryl well would be assigned to stemming work.[150] These operators worked from outside a hood or "lighthouse" that vented to the outside and could accommodate six or eight operators.[151] When GECO first got underway, each filling shop did their own stemming according to English peacetime practices.[152] However, as the war progressed, a dedicated stemming shop — "60B" — Building No. 60, Workshop B — was opened.[153] Segregating and merging these two operations helped confine tetryl dust to one location and greatly reduced the incidence of rash and tetryl-related ailments.[154] GECO management was able to assign operators to 60B who were essentially immune to the effects of tetryl.[155]

Last, but certainly not least, GECO kept meticulous records of each shift, breaking absenteeism down by category and sub-category. Staff tracked how many operators were absent, not only due to every type of illness imaginable — cold, upper and lower respiratory, gastro, genito-urinary, rheumatic, fainting, nervousness, eye trouble, dental, headaches, and night shift complaints — but also accidents, both explosive and other, and occupational illnesses like tetryl poisoning.[156]

Through these initiatives GECO management was able to greatly reduce, if not eliminate altogether, the threat of toxicity among their female operators.[157] The Toronto East Medical Association's Official Bulletin in February 1944 acknowledged GECO's attempt to minimize the hazard of tetryl exposure: "The only girls exposed to the bleaching effect of powder are those filling fuses, and they work directly under suckers (exhaust hoods). This is a very small percentage and the great remainder do a multitude of duties such as assembling, inspection, etc."[158] GECO did not record one death associated with toxic jaundice, and there is no record of any women needing treatment after the war ended.[159]

If women were leery about working with tetryl, they needed only look to their history, and the Great War for motivation. "Stained hands and coppery hair — what are these?" asked a Great War worker. "Do we fear temporary disfigurement when men, for the same cause, are facing death and the horrible and permanent disfigurement of maimed limbs or blinded eyes? Munition life is the greatest chance that has ever come to us women."[161]

Conclusion

Early in GECO's history, in July 1942, Ross Davis, editor of the plant's newspaper, made the following observation: "Where in some industries the emphasis is placed almost entirely on maximum production and the worker left to look after his own safety, here the stress was placed — and remains there — on safety. It has been good insurance in the past as "Scarboro's" record proves — it is good insurance now — and will continue good insurance in the future. All that is needed to keep our record clean is continued good teamwork on the 'clean side.'"[162]

Major Flexman, in the last issue of the newspaper, summed up GECO's exemplary safety record: "Suffice to say that in all the period from 1941 to the present not one serious accident occurred in the production shops of the Plant. This is a unique record and speaks volumes for the efficiency of our Safety Department and for the loyal co-operation of all engaged in the filling shops in carrying out the rules which they all realized were made for their own protection and for the uninterrupted operation of the Plant."[163] Major Flexman's opinion reflected a huge shift from Bob Hamilton's early days when he had stated that Scarboro had been "conceived, constructed, organized and operated for but one purpose — production," where even the safety of their employees did not take precedence.[164]

When designing the plant at Scarboro, production was foremost on everyone's minds, however, safety was on the tip of everyone's tongue. GECO's safety record was exceptional and unrivalled in wartime munitions plant operations. Despite the odds and the history that preceded them, thousands of women worked with high explosives over four years at GECO and filled over a quarter of a billion units of munitions without one fatal occupational accident.[165] From plant design to site security, from burying "igloos" to "super structures," from windowless workshops to heavy fire doors, from enforcing strict workshop rules to calling out "All Clear!" GECO made every decision with safety in mind.[166]

9

Whistle While You Work: Industrial Relations and Personnel

Industrial Relations

While everyone who worked at GECO agreed that peace in the world superseded any personal agenda, both management and employees had their own particular motivations, problems, and expectations. GECO created their Industrial Relations Department as a liaison between its employees and management.[1] Industrial Relations staff handled employee queries pertaining to employment, working conditions, fair wages, recreational activities, and they were responsible for publishing GECO's employee newspaper.[2] The department also dealt with any complaints or grievances that could not be resolved to the satisfaction of employees and management at the production level of the organization.[3] The adage "whistle while you work" rang true for GECO workers. Instead of the grime and roar of machines found in other war plants throughout the nation, songs sung by female operators filled the air at "Scarboro" in surroundings that were just as clean and quiet as their own homes.[4]

Personnel

The Personnel Department, housed in Building No. 2 on the dirty side of the plant, and in the clean-side office in Building No. 153 in the Danger Zone, was mandated to hire the very best employees that could be found, and to make their stays at GECO as "pleasant, profitable, and prolonged as possible."[5] The three "P's" sounded easy, but it took a constant and applied effort to retain employees who were willing to stay regardless of other perhaps more lucrative employment elsewhere, including other war industries. "Workers who move from one plant to another lose time from work," Bob Hamilton said.[6] "Time is wasted in training them for new jobs. This is a hindrance to Canada's war effort and a help to the enemy."[7] There was an initial period of employee flux early on when GECO struggled to replace employees who could not adjust to the conditions of war work.[8] Thankfully, for all concerned, the workforce stabilized in the latter half of 1942.[9] In August 1942, GECO reached its highest level of employment with 5,324 men and women working around the clock.[10]

Department staff handled employee questions, resolved problems, and provided information on all company and community resources.[11] The personnel team also welcomed constructive suggestions that could help improve morale or production.[12]

There's Got to Be a Better Way

Management encouraged and welcomed constructive suggestions from employees on all aspects of plant life,[13] and was particularly interested in ideas that could save time, labour, or material.[14] Listening to their largely female employee base for suggestions was innovative and a huge improvement from the attitudes around women's war work in the Great War, when women were treated like children, thought incapable of advanced thinking. "Engineering mankind is possessed of the unshakable opinion", a First World War worker stated, "that no woman can have the mechanical sense."[15] If women challenged the men, however humbly, during those years, they were told gently that if any improvement could be made, a man would have made it prior to her arrival. "As long as we do exactly what we are told and do not attempt to use our brains, we give entire satisfaction, and are treated as nice, good children. Any swerving from the easy path prepared for us by our males arouses the most scathing contempt in their manly bosoms."[16]

At Scarboro, to help employees offer suggestions for improvement at GECO, suggestion boxes were set up at convenient locations around the plant.[17] When an employee saw an opportunity to create a better tool, a more efficient way to fill fuses, a way to make a "better" (more deadly) fuse — anything that would help to move an "empty" through the plant more cost-effectively, or shorten the steps to fill it — they were encouraged to write the suggestion down and place it in the box. By April 1944 more than one thousand suggestions had been received, and more than half of those had been implemented and their owners suitably rewarded.[18] Names of award winners appeared in GECO's newspaper; however, only names of the winners were listed because "details of the nature of the work done in this plant would be revealed which come under the heading of military secrets."[19]

Show Me the Money

During the time Scarboro operated, the Canadian government established all policies regarding wage rates and employee benefits.[20] However, Bob and Phil Hamilton were eager to facilitate training and advancement of their employees so that they could qualify for and receive the highest authorized pay rates as quickly as possible.[21] In 1943, wages started at thirty-five cents per hour.[22] A Cost of Living Allowance wage adjustment occurred annually. The Cost of Living Allowance during the war reached 17 percent at one point.[23] A typical GECO operator could expect her average weekly pay to be from $17–$19.62 to start.[24] Remarkably, handling explosives in munitions work paid less than other wartime industries such as aircraft manufacturing.[25] Unlike their American counterparts, Canadian munitions workers did not receive an additional six cents per hour in hazard pay.[26] Dorothy Cheesman, in her opinion, received very attractive wages for her age, earning between $15 and $17.50 per week.[27] Typical wages for a female clerk in 1941 were $731 per annum, or $14.06 per week.[28]

As for GECO's executives, the Canadian government needed the very best available men and women to fill the top-level positions. It awarded the plant's chief staff healthy monthly salaries. Dr. Jeffrey, head physician, earned $450; Mr. Flexman, plant manager, made $625; E.H. Smith, plant consultant, earned $516; and Mrs. Florence Ignatieff, cafeteria manager, received $350 monthly.[29]

The Canadian government granted six paid days of vacation — an important dispensation established during the war — to employees after they had completed one year of service, according to terms set out by the government's National and Regional War Labour Boards.[30] However, if the employee took an unauthorized absence from work, their vacation was docked one half day for each transgression.[31]

GECO and Its Books of Many Colours

As a top-secret munitions plant, security and safety were paramount at Scarboro, not only to GECO's success as a producer of ammunition, but also to victory overseas. GECO, like other Canadian war plants, issued many small booklets — small enough to fit in handbags and men's shirt pockets — which outlined rules and regulations relating to particular aspects of plant life. Each employee could count on receiving one or several guides, depending on their responsibilities. The front cover of each booklet was a different colour for easy identification.

The Employees' Guidebook — brown in colour — presented a series of "articles" covering everything from secrecy, ID passes, and change house regulations, to attendance expectations, pay regulations, vacation plans, and training.[32] It further addressed safety directives, industrial relations, medical help, cafeteria services, awards, service badges, and enrollment in the plant's Recreation Club.[33] The book outlined processes and procedures that would help make employees at GECO more comfortable and positive.

The Hamilton brothers and the Canadian government were eager to instill a sense of loyalty and pride in their workers from the moment they were brought on board. "The products of this Plant constitute a vital portion of Canada's war effort," wrote Bob and Phil Hamilton in the guidebook's introduction.[34] "They are now being used by the Active Service Forces of the United Nations. Your work in this Plant is therefore a real contribution towards the winning of the war. Attend regularly and put your best effort into your job so that YOUR war effort may be a source of pride and satisfaction to YOU."[35]

100 Percent Club

Despite encouraging patriotism and dedication, the Hamilton brothers and their management team struggled with chronic employee absenteeism at Scarboro. Major causes of absenteeism included sickness, childcare needs, household duties, shopping, and shift fatigue.[36] GECO's absenteeism rate in 1942 was more than 25 percent, three times higher than that of the War Industry Average (WIA) of just over 7 percent.[37] GECO's absentee rate dropped over the next three years, to its lowest point in 1945 at slightly over 10 percent, but remained almost double the WIA.[38] Bob and Phil Hamilton emphasized that the high percentage of absenteeism was due to "employing a very large proportion of women with home duties.[39] It was necessary to do this in order to absorb all the labour available," they explained, "and due allowance was made for this in determining the force required."[40] Was this explanation reasonable and legitimate? Absolutely. Even if there was any question as to the loyalty of their employees, the Hamiltons defended them, nevertheless.

GECO management employed both the "carrot" and the "stick" approach to absenteeism. Posters hung up around the plant "shamed malingerers," pointing out that taking a day off meant one more "round our Boys Won't Get."[41] On the other hand, instead of focusing on the negative — berating those who did not show up for shifts — management also adopted a more positive and proactive approach. In 1944, the plant introduced the "100 Percent Club."[42]

Admission into the club was simple — show up for every shift. For each three-month period of perfect attendance, management awarded an operator a blue chevron badge she wore on the left sleeve of her uniform at her wrist.[43] A thin red chevron replaced four blue chevrons, earned non-consecutively.[44] Workers who "put in full time without absence, misconduct, or lateness, for twelve consecutive months"[45] merited a wide red stripe, the highest awarded emblem.[46] The 100 Percent Club was exclusive, and the fifty GECOites who earned their wide red stripes wore them with pride.[47]

An Urgent Need — the Guns to Feed

War plants in Canada faced several hiring crises during the Second World War.[48] Despite Toronto's large population being situated only a few miles away, severe worker shortages kept GECO striving to meet their production quotas. The Hamiltons and their staff, never shying away from a challenge, strove to overcome the persistent unavailability of labour.[49] Every year, the munitions-filling factory ran massive hiring campaigns in tandem with Canada's National Selection Service.[50] They made provisions to address worker childcare needs and to offer flexible shifts. The plant relaxed their employment standards, allowing anyone from seventeen to seventy to apply, and hired part-time and lower-graded workers.[51] With the introduction of bulk assembly line production, increased efficiency was evident on many fuse-filling lines, calling for fewer trained personnel.[52] They expanded their hiring radius as far as British Columbia.[53] Management educated their entire workforce about the plant's need for more women.[54] Plant manager Major Flexman spoke to every shop on every shift to communicate the need for more employees, and handed out referral cards and "GECO News" pamphlets.[55] GECO even went so far as to offer its employees GECO bumper stickers to help advertise. The stickers apparently had "a smart appearance."[56] Robert Simpson Co. set up a pair of window displays at its store for two weeks to promote both GECO and D.I.L. at no cost to the plants.[57]

In addition, at the end of June 1944, the *Toronto Daily Star* ran generous articles highlighting GECO's pressing employment needs. In the first of a three-series set of articles, the *Star* considered GECO workers "life savers," equating them to a battlefield nurse in her crisp white uniform who saved lives with her tender care.[58] Of course, GECOnians were saving Canadian lives by "nursing" deadly fuses that would blow up the enemy.

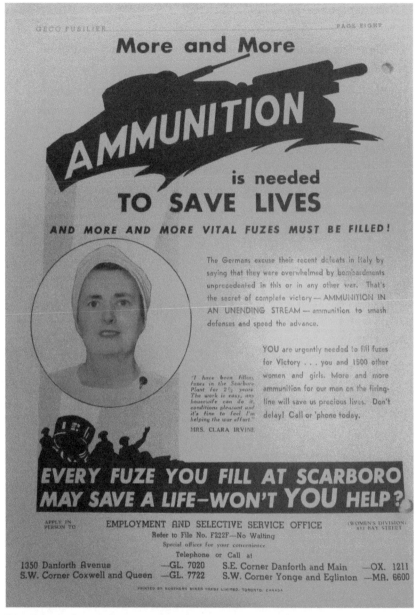

War plants in Canada faced several hiring crises during the Second World War. GECO geared employment advertising toward women, and appealed to their sense of patriotism. "Ammunition Saves Lives," one ad read. "GECO Needs 1500 More Women to Fill Fuzes [sic] to Save Lives. Tell Your Friends. Tell Your Friends to Tell Their Friends." *Courtesy of Barbara Dickson and the Scarborough Historical Board.*

Bob Hamilton is quoted in the article:

> Unless we in Canada can tremendously increase our production
> of shells, our Canadian soldiers are going to find themselves
> short of artillery ammunition, and when they haven't enough
> artillery they have to attack with bayonet or rifle alone, and
> that means heavy casualties. Artillery saves lives. Every girl at
> General Engineering feels that the lives of her brothers, or sons,
> or husband, is in her hands, and they really are. If we can keep a
> steady stream of shells going overseas, we will bring back many
> more of our boys alive and sound.[59]

10

Service with a Smile: Departments Serving Employees

Medical: An Ounce of Prevention

Within a month of breaking ground, in March 1941 Bob and Phil Hamilton already were considering the needs of their future employee base, and organized GECO's Medical Department.[1] They estimated that the department would need to service 3,000 employees, of whom two-thirds would be women.[2] Little did they know, over 21,000 employees eventually would pass through GECO's clock house,[3] and that as the war wore on, the percentage of women employed versus men would reach 95 percent.[4] They had no way of anticipating how heavy the cost to property and human life would be, due to chemical poisoning, fire, and explosions, but they did know full provision had to be made for any such emergency.[5] As in all other decisions, the Hamiltons took a pro-active approach, and prepared as best they could for the worst possible outcome, and then regularly tested their progress, adapting new, better, safer, and more efficient methods to ensure they minimized risk and maximized ammunition output.

In addition to preparing for the worst, as part of Bob and Phil Hamilton's proactive strategy, they wanted to care for all non-occupational illnesses among their employees while they were on plant property.[6] That meant GECO's medical team would treat everything from runny noses to mysterious rashes. Medical Officer Dr. A.H. Jeffrey anticipated the health requirements of future GECOnians. He helped design the change houses and uniforms; he selected soap, skin cream, and towels, and helped choose sinks and toilets.[7] In fact, input from GECO's Medical Department went well beyond the change rooms. From the frequency of laundry service to the maintenance of washrooms, from ensuring buildings were ventilated properly to the proper installation of air conditioning, Dr. Jeffrey was involved with all personnel health-related decisions.[8] He also spearheaded the decision to chlorinate GECO's water supply, to preclude potential contamination from explosive dust, a serious problem at other war plants.[9] Medical personnel also made careful physical examinations of all applicants, setting a high standard of physical fitness for prospective employees.[10] In addition to looking for pre-existing skin conditions and chronic respiratory illnesses that might harm operators working with tetryl powder, eyesight and nimble, steady fingers were important factors as well, since good vision was required for precise filling procedures; unsteady hands could have spelled disaster.[11]

Bob and Phil Hamilton and Dr. Jeffrey embraced the adage, "An ounce of prevention is worth a pound of cure." Industrial medicine, as it was practised at Scarboro, was preventative in nature, designed to keep each individual healthy and capable of productive work with minimal time lost through illness.[12] Records show that 85 percent of medical cases treated over the life of Scarboro were non-occupational in nature, mostly minor complaints like contending with a cold or flu.[13]

However, even minor illness was of concern to GECO management. Viruses had the potential to keep employees away from work, with a subsequent loss in munitions production; and yet, women who continued to work through their illnesses could spread germs within the close confines of their workshop, potentially causing an even greater loss of output. The simple common cold virus demanded diligence and required a delicate balancing act between keeping a dedicated GECOnian on the job and sending her home.

The staff of the Medical Department originally consisted of three full-time physicians on salary and two nurses, but by May 1942 five full-time physicians were on staff to help give pre-employment medical examinations to several thousand applicants.[14] A doctor was on duty on the clean side during specified hours, and employees could see him there or could drop in to the medical building during their lunch hour, or at the end of their shift.[15] As the war dragged on, however, a scarcity of doctors threatened this extra service.[16]

In case of an emergency, an employee could obtain a "barrier pass" from their workshop supervisor and go directly to the medical building.[17] An employee working on the dirty side of the plant could go to the medical building at any time. GECOite Dorothy Cheesman recalled fainting once and having to seek medical help. "I was treated very well," she said.[18]

Nursing staff at GECO increased to twelve by the end of 1943, with six stationed throughout the plant, including in the change rooms at the start or end of shifts.[19] The nurses advised female employees about

GECO nurses enjoying a round of horseshoes on their lunch break. Medical staff at Scarboro included five full-time doctors and twelve nurses. *Courtesy of Archives of Ontario.*

health matters, particularly about skincare and the prevention of tetryl rash.[20] Following the introduction of this proactive nursing service, the incidence of tetryl rash dropped, and other munitions plants nation-wide adopted GECO's approach to managing this occupational hazard.[21] Close supervision in the change houses also helped to limit the spread of contagious diseases; nurses sent women home if they were too ill to work or seemed contagious. Through close daily association with GECO's women operators, nurses gained enough confidence to be of invaluable help in counselling women on non-medical problems as well.[22] In April 1943, GECO's Medical Department introduced a "Visiting Nursing Service" to follow up on serious occupational and non-occupational illnesses at an employee's home.[23]

Between 850 and 1,500 employees — about one in five — visited the Medical Department or the First Aid units each week during GECO's operation, a reflection of the high degree of confidence and trust placed in GECO's medical team, not an indication of poor health among workers.[24] The medical staff probably welcomed employees warmly; there were relatively few munitions-related injuries to keep staff busy. With time on their hands, and with thousands of potential "guinea pigs" on which to experiment, medical staff tried out several innovative investigations in a sincere attempt to improve the overall health of their employees. Doctors measured employees' hemoglobin counts to treat cases of anaemia that potentially could affect a worker's efficiency.[25] They surveyed and documented women's menstrual histories; they also tested the effectiveness of taking daily multivitamins.[26] Unfortunately, vitamin therapy resulted in no lessening in rates of absenteeism or sickness.[27]

During Scarboro's history only two major events occurred that strained GECO's medical facilities.[28] The first happened overnight between the eleventh and twelfth of December 1944, when the entire night shift at the plant became "stormbound" during a blizzard with a record-breaking snowfall and freezing temperatures.[29] No one was able to leave the compound until late afternoon the next day.[30] The second incident occurred on January 26, 1945, when a Hollinger bus carrying employees from the afternoon shift collided with a large truck in GECO's parking lot.[31] The crash resulted in the injury of many employees, some needing hospitalization.[32] One woman, GECOite Mrs. Parkes, died four days later.[33] This woman's passing, while tragic, was remarkable in that it was not munitions-related and was the only fatality recorded at GECO's entire operation at Scarboro.[34]

In February and March of 1942 the Division of Industrial Hygiene, Ontario Department of Health, conducted a chest X-ray evaluation of all employees — the first industrial analysis of its magnitude to be undertaken in Ontario.[35] Dr. Jeffrey explained that "the number of Scarboro employees working in close contact with each other and, in particular, the presence of a large group of young women from eighteen to thirty years of age made such a survey desirable and knowledge was also required as to what extent pulmonary diseases might be an occupational hazard."[36] This first check comprised 5,424 employees, with another round of X-rays nine months later encompassing 2,281 individuals, including all new employees hired since the first analysis.[37] In January and February of 1944 another assessment was made of all employees.[38] Staff paid special attention to X-rays of operators who worked with explosive powders.[39] It was found that these powders had no negative effects on the lungs, which was a relief to all.[40] It was not all good news, though. The first round of X-rays showed nineteen employees with active pulmonary tuberculosis, of which fifteen were sent to a sanatorium for treatment.[41] Another thirty-one cases were questionably active.[42] The prevalence of active TB among GECO's population was 0.54 percent for men and 0.28 percent among women employees.[43] From a contagion and health perspective, government and health experts considered these rates very satisfactory in view of the age groups involved.[44] Questionable cases worked only during the day and learned about disease control.[45] In the second assessment at the end of 1942, only one active case of tuberculosis required treatment.[46] While they wanted to be helpful in conducting the health survey, in an ironic twist, both the Medical Department and management had to dispel rumours that a worker could "catch" tuberculosis from being in close contact with fellow fuse-fillers in windowless air-conditioned workshops.[47]

In April 1943 GECO introduced an employee Sick Benefit Plan.[48] Employees could receive $10.00 per week for female workers and $15.00

per week for male employees, due to illness or accident, up to 13 weeks.[49] A doctor's certificate was necessary to apply for benefits.[50] The monthly cost to the employee to enroll in this plan was $1.13 for female employees and $1.73 for men.[51] Employees could also purchase hospital insurance for stays of up to twenty-one days per year.[52] Coverage was split into three categories: single men and women; married women with or without children and married men with children; and wives of members of the armed forces without children.[53]

Food Services: Eat, Drink, and Be Healthy

When Bob Hamilton brought Mrs. Ignatieff onboard to take care of Scarboro's dietary needs, he gave her full autonomy except for one important stipulation: the cafeteria was to run on a non-profit basis.[54] She was to keep prices down, regardless of inflation, and base every nutritional decision on quality, quantity, and service.[55]

Florence oversaw all operations of the massive lunchroom that sprawled across three-quarters of an acre — one of the largest of its kind in Canada with a seating capacity of two thousand — and directed a staff of 120 workers, including chefs, dishwashers, servers, and cleaning personnel.[56] In fact, GECO staff served more "customers" daily than all the big hotels in downtown Toronto combined.[57] During rush-hour periods, cafeteria staff handled nearly forty customers every sixty seconds.[58] Their cutting-edge dishwashing equipment — another GECO invention — met stringent bacterial counts imposed by the Medical Department, and satisfactorily washed away stubborn egg and lipstick from glassware.[59] Dishwashing staff daily washed and sterilized about 18,000 plates, 5,000 glasses, and a seemingly unending stream of cutlery.[60]

In a review of GECO's operation in 1943, cafeteria manager Florence Ignatieff wrote, "The dining-room was planned and built to enable the employees to secure attractive, nutritious, well-balanced meals, and was arranged large and airy to provide relaxation and pleasant surroundings."[61] A visionary in the science of nutrition, and decades before the "100-Mile Diet" would gain popularity, Florence was convinced local was better, and instructed her staff to buy produce from neighbouring farms whenever possible. Fresh fruit and vegetables harvested from nearby farms at night were on the cafeteria menu the next day. Often ears of corn had been plucked from the fields only a few hours earlier.[62] Educated extensively in nutritional sciences, Florence served wholesome meals and espoused healthy eating habits.[63] In 1944 she offered diet and nutrition lectures to GECO employees.[64] Philip Hamilton, P.D.P. Hamilton's son, remembers Florence as "a wonderful person" who prepared "wonderful meals."[65]

In one day, hungry GECOites consumed up to 1,500 pounds of beef.[66] In a typical month, cafeteria staff bought, cut up, prepared, and served twelve tons of meat.[67] However, a meat shortage in September 1942 meant a few meatless days in the cafeteria.[68] In an amusing GECO cafeteria story, staff mistook salt for sugar while baking a large batch of blueberry pies.[69] The staff did not discover the mistake until eight hundred pieces had been cut.[70] To complicate things, only half of the slices were salty.[71] With only one sure way to ferret out the offending slices, Florence and her assistant Barbara Holmes taste-tested eight hundred pieces of pie.[72] It would be a long time before they wanted to eat blueberry pie again.

Florence and her staff believed the large, comfortable cafeteria contributed in good measure to GECO employees' high morale.[73] From the president to the lowliest position at the plant, everyone gathered in the spacious canteen to eat a hearty meal and meet and mingle in informal surroundings. Frequently the large room also functioned as an auditorium and hall, bringing thousands together to hold Victory Bond drives, musical events, talent nights, judging for Miss Scarboro War Worker competitions, and other plant events.

Uniforms: The Mechanical Laundry Mangle

GECO offered free laundering services to employees, mainly to ensure that no explosive dust lingering on dirty uniforms left the property, posing a hazard not only to workers but to their families and the general public.[74] Early on, staff sent the plant's laundry out for cleaning commercially.[75] However, transporting dirty uniforms contaminated with explosive dust posed a threat to civilians.[76] Opening laundering facilities onsite eliminated a hazard to the public and saved the government $2,000 per week, or more than $100,000 per annum.[77] Fortuitously, there were other benefits to washing linens at the plant. Original GECO uniforms, expected to last about eight months, were still in "active service" after more than a year of wash and wear; a conservation initiative decades before a "Reduce, Reuse, and Recycle" would become a global mantra.[78]

Laundry facilities were housed in Building No. 9, one of the "cleanest" buildings on the dirty side of the plant.[79] Laundry staff were in charge of cleaning all linens used in the plant, from shop, cafeteria, and medical uniforms, to towels and hospital bedsheets.[80] Staff handled between 65,000 and 75,000 pieces of laundry per week,[81] more than Toronto General Hospital at that time.[82] Soiled laundry arrived by "trucks" from around the plant, and were sorted, then washed in industrial-strength washers for about an hour.[83] This wash included a rinse in a mild solution of sodium sulphite, then a mild bleach to remove dirt, germs, and "tet" — tetryl dust.[84] The washing process took seven changes of water.[85] Laundry workers put wet clothes through "extractors" — early versions of the modern dryer — to spin out excess water.[86] They then pressed clean, dry laundry at the rate of one thousand items per hour in the "mechanical mangle," a gigantic "ironing" machine.[87] Mending happened where needed, and then staff sorted and redistributed clean linens to their appropriate departments.[88] Slacks bearing a worker's employee number were matched to her numbered jacket, a clean turban was added, and then her complete uniform was bundled, tagged, and sent back to the change house, all done within an eight-hour shift.[89] By July 31, 1945, GECO's laundry facilities had handled 10,171,989 pieces of clothing.[90]

Transportation: Where the Rubber Hits the Road

With the closest streetcar stop located four miles from the plant, the Hamiltons recognized the need to provide sufficient (and free) transportation for their employees.[91] Management hired Danforth Bus Lines Limited and Hollinger Bus Lines Limited to pick up and drop off workers at designated stops in Toronto.[92] A gentleman's agreement was the only contract between GECO and the bus lines for almost two and a half years until they signed a formal contract in September 1943.[93] Bus stops were situated at the corners of Danforth Avenue and Coxwell Avenue, Danforth and Dawes Road, Yonge Street and Eglinton Avenue, Victoria Park Avenue and Kingston Road, and at Main and Gerrard Streets; there were seven stops in total.[94] Buses ran from 6:00 a.m. to midnight six days a week, with an additional bus at 3:00 a.m.[95] Up to twenty-six buses were needed each shift.[96] Seven additional buses served office staff.[97] As the war progressed and part-time work was introduced, ten more buses were brought online between 11:30 a.m. and 1:00 p.m. daily.[98]

In a typical twelve-month period, not counting holidays or Sundays, GECO's fleet of employee buses transported about 2.7 million passengers — the equivalent of carrying a quarter of Canada's population — about 600,000 total miles, or approximately twenty-four times around the world.[99] By 1944, with additional routes added, GECO buses had made seventy-eight thousand trips, or travelled 780,000 miles, the equivalent of circling the Earth thirty times.[100]

About one thousand operators lived outside GECO bus service routes.[101] Management solved this problem with carpooling. Privately owned cars — about 240 vehicles — that were registered with the War Identification Transit Plan picked up and dropped off those employees who truly lived in the wilds of Scarboro.[102]

During GECO's "rush hours" more than fifty people per minute boarded buses to head home or disembarked before starting their shifts.[103] Mr. Earl Freeland, who was responsible for all bus services, worked tirelessly to keep vehicles on schedule and in good repair.[104] He had no control over Mother Nature, however, when a wicked thunderstorm, a sleet or snowstorm, or frigid temperatures tested the mettle of employees and bus drivers alike. Managing this volume of human beings in a tight space could leave tempers and patience in short supply. Transporting thousands of employees each day sometimes caused anger and frustration for non-war workers along the bus route. In a letter to the editor of the *Toronto Daily Star* on Saturday, February 14, 1942, one such gentleman — a war worker at Research Enterprises Ltd. near Laird and Eglinton, which at its zenith employed more than 7,500 employees — had this to say in reaction to a previous editorial from "East Ender":

Sir: I read with disgust the letter by an east ender. I thought that we had more war conscious people in the east end. I am an employee of Research Enterprises Ltd. I know, as do a great many others, the conditions on the Pape Ave. bus line.

We, too, have seen six and sometimes eight buses one after another coming down Pape Ave. But East Ender does not say that each one is crammed to the doors with people who work in war plants. East Ender does not say that the war workers have to line up to Danforth Ave. to get on these buses. There are usually hundreds late every morning because they cannot get on the buses, they are so crowded.

AN R.E.L. MAN[105]

While "R.E.L. MAN" doesn't say if Research Enterprises Ltd. had their own set of dedicated buses, he makes it clear that war workers — who are striving to end the war — should, and do, get preferential treatment. GECO management reminded their employees that there were other wartime plants that "would give their eye teeth" to have a free ride to work.[106]

Material rationing and shortages, of car parts, rubber, manpower, and gas easily exacerbated an already complicated endeavour subject to scheduling headaches in the best of times, let alone when the nation was at war; somehow, however, GECO's fleet of thirty-five buses diligently stayed on the roads "come hell or high water" and made 245 trips daily.[107]

GECO buses, over the life of the plant, transported between 190,000 and 225,000 riders per month.[108] Although the service was free to its employees, GECO's average cost per passenger per month to run the service was 10.53 cents, a total of approximately $24,000.[109] At the end of July 1945, when GECO closed its doors, the buses had carried more than 8.5 million passengers to or from the plant at a phenomenal cost of approximately $895,000.[110]

11

Rolling Up Their Sleeves: Departments Contributing to Munitions Production

The construction, design, and operation of a wartime munitions plant took the efforts of thousands of men and women over dozens of departments dedicated, directly or indirectly, to the production of GECO's lethal product line. Management established departments to oversee every aspect of production, ensuring the safety of personnel and property, researching and developing new and improved ways to fill munitions, and supporting the myriad needs of women, who represented the vast majority of their employees.

Production Department: The Buck Stops Here

The Production Department — the heart of GECO's operation — was responsible for training every clean-side operator, supervisor, and assistant foreman.[1] Proper training was critical not only to GECO's success, but could mean the difference between life and death. Staff managed employee work record cards that contained worker histories, including information pertaining to raises, transfers, and warnings, as well as evaluation statistics for desirable occupational traits such as efficiency, proper deportment, and attendance.[2] Meticulous production reporting was crucial to anticipate future munitions-filling schedules.[3] The depart-ment also addressed any technical production issues that arose.[4]

Planning and Records: A Juggling Act

Expecting everything to run smoothly in an industry without a precedent in Canada was unrealistic. A new enterprise such as GECO was depen-dent on supplies from numerous other factories that also were charting unmapped wartime waters. One of the assembly and filling plant's great-est hurdles to overcome lay in the dependable supply of components. Often production for filling one fuse would ramp up, only to have work suddenly stop and operators switched to other natures.[5] This occurred in large part because supplies had not arrived in time.[6] These stoppages, while disruptive to the operators in the fuse-filling workshops, and detrimental to the efficiency of production, were all part of the bigger problem of supply. To overcome unreliable component supplies, GECO filled on its own schedule, not based on what production was authorized to fill.[7] For example, GECO was authorized to fill four million Primer 15 Mark IIs, but filled over eight million.[8] There were no idle hands at GECO. If the parts needed to fill one type of fuse had not arrived, they filled and stockpiled other munitions.

Planning and Records (P&R) provided weekly inventory and require-ment sheets to management and supervisors to help anticipate daily, weekly, and monthly component requirements.[9] They also managed the Inspection General — a dedicated independent group of people who worked for the Canadian government and were responsible for inspect-ing fuses, ensuring Canada's armed forces used top-notch ammunition in theatres of war.[10]

Just Where Do You Test Explosives?

The only real way to test a fuse's capability and reliability was to use it in as close to actual battlefield conditions as possible — in Scarboro's case, at a proofing range. Of course, proofing ranges had to be located where there was no danger to life or property.[11] When war broke out,

Valcartier, Quebec was home to the only proof range in Canada.[12] Valcartier's proof range strained under the increased demands for testing as D.I.L. in Pickering and GECO in Scarboro ramped up production.[13] A second proof range was set up near Hamilton, Ontario, to ease the backlog.[14] The Hamilton site, under the direction of retired British artillery officer Colonel Douglas Clapham, was regarded as "one of the most efficient in the British Empire … and the largest establishment of its kind in Canada."[15] D.I.L. at Pickering eventually set up a range, too, which GECO used extensively.[16]

In addition to testing munitions in a war-like environment, ammo was also tested on a smaller scale at GECO in its proof yard. There were two proof yards within GECO's confines. Current arsenal practice required keeping separate, unbiased proof yards for both inspectors with the Inspection Board (I.B.) and contractors like GECO.[17] In an initiative to calm ruffled feathers between the I.B. and GECO workers, the Canadian government allowed GECO to merge its two yards, jointly operated between the two parties.[18] The Proof Yard's mandate was to test, or "proof," small samples of filled fuses randomly selected from each lot to determine how well they performed under controlled conditions and then "sentence" — accept or reject — the lot.[19] Proof Yard staff were also responsible for testing samples by gunfire or "gun proof;" they tested empties to ensure their safety and capacity to be filled satisfactorily; they experimented with new methods and components; and they tested safety devices for use in filling workshops.[20]

Speed of proofing was essential — if units failed, shops had to find not only the cause of the rejection, but a quick, safe solution.[21] In GECO's unique "proofing" situation all proofing was done to the satisfaction of the I.B., who reserved the right to carry out their own proofing at any time.[22] At GECO's peak of production, proof yard personnel proofed forty-two thousand units in one month, equating to about 1,750 explosions daily.[23]

Workers in the Destroying Ground, situated at the southernmost end of the plant, ensured that munitions waste and/or rejected explosives, such as gunpowder, gun-cotton, TNT, tetryl, tracer compounds, caps, detonators, and filled stores were destroyed safely.[24]

An Explosive Conflict

The conflict between independent inspection personnel and the production team, including workshop supervisors and operators, was, at times, volatile. This was not a problem unique to Scarboro, but one suffered by other wartime manufacturing plants.[25] With wartime industry burgeoning in Canada, up to one thousand Inspection Board (I.B.) examiners with little training, and that training based on British requirements, had absolute authority to sentence the quality of work by skilled munitions operators working in Canada.[26] GECO employees, for their own safety, were well-versed in working with high explosives and recognized the vital need to get filled munitions quickly to the Allied troops — fuses' ultimate end users. Within filling shops, work approved by government inspector (G.I.) staff was inconsistent and unreliable. Filled fuses accepted by G.I.s on one shift were rejected on the next, or the quality of work previously rejected suddenly passed inspection.[27] Distrust grew between the operators and G.I.s.[28] There were glaringly obvious inconsistencies in standards and undependable product quality assurance. This was no small problem given they were dealing with high explosives. GECO offered training classes to Inspection Board personnel, but they declined, perhaps as a matter of principle to maintain an arms-length relationship.[29] This exasperated GECO's employees. In addition, the Inspection Board would not approve changes to filling conditions that had absolutely no impact on the quality of the filled fuse.[30] Worse, when they did refuse the changes, they were unable to provide any adequate technical solution to the original problem that triggered the request for a deviation.[31] And the final straw? Any changes that GECO convinced the I.B. to accept had to go through official channels in Ottawa, then, in turn, back to England for final approval.[32] This was "red tape" at its finest, causing delays neither GECO nor the Allied forces could afford.

With no relief in sight, a New Year on the horizon, and a long war before them, the Hamilton brothers, in December 1941, engineered a unique proposal to mend the ongoing and sometimes hostile relationship between G.I.s and GECO employees. Put simply, Bob and Phil Hamilton obtained approval from the Inspection Board of the United Kingdom and Canada to take over responsibility for all fuse proofing and sentencing.[33]

On February 15, 1942, GECO established a Factory Inspection (F.I.) Department to act as liaison between Government Inspection and GECO Production.[34] The F.I. Department set up checkpoints directly on filling lines to catch potential problems as they happened, to examine empties in order to reduce their rejection, and to negotiate standards agreeable to all parties.[35] The department would also oversee inspections in which the Inspection Board delegated responsibility to GECO personnel, or where GECO desired an inspection that was not required by the Inspection Board, to assure quality of product and economy of scale.[36] The new department was staffed with a handful of GECO personnel, but more importantly, a considerable proportion of government inspectors moved into the department.[37] Enmity and mistrust between G.I.s and GECO workers did not disappear instantaneously. Absolute diplomacy of F.I. staff was needed when interacting with the I.B. Although G.I.s were not paid by GECO, everyone, from that point forward, viewed G.I.s as GECO employees and welcomed them into the GECO family.

Establishing Factory Inspection represented a turning point at GECO, validating management's drive to produce top quality production while working amicably with all external parties. Inspectors, by working alongside GECO operators, gained confidence in their abilities and personal integrity.[38] This helped GECO gain a high degree of co-operation from inspectors of the Inspection Board.

A year later, by February 1943, Factory Inspection had evolved to such a point that the department submitted a plan to management to place newly designated F.I. Examiner-Operators at carefully selected points in the assembly lines. Workers wanted to involve inspectors not only through having them visually examine the fuses, but also during the actual filling — getting their hands dirty, as it were — to ensure the inspections were as accurate as possible.[39] GECO staff estimated that 136 fewer operators and I.B. inspectors would be required, while at the same time the efficiency of inspection, and, perhaps more importantly, the authority and prestige of the Inspection Board would remain sound.[40] Several highly skilled GECO operators transferred from Production to Factory Inspection later that spring; they received their new titles of F.I. Operator-Examiner and took over inspection points relinquished by the I.B.[41]

Government inspectors examine filled Primer 15 in Shop 35A. Government inspectors, while paid by the Canadian government, were considered an integral part of the GECO family. *Courtesy of Archives of Ontario.*

The amalgamation between separate proof yards ultimately saved GECO 40 percent in operating costs and capital savings, as only one "proof" was needed from each lot with acceptance or rejection agreed to by both the I.B. and GECO.[42] In March 1943, seventy GECO workers proofed 46,377 natures at a cost of $13,959.61 in salaries; six months later, thirty-nine proofers tested 46,756 natures at a cost of $6,220.17 in salaries.[43] The merged proof yard also greatly increased the degree of co-operation between the I.B. and GECO employees, and saved time and equipment.[44]

New inspection points resulted in savings in labour and materials.[45] By moving G.I.s directly into filling lines to inspect fuses immediately, GECO ensured quality control as it happened, not as an afterthought.[46] "Bench leaders" and assistant foremen observed operators' work, making changes in procedure quickly and easily.[47] GECO was able to reduce their operator headcount by eighty-five through this initiative.[48]

Quality Control: Impressing the Enemy

Ironically, GECO did not formally establish its Quality Control Department until the end of August 1943, a full two years after production commenced.[49] Even then, the department was set up only to address new fuse-filling requirements for the Flame Tracer Bullet .303 G II, which called for a much higher degree of mechanization than had been possible on any component filled to date, and for which current inspection protocol did not apply and could not be adapted.[50]

A lack of a formal Quality Control Department was of little consequence to Scarboro's quality standards. The plant already had set robust quality assurance standards which were the product of myriad rules and regulations, and the inspection expectations of both Canadian and British governments.

Every fuse that left Scarboro was etched with "Sc/C."[51] Over the course of the war, battlefronts around the world came to recognize Scarboro's stamp of quality.[52] Armed forces knew ammunition marked with "Sc/C" would do the job for which it was designed, filled, and assembled: blow up the enemy. In an ironic twist, German soldiers came to appreciate Scarboro's symbol and the quality it signified, too. During fierce battles in Italy, when land and equipment switched sides frequently between Allied and German forces, word got back to GECO that German forces were impressed with the quality of ammunition that came from the plant.[53]

Scarboro was fiercely proud of meeting the highest quality standards set by Government Inspectors, proudly claiming that a rejection rate of just over 1 percent by inspection personnel "was proof of a job well done."[54]

"When one considers the magnitude of the task that Canada undertook to do," wrote Major Flexman in retrospect, "it is surprising that we came through so well."[55]

Scarboro's emblem "Sc/C," which was etched into every fuse, became a symbol of quality for friend and foe on battlefields around the world. *Courtesy of Scarborough Historical Society.*

Shipping: We Got Ourselves a Convoy

GECO established its Shipping Department in August 1941.[56] The department oversaw all aspects relating to the shipping of filled munitions. The Canadian government prohibited the shipment of explosives via rail, so A.W.S.C. established a "proof truck" service; a convoy of heavy-duty munitions trucks shuttling between munitions plants and proof ranges twenty-four hours a day.[57]

Research and Development: Safer, Faster, Deadlier

The Research and Development (R&D) team consisted of representatives from several production departments, including Chemical Investigations, Engineering, Factory Inspection, and Experimental

Work.[58] Finding solutions without the aid of previous experience led indirectly to the adapting of available equipment or the creating of new equipment, which, fortuitously, in many cases, was cheaper than the unavailable equipment.[59] Scarboro saw a potential savings in many of their tooling solutions and seized every opportunity to design and manufacture tools that not only saved money but time and labour, and extended longevity as well.

Achievements attributed to GECO's R&D Department included the invention of an electrical hygrometer.[60] The new hygrometer helped GECO personnel control humidity in the air to a strict 55 percent, which previously had been very difficult to measure and helped fine-tune humidity standards in Canada.[61]

R&D also helped create "stemming" hoods to minimize hazards associated with tetryl dust.[62] With the installation of these hoods in workshop 60B — a shop segregated for stemming purposes — operators could work from outside the apparatus, which had built-in ventilators that suctioned air and dust away, greatly reducing deadly airborne tetryl dust.[63] Over the course of its operations, GECO saw a continued improvement in stemming tools and equipment. Early on, operators had to hand-pack high explosives into detonators, which exposed everyone to potentially disastrous consequences should a worker pack too much of the deadly powder.[64] Through new technical endeavours in Canada and Britain, in 1943 GECO acquired their first automatic stemming machine.[65] The new equipment performed three times as fast as hand stemming, and for safety's sake, more accurately.[66] By 1944, GECO had discontinued stemming by hand.[67]

In August 1942, management established a separate Experimental/ Development Department as a sub-group under R&D, located in Building No. 14.[68] Employees involved in experimental work easily had the most secretive and deadly job at the plant. Not only did these highly trained engineering and chemical experts handle high explosives every day, they searched for better, more deadly ways to blow things up. This was not child's play — harkening back to high-school days in a science lab armed with a Bunsen burner and some odourless, powdered concoction a teacher had whipped up. These specimens, if even slightly compromised

"Stemming" referred to the act of pressing a specified quantity of high-explosive powders into certain areas within a fuse without causing an explosion. The plant introduced a dedicated stemming shop — Building No. 60 — which allowed dangerous tetryl dust to be confined to one building and greatly reduced the incidence of rash and tetryl-related ailments. A further refinement to the process involved the introduction of ventilation hoods, which removed the tetryl dust to the outside of the building. Six to eight women could work outside these hoods, keeping air-borne tetryl dust to a minimum. *Courtesy of Archives of Ontario*

in handling, had the potential to cause catastrophic destruction to life and property.

During its first year, R&D handled more than 650 problems, big and small, of which approximately four hundred involved work carried out by the Experimental/Development Committee.[69] By mid-1943, GECO had registered twenty-two new or improved pieces of machinery for use by the United Nations.[70]

Purchasing: Axes, Apples, and Ammo

In late January 1941, GECO filled out its first purchase order for the future munitions plant: one small and two medium axes to drive survey stakes into frozen ground at the newly chosen site in Scarboro.[71] Bob and Phil Hamilton established their Purchasing Department at GECO four days after construction workers broke ground.[72]

The need for abundant amounts of construction materials to build more than 170 buildings began in earnest in early 1941, and included estimates for 14 billion board feet of lumber, wallboard, rock wool for insulation, material for electrical, plumbing, and heating installations, roofing, flooring, and hardware.[73] Once construction was well underway, by May 1941, the emphasis for the Purchasing Department shifted to buying supplies to equip plant services, such as two fire halls, a hospital, the cafeteria, and the laundry.[74] Emphasis shifted again, in July and August 1941, when purchasing for initial production commenced.[75] While the Planning and Records Department made purchases for components and materials directly related to actual production, the Purchasing Department was responsible for appropriating the extensive variety of materials, equipment, and supplies needed to manage a sprawling military complex.[76]

Materials and equipment were regularly in short supply, often causing delays in delivery.[77] Slowing things down further was the fact that purchase orders could not be made by telephone, just in case the enemy had infiltrated the phone lines[78] This requirement precluded the possibility of speedy delivery of any purchase to Scarboro, whether it was gunpowder or apples. As a result, the Purchasing Department had to anticipate requirements well in advance, so as not to hold up production.

In the end, staff placed 36,344 purchase orders with nearly 1,300 firms for about ten thousand different items.[79]

Engineering General Office: Ground Zero

The massive Engineering General Office handled all plant construction, maintenance, transportation, (including trucking and roads), fire fighting needs, and mechanical services.[80] Crucial co-operation and a congenial relationship between the General Office and all other departments at the plant was fundamental to GECO's success, with their decisions affecting the health, efficiency, safety, and welfare of everyone at the plant. One of the first departments to be established, Engineering was responsible for everything from supplying water and power to changing light bulbs, from controlling air conditioning to servicing toilets, from creating special tools to building office furniture, from providing fire protection to keeping the roads in good repair.

GECO's munitions production ran around the clock, six days a week, which put a tremendous demand on equipment and tools within fuse-filling workshops. Tools broke and small parts were lost. With strict communication protocols placed on GECO as a wartime government plant, a potential three- to eight-week delay was possible if broken parts had to be shipped out to be fixed or new parts ordered in.[81] GECO management anticipated this problem and "fixed" it early by strategically incorporating a tool and machinery shop into its original plant design.[82] In fact, Building No. 7 was the first building to be completed and equipped within weeks of breaking ground.[83] Filled with lathes, drill presses, shapers, steel hardening and tempering equipment, and other machines, GECO's Tool and Machinery shop was one of the best in the country at the time.[84] Highly skilled mechanics replicated or repaired parts within a precision of 1/10,000th of an inch.[85] With the repair shop right on the premises, employees often enjoyed same-day service in GECO's "tool hospital."[86] The shop handled more than two thousand repair jobs per week.[87]

Maintenance workers at GECO looked after the site's buildings as well as the plant's extensive grounds and transportation needs.[88] Grounds Maintenance was responsible for GECO's tunnel system.[89] The Transportation Department managed all plant vehicles, which included taxis, explosives trucks, station wagons, general-purpose trucks, and snowplows.[90]

The Sawdust Brigade

The carpentry shops at GECO, housed in Buildings 8 and 142, were a woodworker's dream.[91] About seventy-five older men, affectionately called the "sawdust brigade" and mostly First World War vets from the "Old Country," worked tirelessly, producing everything from boxes for shipping filled munitions to fine desk furniture, from station wagons to hat racks.[92]

Once construction of GECO was completed, seventy-five older men, with 2,300 years combined construction experience, stayed on in GECO's carpentry shops working tirelessly producing a wide variety of wooden treasures: boxes to ship filled munitions, fine desk furniture, toys for war-time nurseries, and playground equipment for GECO's employee field days. Carpenter Alexander Licorice Waddell is seated in the front row, third from the left. *Courtesy of Barbara Dickson, from Scarborough Historical Society.*

One of the department's proudest accomplishments was the design and manufacture of a fully functional station wagon from scratch, using no blueprints.[93] This wagon, "resplendent in its varnish and new paint,"[94] eased the burden of proof yard personnel having to walk almost half a mile each way in all kinds of weather to and from the southern end of the plant for their shift. It also offered quick relief to fence guards.[95] A second station wagon emerged from the shop later, bigger and sleeker, with all the bugs worked out.[96] By war's end, GECO had amassed a fleet of more than thirty vehicles, including two blue firetrucks — one without a speedometer — an ambulance, munitions trucks, tractors, a jeep, and the big blue twelve-passenger station wagon fondly dubbed the "Blue Goose," which operated as a shuttle between Scarboro and Pickering's proof range.[97]

While the "boys" in Shop 8 built toys to donate to wartime nurseries, and built playground equipment for GECO's Field Days, their most important contribution to the war effort was shipping boxes.[98] After empties had been unpacked, the boxes were revamped to house filled munitions, fondly referred to as "Hitler's headaches."[99] "Booster" boxes built at GECO numbered in the thousands, but due to the secretive nature of GECO's work, total boxes built was just one of countless statistics that were not divulged.

Every man on the sawdust brigade felt he did "his bit towards bringing the war to a successful conclusion."[100]

Other Departments: Smaller but Just as Deadly

Several other departments supported production at GECO. The Chemical Investigations Department (C.I.D) started with just one man, Mr. E. Littlejohn, but over the course of Scarboro's operation, C.I.D. would grow to a staff of thirteen working in a well-equipped modern laboratory.[101] Staff in the Time and Motion Department worked to increase efficiency and speed in fuse-filling operations.[102] Through extensive evaluation and study of fuse-filling methodologies, personnel introduced processes that saved $15,942 per month, the equivalent of constructing a new 5,700-square-foot GECO building every month, with money to spare.[103]

The Textiles Department's mandate at GECO was to produce paper and cloth components, which to the casual observer may have seemed like dull work. Textiles manufactured at GECO were anything but dull. These creations encompassed washers, discs, tabs, patches, strips, and paper capsules needed in the filling of deadly ammunition such as fuses, tubes, primers, and gaines.[104] These small yet potent "textile" components were essential in maximizing the potency of GECO's product line.

The Pellet and Magazine Group took care of GECO's most deadly inventory: explosives, initiators such as caps and detonators, and pellets.[105] Workers received, stored, prepared, and released all explosives and components to workshops as needed. They also were responsible for producing pellets needed for most percussion and time fuses.[106] Small pellets, filled with tetryl, were positioned within the fuse, which, once detonated, set off the substantial bulk of explosives housed within a shell or other large armament. Pellets filled with gun powder were also used in some munitions filled at the plant. Their safety record was exemplary, despite their dangerous stock: "The great mounded magazines," management recorded proudly, "in which hundreds of tons of high explosives, gunpowder, and fuse powders would be stored, were processed without accident during Scarboro's history ..."[107]

12

Nothing Less Will Do —
Employee Morale

The Situation Room

By the time GECO launched its massive hiring campaign during the
fall of 1941, the war in Europe was well into its third year. Hitler had
seized Austria, Czechoslovakia, Poland, Norway, Denmark, Netherlands,
Belgium, Luxembourg, and France, and was doggedly determined to
annex Britain and Russia. The need for munitions was acute. It would be
only three months before Japan launched its assault on the U.S. Navy at
Pearl Harbor.

The free world was at war and no life in Canada, or overseas, was
exempt from its troubling effects. GECOnians lived, worked, and prayed
on the home front. They read the evening newspaper filled with grim
war news. They gave up sugar in their tea, and precious dollars for
war bonds. They watched as sombre staff delivered telegrams to fellow
GECOnians in their workshops, announcing the saddest news of all —
that a loved one was missing in action, had been taken prisoner, or had
been killed while fighting the enemy.

The women of GECO gave every fuse their full and undivided attention, not only because they were handling high explosives, but also
because they wanted their men home. Great Britain, homeland to many

women at GECO, was taking a pounding Luftwaffe-style. Besides, what was the alternative? Ominous words appeared in GECO's employee newspaper less than a year after plant productions got underway:

> It's hard to stick at a job we may not like, to work under people we may not like, and harder still to contemplate handing over to the government the major portion on one's surplus earnings.
>
> The fact is that the whole grim business is hard — but it will be harder still if we do less than everything we know how — and lose the war.
>
> If anyone thinks otherwise, let him read and digest what is happening in Poland, Holland, Czecho-Slovakia, Jugo-Slavia, and Greece. The folks in these countries would give their souls to be in our shoes today."[1]

The GECO Diamond Is Their Badge

There were no shift quotas at GECO.[2] They weren't needed. The deaths of Canadian soldiers steeled the women's resolve to fill as many fuses as fast as their deft fingers could manage. Instead, Bob and Phil offered service badges, rewarded for completing years of faithful service.[3] Operators strived to achieve this simple yet solemn mark of distinction, which they wore on their left sleeve.[4] Workers earned a red diamond-shaped badge after one year, green after two, blue after three, and a large gold badge after four years of service, which replaced the former three and had the number "IV" embossed on it.[5] Inspector Carol LeCappelain was disappointed that Germany surrendered when it did; she had just weeks until she would have received her gold badge.[6] Management issued letters of congratulations for faithful service as well,[7] and these became treasured keepsakes for employees and were used as references after the war.[8] GECO also offered employees the chance to join their "100 Percent Club" for exemplary attendance.[9] GECO employees proudly wore their company's insignia on their uniforms, and GECO flags flew from the company's mast and hung in the cafeteria. Other visible symbols of pride for employees included GECO pins worn proudly on civilian clothing.[10]

With each worker's individual employee number etched on the back, every pin depicted a maple leaf and beaver symbolizing Canada, the GECO diamond indicating the company's trademark, and in bold lettering the words, "Munition Worker."[11] "This pin not only identifies the wearer as an employee of the Company," wrote R.M.P. Hamilton in a review of Industrial Relations mid-1943, "but also symbolizes his (or her) part in the Canadian war effort. It is worn with pride and is most helpful in its influence on 'esprit de corps.'"[12]

GECO Fusilier: A Powder Magazine

The Hamiltons and the Canadian government appreciated the far-reaching positive ramifications an employee publication could have on its readership. Management gave Mr. Ross Davis the mandate to promote loyalty, morale, and unity amongst its employees through their "powder magazine."[13] Each issue of the *GECO Fusilier* not only kept the GECO community informed of "all things GECO" but encouraged a dedicated work ethic and an unparalleled safety standard within wartime industry as well. Ross put together an enjoyable read that left women's heartstrings suitably stirred, chock-full of cartoons, inspiring stories, birth, engagement, and wedding announcements, and friendly inter-department competitions. The plant issued eighty-four editions and it had expanded to eight pages from its original four after its first year of publication.[14]

GECO workers were reminded by editor Ross Davis that while they couldn't be "the man behind the gun," they all could be "the man behind the man behind the gun," and that "it is up to us to be good and sure that 'the man behind the gun' has plenty to put in his weapon when he brings his sights to bear on the hordes of Axis assassins."[15] In fact, in just the second issue of the newspaper, printed in April 1942, Ross wrote, "The storm signals are up. There is no question but that the Axis powers are all set for a 'knockout' this year. Millions of men armed to the teeth are on the march. The hurricane is about to hit in all its fury and soon. Let us not delude ourselves — we can lose."[16]

When it came to patriotism and commitment to the war effort, Davis didn't mince words. The newspaper pointed out that those who did not

Cartoonist Lou Skuce created cartoons during GECO's early days using humour and wit to foster patriotism and a dedicated work ethic. In this drawing Mr. Skuce likens munitions workers' war effort to that of servicemen, deserving of a medal. For a GECO worker her medal was her company pin worn proudly on her civilian clothes. *Author's photo.*

have perfect work attendance were "Hitler's Helpers."[17] Ross posed the question, "... what essential difference is there between a fighting man deserting his post in time of danger — and a worker in a munitions plant?"[18] In fact, quite regularly, the newspaper employed guilt tactics to motivate its readers. The following text appeared in the "Editor's Column" in the paper's inaugural edition in regards to shortages in supplies: "... these materials have been brought across sub-infested seas and brave men are daily risking and losing their lives to ensure that we get them. What a pity if we should be found guilty of improper or wasteful use of things so costly."[19]

GECOites with a penchant for poetry wrote about the men who were dying overseas, of their bravery in the face of death, of their sacrifice, and of the shame the nation should feel should the men die because citizens didn't do their very best to supply fighting men with the "tools" needed to get the job done. Mr. William "Bill" Taylor wielded an especially sharp pen, and was a regular contributor of poems to the newspaper.

"A Young Canadian Died!"

For want of a shell a gun was still;
For want of that gun on a Flanders hill
A Hun in a foxhole was free to kill—
And a young Canadian died!

For want of a fuze that was yet unfilled
A shell was lost and a gun was stilled;
And a Hun was alive that it should have killed—
And a young Canadian died!

For want of the hands of a worker skilled,
The task of a fuze was unfulfilled;
And a gun was mute, and a Hun was thrilled
As a young Canadian died!— Bill Taylor[20]

Skuce's Goose

GECO hired "Canada's Greatest cartoonist" Lou Skuce to create posters and cartoons for the *GECO Fusilier* during the first year of the plant's operation.[21] *Taddle Creek Magazine*'s Conan Tobias called Skuce "… something of an international celebrity throughout the thirties and forties, achieving a level of fame unthinkable for a newspaper illustrator today."[22] Lou Skuce relied heavily on humour to convey serious messages. His iconic goose — the infamous Skuce Goose — showed up in many of his cartoons. The goose became almost as famous as his creator, with his tiny top hat balanced on his head. Mr. Skuce presented his goose in a "Jiminy Cricket" role, reacting to and offering sage counsel to his audience.

Cartoonist Lou Skuce drew unabashed anti-Nazi cartoons to send a crystal clear message to Hitler and his minions. This drawing features an Allied soldier shoving "bitter pills" — ammo produced by GECO — down Hitler's throat in retaliation for the massacre at Dieppe in 1942. *Courtesy of Barbara Dickson, from Archives of Ontario.*

A Little R & R

With the payment of dues of $1 per year, GECOites could join the company's Recreation Club, which sponsored a variety of sports, dances, and entertainment throughout the year.[23] Diverse and plentiful social activities catering to men and women, old and young alike, were available, making it a challenge for any GECOnian to partake in every activity. Within GECO's environs, workers could play volleyball, horseshoes, lawn bowling, croquet, and softball.[24] Employees even found space to set up a nine-hole mini golf course between Building Nos. 144 and 23.[25] An area set up in the cafeteria provided room for table tennis, badminton, shuffleboard, cribbage, checkers, bridge, euchre, and dramatics.[26] Away from the plant, people could enjoy bowling, trap shooting, horseback riding, swimming, and tennis. The men established six hockey teams and the women pleasure-skated on two skating rinks set up each winter at the plant.[27] GECO's Saddle Club included sleighing during the winter months at Three Gaits Stables, also known as Hilltop Boarding and Riding Stables near Wardin and St. Clair Avenues in Scarboro.[28] Bingo was so popular that sessions had to be limited to five hundred people.[29] Monthly dances had upwards of one thousand in attendance. Various lessons were offered, including dance classes, health and beauty tips, nutrition sessions, and sewing classes. The plant also had a Glee Club.[30] Finally, if employees were looking for something more, they could purchase memberships for up to 25 percent off to the YWCA.[31]

Sing a Song of Softball

GECO installed four baseball diamonds on the northeast corner of Eglinton and Wardin Avenues, with eighteen men's teams in three leagues and fourteen women's teams in two leagues launched.[32] Fierce competition ruled the day between fellow GECOites. Recognizable team names such as "Stores," "Pellets 'A'," "I.G.," and "Time Office" easily identified where the players worked, whereas more ingenious names such as "Geco Aces," "Commandos," "Tank Busters," "Woodbutchers," and "Gecolettes" spoke to an individual team's pride and imagination.[33] GEOC's most

GECO installed four baseball diamonds on the northeast corners of Eglinton and Wardin Avenues. Fierce competition ruled the day between fellow GECO teams, as well as against other war-time plants. In this photograph, a couple of softball players are wearing GECO's colours on their shirts. The plant's administration building and signature smokestack can be seen in the background. *Courtesy of Archives of Ontario.*

recognizable pair, "Dazzy" Bob Hamilton and his brother, "Drop'em" Phil Hamilton, played on the "Whirlwinds" team.[34]

Bombs Away, Beautiful!

The Toronto Police Amateur Athletic Association sponsored the Miss War Worker Contest annually; open to women sixteen years of age or older and engaged in war work in the city.[35] GECO participated each year, with several dozen entrants vying for the title of "Scarboro Miss War Worker."[36] Six to eight finalists from this competition went on to next round held typically at Acorn or Sunnyside Park.[37] While many lovely GECO ladies entered each year, with several of their "Miss Scarboro" finalists placing at the semi-final and city-wide events held at

Miss War Worker Finals, July 1942. Every year GECOites competed in Toronto's Miss War Worker Contest, open to any woman over sixteen years of age engaged in war work. GECO held its own competition each year, sending several lovely "Miss Scarboro" finalists to the semi-final and city-wide events held at Exhibition Park. This photograph offers a rare glimpse into the plant's massive cafeteria with its freestanding "laminated beam" construction, a GECO engineering innovation. *Courtesy of Archives of Ontario.*

In 1943 GECOites Margaret Miller, Grace Bollert, Eunice Harrison, Alma Campbell, Kitty Russell, and Alice Newman represented Scarboro in the Miss War Worker Contest at the Toronto Police Amateur Athletic Association's Annual Field Day. Five GECO women remained in the final ten chosen at the city-wide event. Alice Newman came in second, winning $150 and a chest of silver. *Courtesy of Archives of Ontario.*

Exhibition Park, the coveted first-place prize remained elusive, although several beauties finished in the contest's top ten.[38] GECOite Kathleen Russell took fourth prize in Toronto in 1942, and Mrs. Alice Newman and Eunice Harrison took second and fourth place in 1943.[39] In 1944, GECO's Lottie Walsh placed third at the city event, and Grace Bollert and Sylvia Jenkins ranked in seventh and tenth place respectively.[40]

Major Flexman, GECO's operations manager, added a sombre note during the preliminary event in 1944 when he stressed the need for more and more ammunition, and made an urgent appeal for employees to find more recruits.[41] In fact, R.M.P. Hamilton allowed GECO to participate in the beauty pageant in 1944 — held within weeks of the Allied Normandy invasion — only if there would be no interference with production.[42] "The necessity for this condition," stated Mr. Hamilton in a formal notice to all employees, "will no doubt be realized in view of the fact that the demands for ammunition at this time are urgent and must take precedence over everything."[43]

To celebrate the beauty of GECO's feminine side, in March 1944 management introduced a new morale booster — pin-up girls.[44] Each shop on each shift had the opportunity to select one "pin-up" girl who best represented their shop.[45] Selected women appeared in future issues of the employee newspaper.[46] Beauty and health classes were also popular at GECO.[47] The men, who enjoyed "pin up" girls, did not think so much of beauty lessons, and were known to tease their female counterparts. Their attitude was adjusted via a smart article in the *GECO Fusilier*. The plant's men were reminded that there existed a serious problem with distribution of coal in major cities due to a labour shortage.[48] The scuttlebutt around the plant hinted that men from munitions plants might be "utilized" to shovel coal.[49] The employee newspaper reminded men it would be to everyone's benefit if the teasers kept their beauty comments to themselves, since "he laughs best whose face is unsullied by coal dust."[50]

Victory Gardens

In 1943, on the northeast corner of Wardin and Eglinton Avenues, GECO established a "Victory Garden."[51] Workmen plowed twenty-six acres of farmland, preparing more than six hundred plots, each measuring twenty by sixty feet.[52] More than five hundred employees took advantage of the opportunity to try out their green thumbs.[53] They undertook their sowing with eyes wide open. Should the winds of war change, the gardens would be taken to accommodate Canada's war needs.[54] Management encouraged workers to plant vegetable gardens, since a food shortage was a constant worry throughout the war. The more food cultivated by citizens, the more foodstuffs could be sent overseas to help feed the troops. In fact, in anticipation of the upcoming gardening season in 1945, the plant newspaper warned, "Food may be in short supply this year. Better arrange to have a garden."[55]

More Mistletoe and Less Missile-Talk

During each annual Advent season, employees savoured a full-course turkey dinner with all the trimmings in their spacious cafeteria for "two bits (twenty-five cents)."[56] The repast cost GECO fifty cents per employee.[57] The meal, meant to serve upwards of five thousand employees, included (approximately, depending on the year) 400 turkeys (from 1.5 to 2 tons in weight), 300 loaves of bread (for stuffing), 80 gallons of gravy, 25 to 30 bags of potatoes, 25 cases of canned peas, 12 gallons of cranberries, 27 gallons of apple jelly, 1,200 pounds of pudding, 300 pounds of brown sugar, and 200 gallons of coffee.[58] In 1943, cafeteria staff clocked 846 hours of regular time and 118 overtime hours to plan, procure, prepare, and serve the festive holiday meal.[59] GECOite "chef" Karl Markovitch worked twenty-four hours straight preparing turkeys.[60]

In 1944, due to significant snowfall, the turkeys were three days late arriving at the plant.[61] Mrs. Ignatieff, anticipating thousands of sad faces, procured hams — just in case.[62] The turkeys arrived in the (St.) Nick of time. They even managed to enjoy cranberries, which had turned up after being lost somewhere between Montreal and Toronto due to heavy snow.[63]

Each year, GECO held a Christmas party for the children of their employees.[64] The official program consisted of a festive hour of entertainment, with a magic show, musical performances, and clowns, and was offered three times over the course of an afternoon. Overcrowding was a concern, so management gently told their employees to bring their children, enjoy the show, and then leave promptly.[65] Record snow from the "storm of the century" on December 12, 1944, made the munition plant's Children's Christmas Party, held only four days later, even more festive. A record number of guests — more than 2,500 youngsters and their happy parents — partook in the festivities, eager to receive a toy from Santa.[66] Local bus lines carried 12,574 excited and happy passengers to and from GECO that afternoon.[67]

The Kids Are Alright

Daycare was virtually non-existent before the Second World War. With the war's outbreak, tens of thousands of women took up war jobs, working six days a week, and could no longer care for their pre-school children at home. To ease the burden, the Canadian government introduced a "wartime day nurseries" program developed with the joint sponsorship and financial support of the provincial governments, which commenced in earnest during the fall of 1942, offering childcare to children two years of age and up.[68] War factories offered the service to mothers at a nominal daily charge of thirty-five cents for one child, or about the equivalent of the women's first hour of work at GECO each day, and fifty cents for two.[69] This fee did not meet the expense of providing for the children. The balance of the cost was made up by Canada's federal and provincial governments.[70] The intent of the program was "to relieve mothers of smaller children, who are employed in war industries, of the responsibility and the worry of locating someone capable of and willing to look after her progeny while away at work. It should furnish the answer to a major problem of a great many 'working' mothers."[71]

Before children were admitted to the day program they had to undergo an extensive medical exam, including a throat swab.[72] A Public Health nurse visited the facility three times each week and a doctor paid a visit weekly, hoping to ward off the spread of viruses that could overwhelm the nursery, cascading into lost days of work for mothers.[73] GECO was affiliated with "Unit No. 7" Day Nursery, which operated out of the basement of Dentonia Park United Church and at 125 Rose Avenue, near Parliament and Bloor Street East.[74] Women engaged in war work comprised 75 percent of the parents who used day nurseries during the early 1940s.[75] Women saw the nursery as an excellent avenue to expose children to social interaction and to learn how to be kind to others. Women had peace of mind knowing competent nursery staff cared for their children.

Big Business Unions

By December 1941 GECO's management had employed and trained more than three thousand operators.[76] With hundreds more expected to join the ranks over the ensuing months, Bob and Phil Hamilton quickly recognized that they needed some systematic way to acknowledge merit and control wages. Staff introduced a work record card system that contributed to an enduring amicable relationship between the plant's "labour" and "management."[77]

GECOites recognized a need for some sort of intermediary group to take their needs and concerns to management. With Bob and Phil's encouragement, and at their request, employees organized the GECO Munition Workers' Association.[78]

Until Canada's federal government passed legislation in 1944 to enact labour reform — in particular, provisions for union certification and collective bargaining in good faith — the Munition Workers' Association (M.W.A.) was not a union.[79] Even after the association was made more formal and referred to as Local No. 1, there was no other.[80] Unions tried to organize GECO's operators in filling shops during the course of the plant's operation, but, for the most part, workers were happy with their M.W.A., with management's commitment to keep the lines of communication open and to maintain a high standard of working conditions and boost morale.[81] This dampened any desire to form a union. Unions formed at other war plants, especially when the labour situation grew graver after more and more men shipped out, allowing workers to demand higher wages.[82] Unionized shops received a 10 to 20 percent pay increase; non-unionized plants like GECO had to strive diligently to keep their employees happy to remain competitive.[83]

The M.W.A. worked with management. They found ways to conserve materials.[84] They helped eliminate sources of operator "irritation" to reduce absenteeism, and they introduced changes that would have a positive effect on working conditions and relationships.[85] The association issued an off-white booklet entitled *What the M.W.A. Can Do*, describing the role and responsibilities of the association.[86] The M.W.A. guaranteed a "no strike" policy to give workers peace of mind.[87] It guaranteed that it would not get involved in "big business unions."[88] The association would bargain collectively for fair wages and working conditions, ensure seniority and overtime rights, negotiate for legal holidays with pay and double pay, and obtain extra pay for afternoon and night shifts.[89]

Elections occurred annually.[90] The M.W.A. represented all workers below the rank of assistant foreman on the clean side and foreman on the dirty side.[91] Employees nominated candidates from within their shop or department.[92] Each department elected a representative — approximately one for every fifty employees.[93] Those representatives appointed an Executive Plant Council — one for every two hundred employees — who met with management knowing they took any grievance from the M.W.A. seriously.[94]

The only labour strife Bob and Phil Hamilton encountered at GECO occurred over the course of one shift on September 11, 1942.[95] The operators in Building No. 63 refused to work due to "working the worst shift without relief."[96] The operators had worked many days without a day off due to demanding production schedules attributed to fierce fighting overseas. The women were exhausted and feared they would make a fatal mistake borne of crushing fatigue. The M.W.A. got involved immediately, the employees returned to work, and shortly thereafter operators in three other buildings, in solidarity with their fellow fuse-fillers, agreed to go on rotating shifts.[97] Within weeks all workers on the clean side of the plant adapted to shift rotation.[98] GECOnian Sylvia Nordstrand said the only aspect she did not like about working at GECO was doing shiftwork. It "played havoc with your sleep. You no sooner got used to sleeping on one shift when you had to change to another. The night shift was the worst. You couldn't sleep when you got home in the morning. Then while working at 2:00 a.m., you would give anything for sleep."[99]

In another less serious incident, workers in the Pellet and Magazine Section threatened to strike because they felt they deserved higher wages given the extraordinary dangers of their work.[100] The M.W.A. took their grievance to management, who moved quickly to adjust their wages accordingly.[101]

Winning the war was, for the vast majority of employees, the motivation behind every fuse filled at GECO. Regardless of striving for optimal working conditions, or crabbing about petty inconveniences, women showed up for work every shift in a dedicated bid to bring their loved ones home quickly. "The war must be won," it said in M.W.A.'s booklet. "A better, more democratic and free M.W.A. in G.E.CO. will help YOU and your kinfolk overseas to win the war."[102]

Blood Is Thicker Than Water

GECO held its first blood donor clinic on December 2, 1942, as part of the Canadian Red Cross Society's new initiative to go to donors instead of donors coming to them.[103] This first blood drive collected sixty-one donations.[104] Word spread rapidly and at the next clinic workers made 111 donations, almost double that of the first.[105] GECO held weekly blood donor drives over the course of the war.[106] By the time Scarboro closed its doors, GECOnians had donated 8,453 units of blood.[107] Additional "on call" blood donors were available at GECO should an emergency arise, such as an explosion.[108]

"We are constantly receiving reports of the value of dried human serum," wrote Mr. G.R. Sproat, Director of Blood Donor Services, in a thank-you letter to GECO workers.[109] "It is being used in the front lines with great results. It must be a source of great pride to the donors to know that their blood is helping save lives of their brothers and human kind throughout the Allied fighting fronts."[110]

I'm Making Bombs and Buying Bonds

Wars cost money. Canada needed $12 million a day to fulfil its military obligations and help Allied prisoners of war.[111] With a promise to give their money back with interest at predetermined rates and redemption dates, the Canadian government, aiming to raise a staggering $750 million through just one victory war bond drive, asked its citizens to buy bonds and War Savings Certificates.[112] By Canada's fifth drive, that individual bond objective had grown to $1.2 billion.[113]

GECO employees purchased almost $4 million in bonds over the course of the global conflict.[114] By the time the first edition of the *GECO Fusilier* went to print, the second Canada Victory Loan campaign — the first for Scarboro — was finished.[115] Management had asked GECOites to meet a $150,000 quota in two weeks.[116] Employees more than doubled that amount with total subscriptions of $327,939 with practically 100 percent participation.[117] Bob and Phil Hamilton wrote, "Although we have learned to expect thoroughness in everything undertaken by the employees of this plant, your effort in this campaign surpassed our highest hopes. We thank you sincerely."[118]

GECO set their next Victory Loan goal at $350,000 but with still a week to go, the plant already had raised $322,500, so GECO raised their quota.[119] "Our real objective is not $350,000 or $400,000 or any other arbitrary figure —" wrote Ross Davis in the employee newspaper, "— it is to do our utmost, whatever that may be, to blast from the earth these beasts who cast little children adrift in open boats in the mid-Atlantic to perish, who glory in the murder of defenceless people. That's our real objective."[120] Employee purchases totalled $384,844.[121]

By the end of Canada's fourth Victory Loan campaign, GECO employees purchased $545,000 in bonds, easily surpassing an already aggressive goal of $504,800, which had been increased from an initial target of $385,000.[122] To maintain employees' enthusiastic drive to give, F.G. Pope, Chairman of GECO's Victory Loan Committee, asked workers to "... show the Madman of Berchtesgaden that we're 100 percent behind the War effort. Why wait another six months till we tell him again? Let's tell him again and again, every single day, by the way we conduct ourselves by sticking to our respective jobs, by the way we produce things to hit

GECO employees purchased almost $4 million in bonds during Canada's Victory Loans campaigns. Stirring poems and articles appeared in the employee newspaper during the bi-yearly bond appeals. Workers were encouraged to bring "their treasure to fill the coffers of the State, denying themselves the trinkets and pleasures of peacetime." *Courtesy of Barbara Dickson, from Archives of Ontario.*

him with — that we're in this struggle with all we have, and for all we can produce till Victory is won and Freedom assured."[123]

During the next bond drive, held in the fall of 1943, the employee newspaper dedicated an issue to encourage subscriptions through heart-stirring articles. Bill Taylor, Engineering, wrote:

> These boys — sailors, soldiers, airmen — they are offering everything they have, even to life itself, as their contribution to the speeding of the victory. Seems ridiculous that we should be asked to contribute — what we have to *spare!* Crazy, isn't it? Home; wife; family; food; comfort; security; and what's left after these have been assured we are asked to loan as our contribution to victory. Not to give; just to loan! Over there, they are willing to **give** everything! Over here, are we willing to **loan** all we have to spare — and that extra that means victory?
>
> There isn't any option — for a Canadian. It has to be every cent that can be spared — every cent that can be squeezed from the savings of the past, the earnings of the present, and the wages of the future. Without these cents and dollars there won't be any future that's worth while; for Canadians. The job of the moment is to Speed the Victory! Our part is to provide the dollars for the material that means Victory.[124]

Neither time nor the hint of the war ending had much effect on the drive to buy bonds. During Canada's seventh bond drive, GECO raised $788,950, 42 percent over their target of $555,000, with a subscription rate of $139.59 per employee.[125] By the eighth Canadian Victory Loan campaign — the seventh for GECO — employees were still eager to help the war effort financially. Victory in Europe was palpable and fund raising now focused on returning, reuniting, and rehabilitating loved ones.[126] GECO's target set at $560,000 was met the first day.[127] They would go on to achieve $682,500 in purchases with an average of more than $150 subscribed per employee.[128] Subscriptions for seven campaigns held at GECO totalled a stunning $3,873,643, or the equivalent of more than $51 million dollars today, assuming 3 percent interest.[129]

The Good Ol' Sally Ann

In yet another initiative, GECO employees raised $2,500 toward the purchase of a Salvation Army Mobile Canteen, above and beyond their support in Victory Loan drives.[130] "Whether it is army manoeuvres in England," Ross Davis wrote in GECO Fusilier's Vol. 2 No. 2 edition, "— commandos returning from a raid on the continent — the navy back in a home port after the perils of the sea — on the landing fields after a bombing raid over Germany — or "blitzed" areas in Britain — everywhere that men and women doing their bit in this war need the lift of a cup of tea, biscuits, hot chocolate, or cigarettes to relieve the strain of war, there you will find mobile canteens."[131]

GECOite Peggy MacKay, on behalf of GECO's employees, presented a cheque to cover the purchase of the canteen to Colonel W.J. Bray, Canadian Secretary of War Services of the Salvation Army.[132] "The story of the mobile canteen is one that comes close to the hearts of all people of humanitarian instincts," Ross Davis wrote, "for it is a saga of help in a most practical form to those who are fighting our battles for us."[133]

The Salvation Army is not a military organization, but rather an evangelical Christian church founded in 1865 in London, England's East End, where poverty, disease, alcoholism, and homelessness ran rampant.[134] Its founder, William Booth, a Methodist minister, felt that a human being's soul couldn't be fed until their stomach was full.[135] The Army's motto is "Heart to God — Hand to Man," and today, according to the organization, it is the largest non-governmental social services provider in Canada.[136]

Pennies from Heaven

Friendly rivalry and competition throughout the plant not only helped build morale, but also helped raise money for various war-related causes. One of the earliest philanthropic undertakings originated with GECOite Ruth Richards, who worked in Change House #17.[137] Britain was in the throes of the Blitz at the time. The plight of its people touched her heart. Why not collect pennies to support the British War Victims' Fund? Each payday, small red boxes marked "B.W.V.F." were set out in the change houses into which operators dropped their pennies, nickels, and dimes.[138] While there wasn't any "prize" for the shift house that raised the most money, fierce competition amongst the women propelled the original and seemingly aggressive target at the outset of one thousand dollars to a considerable chunk of copper.[139] By June 1945 GECOites had raised more than $11,000.[140]

Special Guests

During its four-year lifespan, GECO had many distinguished visitors, especially during Victory Loan campaigns. Special guests of note included His Excellency the Earl of Athlone, the sixteenth; governor general of Canada and his wife, H.R.H. Princess Alice; Lieutenant-General Andrew

GECO played host during the war to many military dignitaries and well-known entertainers. Canadian actress Mary Pickford visited the plant during a Victory Loan campaign. *Courtesy of Archives of Ontario.*

McNaughton; the minister of national defence; Toronto mayor Fred Conboy and his wife; and Ms. Mary Pickford, the Canadian actress ardently dubbed "America's Sweetheart."[141]

Just before Christmas 1942, GECO workers found brightly coloured handkerchiefs tucked next to their paycheques.[142] Mr. and Mrs. Leonard Bernheim of New York City, who had visited the plant earlier that fall, wanted to present a small gift to the women in recognition of their devotion to duty.[143] Three hundred and fifty dozen handkerchiefs were manufactured in the plant with which Mr. Bernheim was connected,[144] and GECOites showed off their gifts with pride. Photographs taken over the course of the war attested to their popularity.[145]

The Songs They Sing Are Preludes to the Voices of the Gun

Unlike other war plants where employees manufactured heavy machinery, women who worked at GECO enjoyed clean, quiet working conditions. As an extension to their pleasant surroundings, and perhaps as an informal indication of plant morale, operators on the clean side regularly sang as they walked through the gallery system or while they filled munitions.[146] Canada's governor general, His Excellency, the Earl of Athlone, witnessed this cheery phenomenon first-hand and remarked that in the "corridors and on the assembly lines, [the women] broke into spontaneous song."[147] Sylvia Nordstrand, a GECO fuse-filler, said they sang to fight sleep and break up the monotony. "Someone would, say, sing 'Deep in the Heart of Texas,' 'There's a Long, Long Trail A-Winding,' or 'I'll Never Smile Again.' Each of us would request a song and all would join in singing. It certainly passed the time beautifully. We never got tired of singing, including our supervisors who joined in."[148]

In a letter to R.M.P. Hamilton on May 5, 1943, L.H. Campbell Jr., Major General, Chief of Ordnance, War Department, wrote: "… it was most unique and enjoyable to hear the girls sing during their work. It certainly was apparent that the morale was exceedingly high!"[149]

Canada's governor general, His Excellency the Earl of Athlone, and his wife, Her Royal Highness Princess Alice, visited GECO in March 1944. *Courtesy of Archives of Ontario.*

Every Fuse You Fill May Save a Life

Women of GECO were reminded regularly that "plenty of ammo" meant a "savings of precious lives" — a dichotomy to be sure and one against which civilized society grappled.[150] Men on the battlefields of the Second World War did not have much choice. Either they killed the enemy, or the enemy killed them. Women at GECO had a different choice. Fill munitions that would ultimately kill, or perhaps die trying.

How did grandmothers, mothers, and young girls justify building weapons that would destroy human life and property? Two hundred and fifty-six million fuses had the potential to obliterate men in not only face-to-face combat, but also to wipe entire towns from the face of the earth.[151] Where did women find the resolve to create the means to kill? Moreover, where did they find the courage to work with high explosives that could potentially explode in their hands, ending their own lives? Each GECOite had his or her own reasons for working with high explosives. Carol LeCappelain spoke of a local regiment stationed in North Bay, Ontario, her hometown. Many men from that regiment — her friends and neighbours — were overseas fighting and she felt compelled to help, even if that meant taking lives to save lives.[152] Carol was diligent in her inspection duties at GECO. "I didn't want any soldiers killed due to faulty ammo," she said, and she hoped that "maybe we had done some good for the men."[153]

"I had too much time on my hands with my men away," GECOite Peggy MacKay said when explaining why she worked at GECO.[154] "I felt too that it would help my country."[155] Molly Danniels, while a young woman at GECO, recognized the dangerous nature of the work she did — handling detonators the size of her pinky fingernail. "If you punctured one, it blew up," she said.[156] In hindsight she couldn't do it today.[157]

Hartley French explained his stint at GECO this way: "There was a war on and you were more concerned about your own future than what GECO was about."[158] He added, "There was definitely no certainty that we would win."[159] Toronto hadn't recovered from the Depression and people were scrambling to find work. Hartley was barely out of his teenage years and his focus was on seeking employment while pursuing an education. He was concerned about what would happen to him after he finished school.

Perhaps the best motivation for GECOites to build instruments of death and destruction was the letters from husbands and sons fighting overseas. The following letter arrived at the home of a GECO worker from her twenty-year-old son who was at sea and had been torpedoed. He had been bombed in the London Blitz as well while on leave.

> … Mum, I am nearly bursting with pride at the thought of the work you are doing; it makes this job seem child's play by comparison. I hear so much both from letters from Canada and fellows I meet over here who have heard about you in their letters from home. If the Empire would follow your lead this war would not last long. This may sound like a line but words are useless to express my thanks that I am your son … you have

given us something to fight for that other people haven't got, (not to mention the wherewithal to fight)."[160]

A young GECOite who worked in Building No. 45 packing filled munitions for shipping felt compelled to send a note of cheer to the men who would receive the shipment.[161] Without permission or management's knowledge, she tucked a note in amongst a box of filled fuses. The note travelled all the way to France where a team of gunners discovered it when they unpacked the ammunition.[162] The soldiers wrote back, thanking her for her note of cheer; one fellow going so far as to ask to become pen pals.[163]

The Whispering Gallery

Rumours and malcontents are a part of any organization. Rumours within a secret munitions factory tended to be tastier, and the tongue-wagging work of mischief-makers was more insidious than their non-military counterparts. Management was eager to squash rumours, knowing the damaging effects gossip — whether there was truth in the tidbit or not — could have on their employees' resolve. "Whispering Gallery," a regular column in *GECO Fusilier*'s early issues, featured poems and cautionary tales that appealed to its audience's tendency to tongue-wag.[164] Ross Davis wrote in the paper's inaugural edition: "If anyone secured any benefit whatever from such rumors as we speak of — if they were harmful to no one — they might be endured with Christian tolerance. But when they produce nervousness in jobs that call for steady hands, it's different."[165] Every employee at GECO had been assigned a job, "a big and increasingly important job," in securing victory for the free world.[166] "It is up to everyone [sic] of us to see that nothing interferes with doing that job to our level best," Ross continued, including spreading, listening to, and taking any kernel of discontent to heart.[167]

Seventy years have passed since operations at Scarboro ended, and even though rumours are usually true only in fancy, tall tales told in a war plant still tickle tongues today. Someone started a story that saltpeter (used militarily and commercially in fertilizer, food preservation, and as a component in rocket propellants, fireworks, and gunpowder) was not only in the tea and coffee served in the cafeteria, but also in the salt tablets that the Medical Department offered to employees to combat ill effects from heat and humidity during Canada's summer months.[168] Yet another worrisome story circulated that workers could "catch" tuberculosis from being in close contact with fellow fuse-fillers in workshops since all buildings on the clean side were air-conditioned and windowless.[169] To stir dissent during Victory Loan drives, people petitioning for Victory Loan purchases were rumoured to receive a commission.[170] Management was swift to squelch the rumour, calling such gossip "slander on patriotic people" and was "unworthy of 'Scarboro.'"[171]

Conclusion

Why did GECO work so well? Because its employees were determined to make it work. Why did they buy in? Because extraordinary times called for extraordinary measures. Uncertain times with a precarious future called for sacrifice, not only from Canada but from every man, woman, and child around the world who lived and longed for peace. Bob and Phil Hamilton, along with their entire management team, tirelessly endeavoured to create working conditions that boosted the morale of their employees. Despite a wildcat strike that lasted a few hours, and a few tight-fisted employees who did not participate in Victory Bond drives, nearly all GECO men and women were engaged, interested, and eager to give their best to their work. From plentiful social activities to social events; from fundraising opportunities to blood donor clinics; from day care to beauty classes; singing, not grumbling, echoed through the galleries of GECO.

13

Disasters at the Plant

Snow Stranded

Only two major events occurred during GECO's operation that strained medical and management staff.[1] Ironically, neither was an explosion or workshop accident.

The first event — the heaviest snowfall in seventy-five years to hit Toronto — began after midnight on Monday, December 12, 1944, and continued well into Tuesday.[2] "Traffic is at a complete standstill," reported the *Toronto Daily Star*, "as one of the greatest snowstorms of Toronto district's history left a blanket of one to two feet on level roads and piled drifts as deeply as seven feet."[3] Twenty-two inches of snow fell in less than twenty-four hours.[4] War plants shut down, including GECO, whose Monday overnight shift became stormbound, with all roads impassable between the plant and the city.[5] Upwards of 1,300 workers — the vast majority of them women — were unable to go home.[6] While a snowfall might have been a good way to stir up some good old-fashioned Christmas spirit, the snowstorm was more than Toronto could handle. Gale-force winds buried cars entirely.[7]

Carol LeCappelain was one of the weary workers who were more than ready for a hot meal and rest. She remembered having to sleep overnight at GECO.[8] It was GECO's first real widespread emergency and everyone in a service or support position — from management to supervisors, from engineers to nursing staff — pitched in. Lines of position and responsibility blurred, with staff and fuse-fillers helping wherever there was a need. Security guards and maintenance workers helped with cooking and serving coffee. Engineers and carpenters shovelled snow. Two men manned the P.A. system and kept workers up to date on war and storm news, and relayed personal messages. Even weary operators helped out. Mrs. Ignatieff, who lived in a pre-war house at the northwest corner of the plant, walked through drifts up to her chin to get to the plant.[9] Along with her tired staff (they had worked all night too) she stepped into the fray and fed the masses.[10] Anyone and everyone cooked, washed dishes, and cleared tables. With their stomachs satisfied, hundreds of tired "soldiers" bunkered down in the cafeteria or in change rooms.[11] Others played cards, sang, and otherwise entertained themselves.[12] The Medical Department, under the leadership of Dr. Jeffery, helped those who had "succumbed to fatigue or worry."[13] Switchboard operators stayed on the job for seventeen hours straight.[14]

Meanwhile, others attempted to get to the plant. Fire chief Tom Benson trekked three hours through the raging storm from his home at O'Connor and Broadview ... on foot.[15] The Hollinger Bus Line struggled to keep their buses moving in the early stages of the storm, but had to give up as the weather intensified.[16] Molly Danniels recalled she waited for the GECO bus Tuesday morning, but only three other women made it to the bus stop.[17] When the women finally were picked up and delivered to the plant, Molly found just six other women in her workshop.

Only three buses made it to the plant that day.[18] One bus became stuck in a snowdrift at Woodbine Avenue and O'Connor Drive.[19] Carol, when she heard about the women trapped inside the bus, worried they would freeze to death if they weren't rescued soon.[20] They waited for four hours in the bitter cold before help arrived.[21]

Greg Simerson, teenaged son of GECOite Zaida Simerson, recalled that with roads and sidewalks impassable, and a temperature of minus 23 degrees Celsius, he and his dad outfitted a toboggan with a big cardboard box.[22] They filled it with blankets and trudged through deep snowdrifts to GECO from their home on Rosemount Drive off Eglinton Avenue East, east of Birchmount Road.[23] While Zaida was a modern-day worker doing men's work for the Allied forces, she still wore dresses and stockings to work; the bitterly cold weather that frosty morning caused her toes to freeze, and the little rescue troupe had to stop at the first house on Rosemount Drive to ask for help.[24] The family graciously helped warm up Zaida's feet with warm water.[25] The determined trio set out again, but by the time they reached home at "the top of the hill," Zaida's toes weren't the only casualty of the war against the storm.[26] Greg had collected his own battle scars — the bitter cold temperatures had frostbitten the tips of his ears and are still waxy today.[27]

By noon on Tuesday, breakfast in the cafeteria had morphed into a full-course free dinner. At one point the bread supply ran low.[28] GECOnian Gord Garrity walked south to Danforth Avenue and hauled 150 loaves of bread back on a toboggan.[29] Garage mechanics equipped a bulldozer with a snowplow.[30] Between the Good Roads Commission and the Provincial Highways Department, along with the tireless work from behind GECO's eight-foot fence, they won the battle against the snow late Tuesday afternoon.[31]

GECO's snowplow led the way and broke through heavy drifting snow while the company's fleet of heavy-duty ammunitions trucks, filled with exhausted employees, formed a convoy.[32] Carol, along with several other women desperate to get home, huddled in the back of one of the trucks. "We felt like a herd of animals," Carol recalled.[33] An hour later, the truck dropped them off at Dawes Road and Danforth Avenue, and from there she still had to walk about three miles home in the raging storm.[34]

Bob Hamilton was forced to cancel four shifts at GECO, suspending fuse-filling for thirty-two hours.[35] Production started up again Wednesday in time for the afternoon shift.[36] Bob wrote a letter of thanks to all GECO employees once the snow had settled a few days later:

> The qualities of mind and character that make good will were genuinely demonstrated by the employees of Scarboro on December the 11th and 12th.

Twelve hundred and fifty finished their night shift to find themselves storm bound for 10 hours. Cheerfully they helped each other to "carry on." Many trudged miles through the storm to look after their special responsibilities and worked long hours — up to 36 — to keep the services going.

Every responsibility was met.

Hundreds of others struggled for hours to get to work and their failure was no fault of their own.

For all these evidences of loyalty and devotion to duty your Management is grateful and more than that — proud.

May you all at Christmas enjoy that good cheer your good will has earned and on behalf of the Management I thank you for what you have done. MERRY CHRISTMAS!

— R.M.P. Hamilton[37]

Death at the Plant

On January 26, 1945, a Hollinger bus carrying employees back to the city at midnight collided with a heavy truck owned by Toronto-Peterboro Transport. The accident occurred at the eastern junction of GECO's parking area and Eglinton Avenue.[38] The bus spun around from the impact and its side was torn out, while the truck careened into the ditch.[39] The truck's driver was uninjured, but the crash demolished his vehicle.[40]

According to newspaper coverage, eighteen workers were injured in the accident, the most seriously being Mrs. M. Parkes, who suffered a fractured skull and a number of other injuries.[41] Others like Mrs. G. Sinclair, Mrs. R. Wolffers, and Ms. Jean Box suffered serious fractures and shock.[42] Hollinger bus driver Mr. Stan York lost consciousness and sustained serious chest injuries.[43] Frightened women jumped through shattered bus windows to escape.[44]

"Drivers of other buses parked at the plant did valuable work in quelling what might have been a panic," said Mr. John Hollinger, head of Hollinger Bus Lines.[45] "There was a rush to the front of the bus where a number of passengers had already been standing beside the driver.

Those who jumped through the windows ran the risk of being cut by glass left around the edges."[46]

The compassionate staff of GECO's medical centre worked diligently to render first aid, and prepared and stabilized ten seriously injured victims for transport to hospital.[47] In the minutes of GECO's staff meeting, dated January 30, 1945, Major Flexman, plant manager, openly thanked Dr. Jeffrey and his staff for "the speedy and accurate diagnosis of injuries received by the passengers and the quiet efficient handling of all cases."[48]

Management made only a terse mention of the accident in GECO's chronological record: "Collision of bus with other vehicle at junction of parking lot exit and highway results in injury to employee passengers, ten requiring hospitalization. One of these (Mrs. Parkes) died four days later."[49]

14

When "Victory" Trumpets Sound the Call

Canada's involvement in the Second World War lasted five years, eight months, and six days. When Germany unconditionally surrendered on May 7, 1945, the need for ammunition dropped almost immediately. Every soul who worked at GECO longed for the war to end, yet when the order to "cease fire" was issued, its declaration was so sudden that GECOites were taken aback. Thousands of women and men quickly had to face the psychological, emotional, and economic implications of impending peace. After four long years in operation, "Scarboro" would close its doors.

Lay Down Your Arms

GECO's day shift was well underway when the official declaration came through on Monday, May 7, 1945. Word rippled first through the dirty side of the plant, then over to the clean side. There were no whoops, hollers, or claps of joy. Women continued to fill fuses. "As a matter of cold fact," Ross Davis wrote in the next issue of the plant's newspaper, "we've seen Scarboro a good deal more excited about a visit by screen celebrities or a military band around Victory Loan time."[1]

"How are they taking it inside?" a woman asked a worker as she stepped over the clean-side barrier to take her lunch break.[2] "I just came from the High Side (high explosives line), and it's very quiet there," was her reply. "A few women are crying."[3]

Women proceeded to the cafeteria for their lunch at noon, and they quietly ordered and ate their Monday choice of beefsteak pie or breaded veal cutlet, the same way they had done for the past four years.[4] Bob Hamilton announced Tuesday, May 8 would be a holiday "with pay."[5]

Management expected a mass exodus after lunch and had buses waiting.[6] The buses left empty.[7] When lunch break was over only a few failed to return to their workshops.[8] Over 90 percent of the afternoon shift showed up for work at 3:00.[9] "To complete this chronicle of devotion to duty," Ross Davis wrote, "a devotion that has become traditional with Scarboro, it is essential to add that when the Plant's operations resumed with the night shift on Tuesday (official V-Day) at 11:00, over 80 percent of the normal number of employees passed through the time clocks — sober and ready for work."[10]

Why was there such a tepid reaction to the end of a global conflict so dreadful, so brutal, and on a scale of human suffering never seen before in the history of mankind? The reasons were as varied, personal, and unique as the women who worked at the plant. Many women had to face a stark and sober reality that their loved one was not coming home. Others, out of respect for grieving women, tempered their own elation at knowing they would be reunited with their loved ones again. GECOites who needed extra money to keep their homes and feed their children feared the impending loss of income. For some women, they foresaw a loss of newfound identity. These women had filled a vital need for the Allied forces — they had become mighty Fusiliers, Bomb Girls, and the Girls Behind the Guns. With the war over, could they be content with the humble title of Mother, Nana, or the Girl Next Door again?

And what of the impending loss of community and friendship? Thousands of GECOites brought together in a united, altruistic, fiercely patriotic purpose were about to scatter, heading back to their pre-war lives, perhaps back to aprons, back to the mundane — and sometimes lonely — duties of the home, back to school, or back to life on the farm.

How could they replace the unique comradery and solidarity forged on fuse-filling lines of a top-secret munitions plant?

"Scarboro has always had an esprit de corps very similar to that found in the armed services," Ross wrote, "and the bonds which tied all sections of the Plant together, forged in the fires of a deep-seated patriotism, have grown stronger than most of us had realized."[11]

And perhaps the most obvious reason of all? GECOites, regardless of their mood or desire to celebrate, knew well the potentially dire consequences of carelessness or distraction — even for the best reasons — while on the job.

As days passed, women warmed to the inevitable ending of their wartime work. "… after the first shock had spent its force," Ross wrote, "individual reactions became more apparent. 'Golly, am I glad it will be over soon', said one supervisor we talked to, — and she really meant it. 'No more night shifts — no more dirty gunpowder.' 'Won't it be swell just to stay at home and look after the housework' was another reaction. 'Am I going to take a good holiday in the sunshine' was still another remark heard."[12]

Less than two weeks after Germany capitulated, the Government of Canada sent out a notification to the Hamiltons from Ottawa on May 22, 1945, stating production at GECO would end June 30, 1945.[13] Within twenty-four hours, Bob Hamilton received a Final Production Plan from the Department of Munitions and Supply.[14] The first round of layoffs would come quickly, scheduled to begin within the week.[15] GECO's photographer, George Rutherford, hastily took workshop photographs, in an effort to capture a moment in time for as many employees as schedules would allow.[16] On May 28, management reduced production shifts from three to two.[17] With layoffs imminent, and with some time to absorb and accept their eventual parting, the spirits of men and women at GECO rebounded.

Thanks for Your Faithful Service

The Hamilton brothers formally thanked their employees in *GECO Fusilier*'s May 28, 1945 edition:

In an organization such as Geco at Scarboro, it is necessary to have many auxiliary or service departments in order to keep the primary or Production Department operating at a high efficiency. It will be of interest to all employees to know that in addition to your remarkable production record the splendid results obtained by the service departments in keeping operations going with no lost time due to mechanical, power, maintenance, or transportation difficulties; the improvements in methods, designs, and knowledge of ammunition problems; the tenor of your housekeeping and the safety record; the results of your medical care and research; the Personnel Departments; and the cafeteria; the activities and co-operation of the Munitions Workers Association; the keen interest developed by the Recreation Club, the war veterans and other charitable groups; your generous response to all war loan and other drives; your co-operation and spirit of give and take with all departments of Inspection Control, and of course the splendid spirit of mutual respect between workers and staff is known and appreciated not only in our locality but throughout Canada, and in the United States, Great Britain and Australia.

Your products have always been of the highest quality and have gained the proper respect of both friend and foe. Truly, this is a record of which we may all be proud.

During the course of our associations these last five years we have made friendships both in the production lines and throughout the staff that will remain with us always. We will never forget such scenes as a production shop at 2:00 in the morning with dozens of workers busily engaged at their respective jobs, or the cheerful greeting of a guard just off patrol on a cold and blustery night, or the enthusiasm of thousands greeting a concert artist during a war bond rally.

In closing, may we express the wish that your future endeavours will bring to you continued happiness and well being. For doing such a grand job at Scarboro, we thank you sincerely.

R.M.P. Hamilton and P.D.P. Hamilton[18]

From Ammunition-Filling Jobs They Proudly Can Retire

Wrapping up and winding down came quickly. *GECO Fusilier*, in its June 11, 1945 edition, acknowledged the sudden and frenetic pace at which the plant was closing.

> Everywhere the *Fusilier* has heard regrets openly expressed at the threatened dissolution of that "all for one and one for all!" spirit which was built up during the months of stress when calls came to "pass the ammunition" in ever increasing quantities.
>
> At the time we were too busy to realize how strong the bonds were that were being forged. Realization has come since. Out of this realization has come, as we said before, a strong desire in many quarters to carry on the tradition that seems to have been a uniquely Scarboro thing.[19]

To help with their transition back to "civilian" life, employees established an "Old Boys' and Old Girls' Association" to foster the friendships and associations formed during their time at Scarboro.[20]

In early June, management formed a committee to determine the best method for desensitizing the plant and equipment.[21] By the fifteenth of June, GECO had terminated its lease at their employment office at 1350 Danforth Avenue.[22] The Medical Department closed its blood donor clinic the same day.[23] Management held their last staff meeting four days later.[24]

Carol LeCappelain completed her dedicated service at GECO on June 23, 1945.[25] In retrospect, she wondered aloud what happened to the thousands of pairs of shoes when the plant closed down.[26] She recalled fondly that the shoes were "the most comfortable shoes I'd ever had."[27]

The Hamiltons reduced production to one shift with another massive layoff of workers on the third day of July.[28] The plant published the last issue of *GECO Fusilier* on July 31, 1945.[29] The front cover depicted Mrs. Eva Needham enjoying the distinction of filling the last, or the 8,604,742nd, 119 fuse at GECO.[30]

Production at GECO ended.

The last layoff of GECO's operators occurred in early August 1945.[31] Because of the continuing need for her skills as tele-typist, and regardless of military conflict, Molly Danniels stayed on at GECO until August, after most employees had already moved on.[32]

Regardless of how women felt about the war ending, losing their jobs, and heading back to their domestic duties, a huge indicator of their "Thank God, it's over" attitude would become evident quickly, about nine months later actually, with the commencement of the "Baby Boom." Many women were happy to be back in the home doing "women's work," and caring for their children. Young women were eager to marry a returning vet and start families.

Rationing stopped, the economy picked up, and Canada's future looked bright, with the winds of change alive across the nation. Women had proven they could perform jobs that had been solely in their male counterparts' realm before the war. Many women were not ready to be just homemakers again. As peacetime lengthened, increasing numbers of women sought work outside the home.

Men who worked at GECO, for the most part, returned to their peace-time occupations, found new jobs within their trades, or retired.

Canada experienced a time of economic growth and prosperity after the war. Industry returned to manufacturing, and consumer goods were readily purchased and enjoyed by ration-weary Canadians more than ready to spend their Victory Bonds. Quickly expanding families of the "baby boomer" generation moved out of the city to affordable new housing in rapidly growing suburbs.

Scarboro's Spoils of War
Production: Collateral Damage

While GECO originally intended to fill seven different "natures," or types of fuses, the plant had been designed to be completely flexible and responsive to the needs of the Allied forces.[33] Good thing, too. The plant eventually tooled up for and filled forty-one types of ammunition.[34]

GECO's production accomplishments were remarkable in many aspects. Perhaps one of its biggest claims to fame was the fact that workers

Example of a timer fuse filled at GECO. *Courtesy of Barbara Dickson, from Scarborough Historical Society.*

filled more than 256 million units of ammunitions without one fatal accident, a feat not only unique in Canada and North America, but globally.[35] This statistic becomes more remarkable when one considers the number of operations that were required to unpack, fill, pack, and ship a single fuse at GECO.[36] Each and every step in the fuse-filling process presented an opportunity for explosion. In particular, 8,604,742 No. 119 fuses were filled at GECO, with seventy-six different operations needed to load just this one type of fuse.[37] Simple math suggests that more than 653 million manual operations were needed to prepare the more than eight million Fuse 119s for service. Fuse-filling workshops reached the height of production in July 1944, when the plant filled 11,466,878 .303 Flame Tracer bullets alone, giving an all-time high production in the plant of 14,753,003 units for that month.[38]

To add icing to GECO's cake, the facility boasted an acceptance record by government inspectors of nearly 99 percent, unparalleled within the munitions industry.[39]

Total products shipped from GECO were valued at $112,692,316.[40]

GECO's impressive munitions display. Over the course of the war, workers filled forty-one types of ammunition, including percussion and time fuses, nose and base fuses, tracer-igniters, and flame tracer bullets. GECO filled an impressive 13,426,587 Fuse 251s by June 30, 1945 — the largest production of any single fuse at Scarboro, or in Canada. *Courtesy of Archives of Ontario.*

Scarboro's War Score: July 1941 to July 1945

Fuses, Primers, etc. filled: 129,066,629

.303 Tracers filled: 127,601,555

Total munitions filled: 256,668,184[41]

Final Headcount

GECO reached its employment peak in July 1943, with 5,324 operators plus an additional 980 Inspection Board personnel.[42] In total, 17,104 operators worked at GECO over four years.[43] Including support staff and Inspection Board personnel (of about four thousand), that number swells to more than twenty-one thousand employees.[44] GECO paid out $27,165,212 in wages.[45]

It's in You to Give

Above and beyond purchasing Victory Bonds, employees managed to raise $34,480 to support many charitable organizations, which included British War Victims' Fund, Canadian Red Cross (including P.O.W. care packages), GECO Veteran's Fund, Sunshine Club (a comfort service for disabled veterans), various local welfare agencies, and the Salvation Army with the purchase of a mobile canteen.[46] More than 250 wallets were given as gifts to enlisting GECOites, four tons of books and magazines were sent to servicemen, and $3,000 was spent to host annual children's Christmas parties.[47] This bounty does not reflect the thousands of dollars donated to various philanthropic organizations for which records were not kept.[48]

Shrapnel

Other curious figures and totals, of no less importance, of a top-secret munitions plant include:

- 2,151 individual employees made 8,453 blood donations to the Red Cross;
- GECO purchased 22,640 female uniforms and 5,266 uniforms for male employees;
- a total of 36,344 purchase orders were placed from about 1,300 different firms for approximately 10,000 different items, not including combustible materials needed for component stores;
- 41,000 messages were transmitted or received by Scarboro;
- buses transported 9,161,258 passengers and covered 3,095,040 miles;
- GECO's cafeteria served 6,854,287 meals;
- the plant consumed 39,841 tons of coal and 357,520,600 gallons of water;
- total Employee War Loan Subscriptions reached $3,873,643;
- GECO's Medical Department treated 173,456 patients — of which the vast majority were suffering from non-occupational injury or illness;
- GECO spent nearly $7.2 million in capital and $102.2 million in operating expenditures.[49]

Before the first stick of TNT ripped up Scarboro's countryside, T. Holmes Bartley, Toronto Industrial Commission, estimated the cost to design, construct, and equip the top-secret munitions plant in the east end of Toronto stood at between $5 million and $8 million.[50] GECO's management team felt they could build the plant for a modest $2.25 million.[51] When all was said and done, the final cost of construction reached $7,181,124,[52] almost three times GECO's original estimate.

They'll Hear ... "They Kept 'Em Firing"

The war decree, "They Kept 'Em Firing," from Canada's fighting sons honouring the faithful back on the homefront, still echoes across the decades since the Allied forces laid down their arms. The story of GECO at Scarboro is an incredible tale, one of which legends are made.

"The record, we think, will stand," wrote Ross Davis, proudly, in the *GECO Fusilier*, "as lasting proof of what can be achieved by a company of purposeful Canadian men and women drawn from all walks of life, when faced with grave necessity."[53]

15

If You Build It, Scarborough Will Come

GECO's story at Scarboro did not end with Germany's surrender.

Decontamination and Desensitization

With GECO's days of production numbered, Bob and Phil Hamilton had more to worry about than just wrapping up payroll and taking down posters. Management had to ensure workmen desensitized the buildings and surrounding land, ridding the compound of all toxic and explosive materials, as well as destroying all drawings, specifications, and sensitive employee data.[1] Most buildings on the dirty side of the complex did not need special attention, except for change houses, where workers had carried explosive dust in on their hair, uniforms, and shoes. However, most everything on the clean side needed decontaminating, right down to scouring cracks between linoleum floor tiles and disinfecting or destroying sink traps.[2]

Workmen treated workshops with a special chemical formula depending on the explosive residue being removed. Water was sufficient for ridding a site of gunpowder, while workers needed a solution of sodium sulphite, water, and acetone to remove tetryl.[3] Some buildings were razed; their lumber burned.[4] Contaminated rock wool, as well as tainted earth and bricks from the Destroying Ground, Proof Yard, and magazines were transported to the "Don Valley Pit" and submerged in nearly ninety feet of water.[5] More than 6,800 pounds of various excess explosives were destroyed by burning in the proofing yard.[6]

The War Assets Department of the Canadian government took over managing GECO's buildings and re-zoned the area for light industry.[7]

Sheltering the Homeless

At the north end of the GECO plant, bordering Eglinton and Warden Avenues, several buildings were acquired by W.H. Bosely, emergency shelter administrator for Greater Toronto from the War Assets Corporation.[8] In many ways, providing emergency housing in the now abandoned buildings of the Scarboro munitions plant made sense. Besides the influx of returning G.I.'s, many families, due to circumstances, some beyond their control, were suddenly without a place to live, or needed to find an affordable place until the economy picked up. In an article in the *Toronto Telegram*, a writer reported, "With the number of evictions increasing, the housing plight in Toronto is reaching a new crisis ..."[9] With other emergency housing facilities cropping up, the city refitted GECO's facility to accommodate some of the neediest. GECOite Helen Leslie and her fine family were the first residents to move into the new housing project, taking up residence in GECO's administration building on July 15, 1946.[10]

"When the housing shortage became almost disastrous after the war's end," reporter Harvey Currell wrote, in an article in *The Telegram*, "Toronto leased some [GECO] buildings, threw up flimsy partitions, put in plumbing and rented apartments to city families who could find no other place to live."[11]

Helen told a newspaper reporter the day they moved in, "We will be rather cramped in our four-room apartment but it is such a relief to know that we will be all together, under one roof until better housing accommodation comes along."[12]

Living at GECO combined the pleasure of living out in the countryside with the convenience of the city within reach by bus. It was the best of both worlds. In the morning, a resident could go apple picking, or swim in a nearby creek; the afternoon could be spent in the city enjoying a movie and shopping along the Danforth followed by an evening sweet-smelling hayride offered by a local farmer.

GECO became a close-knit community brought together through their unique living arrangement. In many respects, it operated much like a beloved campground nestled away amongst the "wilds" of Scarboro, where neighbours knew one another, looked out for one another, brushed their teeth and showered in communal washrooms, and knew everyone's business. Many moms and their small children rarely left the grounds, especially when the family couldn't afford an automobile. Mothers would sit on wooden benches placed along concrete sidewalks to keep an eye on their children as they played. An apple orchard sat at the northeast corner of the property. Children would run across Eglinton Avenue to pick mushrooms where GECO employees had once planted their Victory Gardens. Hundreds of children could be seen running around the compound on any given Saturday. The thrill of (mis)adventure living in Scarboro's farming "playground" only added to GECO's exclusivity.

In addition to enjoying the bounty of nearby farms, GECO residents appreciated some original wartime amenities such as a baseball diamond and a hockey rink. Lawn bowling was available at the corner of Civic Drive and Warden Avenue before the municipality installed a new water tower.

Residents of the GECO housing complex, arguably a unique community within Scarboro Township, had to consider daily life, from performing ablutions to doing laundry, from grocery shopping to keeping children entertained and out of trouble.

Helen Leslie did her laundry in her apartment, using, as her daughter Jackie recalled, an "old clunker" washing machine. She hung out their clothes to dry, year round, on a line rigged up by her husband, Howard, accessed via their second-storey bedroom window. Each building had its own laundry mat complete with washing machines, large tubs, and indoor clotheslines.

Men and women shared separate but communal washrooms situated in the middle of each building and consisting of three toilets, showers, and sinks. Each sex was responsible for keeping their respective ameni-ties clean. If the men didn't bother, the facilities were neglected. The women's bathrooms were better cared for.

Grocery shopping proved a challenge. Women had limited options. They could travel into the city, which took time and was a great incon-venience if they had no vehicle; they could seek out meat and produce in season from neighbouring farms with no guarantee as to selection; or they could walk to the nearest store, which was located at Eglinton Avenue and Kennedy Road. It wasn't long before residents and business owners recognized the need for a store onsite.

A store was opened shortly after people moved in. Remarkably, a blind man ran the shop. When a young customer entered his store, they picked out their merchandise and put their payment in a dish. The chil-dren couldn't figure out how the sightless man knew exactly what they had purchased; he would feel the coins with his fingers to ensure he was paid accurately.

Another shop was set up in an old silver-coloured bus, which housed a fruit and veggie stand. It would be six years before the first big grocery outlet, a Dominion store, would open as part of the new Golden Mile.

The forty-five-minute trip to and from the city was too great a distance for young children to travel, so Building No. 86 — GECO's former medical building — was renovated, and a school opened. At its peak, the housing complex had four school buildings — three public and one Catholic — all run by accredited, competent teaching staff. Classrooms could accommodate close to forty students. Kindergarten classrooms were attached to the recreation centre. Children identified the schools by colour; the "green school" housed the lower elementary grades, while the "brown school" accommodated grades four to eight.

Given GECO's remote location, and with hundreds of children idle on Sundays, churches such as the Salvation Army set up parishes at GECO. Many children attended Sunday School. Scarboro's city council provided the Salvation Army with a large hall rent-free on GECO's premises in March 1952, in which they could hold their various weekly meetings.[13] As of May 1954, the Salvation Army had christened almost fifty children at the housing outpost.[14]

The GECO housing complex operated from 1946 to 1954, with one to two thousand men, women, and children, conservatively, inhabiting more the than three hundred units.[15] It has been suggested, though, that more than six thousand people — upwards of eight hundred families — lived at GECO over its postwar tenure. *Toronto Telegram* staff newspaper reporter Derm Dunwoody adds credence to the latter estimate. During the summer of 1950, Dunwoody wrote, "The shouts of what seems to be more children than anywhere else in the world" could be heard amid GECO's housing units.[16] He estimated 1,100 children lived at the complex.[17] The first residents, Helen and Howard Leslie, added to their fine family while living at the complex, bringing their seventh child, Howard Wayne — "Harry" — into the fold on May 19, 1949.

Unfortunately, by June 1952, the Anglican Synod charged that "intolerable conditions exist[ed] at the Toronto Emergency Housing Unit at GECO."[18]

The Scarboro Police Force set up a precinct on the premises of GECO and ushered in each New Year's Eve rounding up rowdy and quarrelsome GECO men who'd toasted one too many. One year in particular, 1951, brought out more than just happy revelers. One man ended up in hospital with knife wounds, while many others suffered bloodied noses and black eyes. Scarboro police were kept on duty all night with "a continual series of near riots."[19] According to Acting Chief Wilfred McLellan, brawls were yearly events at GECO.[20] The police station at GECO was staffed by one regular officer but the entire Scarboro force showed up New Year's Eve.[21] Former Baptist minister turned politician Oliver Crockford called the riot a disgrace. "They are just running wild," he said. "Children by the hundreds are growing up there in deplorable conditions."[22]

Today, surviving residents who lived there as children, vehemently disagree with the unflattering reputation their housing complex earned. They fondly recall a unique time in their young lives when, due to unfortunate circumstances caused by the fallout of a world at war, they lived in unique conditions never to be repeated in their lifetimes, perhaps never again in the history of Canada.

After the war, from 1946 to 1954, several GECO buildings were acquired by the city and refitted to provide emergency housing to needy families. Conservatively, upward of two thousand men, women, and children lived at the complex. Rent, on average, ranged between $37 and $40 per month for over three hundred, mostly tiny, four-room apartments. Washrooms were communal. *Courtesy of Scarborough Historical Society.*

Scarborough's "Golden Mile" of Industry

The Canadian government's decision not to raze GECO's 173 buildings after the Second World War set the wheels of progress in motion. Less than five years after the war ended industry was setting up shop in and around GECO, partly due to cheap land and low taxes.[23] In 1948 Reeve Crockford said, upon the township's purchase of the GECO property, "This is our golden opportunity. Unless Scarboro steps ahead, we will not make progress."[24] Scarborough's "Golden Mile" was well underway.[25] This notable stretch of formerly quiet countryside transformed into a bustling centre of large-scale manufacturing, and represented hope and prosperity after the war. New housing sprung up to accommodate the need for residences near places of employment like Thermos and Frigidaire.[26] Past GECO women who wanted to stay in the workforce made Scarborough their home to raise their families in the post Second

World War housing boom. The Golden Mile even merited a visit from Her Majesty, Queen Elizabeth II in June 1959.[27]

If you build it, they will come. In a sense, GECO's wartime presence among the gently rolling hills of southern rural Scarboro became a catalyst in a time of peace, stimulating growth and urban expansion and helping Scarborough to become the vibrant, multi-cultural city it is today.

Veil of Secrecy Lifted

More than seventy years have passed since King George expropriated farmland in Scarboro to build a top-secret munitions plant, yet remnants of GECO still stand today, a testament to the incredible workmanship of her builders. Little could the Hamilton brothers or their twenty-one thousand employees have fathomed GECO's enduring presence in Scarborough.[28] Intended to be temporary wooden sheds with an anticipated five years of useful service, twenty-one original buildings still stand today.[29] A walk or drive around the area bordered by Warden and Eglinton Avenues and Sinnott and Hymus Roads will reveal, with a discerning eye, the low silhouettes of original GECO buildings, some remarkably unchanged from their former heyday. The quality of the building construction speaks to the high standards that the entire GECO endeavour strived to not only meet but also surpass. In an odd twist of fate, GECO's buildings have survived longer than most of the men and women who once worked behind the quasi-military compound's eight-foot-high barbed-wire fence.

Some GECO properties are easy to recognize; others take some sleuthing and keen deduction skills to find. Windows, colourful clapboard, aluminum siding, and façades have been added. These historic buildings house restaurants, car repair shops, small businesses, and are used for storage and warehousing. Some owners use the tunnels under their feet as cellars, storing inventory such as beer and car parts. While several GECO buildings are still well-maintained, others are dilapidated and dingy, armed with the latest in security deterrents. Guard dogs, barbed-wire fencing, surveillance cameras, intimidating signage, and iron gates serve to warn trespassers to enter at their own peril. Ironically, some GECO buildings are better protected today than when sabotage was a real threat.

One might argue GECO today is just an empty shell of its former self; ruins really, and a mere shadow of the glory days when it was used for round-the-clock war work. However, almost everyone who has had the unique experience of walking through GECO's tunnels will agree that its ruins both captivate and humble, not only because of the vital job carried out at "Scarboro," but also because of the plant's sheer tenacity in surviving. GECO was and still is a historical treasure trove, not only in its physical ruins but also in its legacy to the future generations of Scarborough and Canada. Its extensive tunnel system remains one of Scarborough's best-kept secrets, sparking puzzled looks on the faces of seasoned citizens at their mention.

In 1967, Reeve Albert Campbell did not think the old (GECO) buildings were worth keeping.[30] He would have liked to have seen most of them torn down. In time, he suspected — and perhaps secretly wished — that even the name "GECO" would be forgotten.[31]

Several miles of tunnels ran beneath the GECO plant at Scarboro, connecting most of its buildings in the Danger Zone. Today, most of the tunnels have been filled in, or have been destroyed by age or neglect. However, there are still some sections of tunnel intact, used as cellars and storage, or, perhaps unknowingly, to shelter feral animals. This tunnel sat under Building No. 67 before it was demolished for commercial expansion. *Courtesy of Rebeccah Beaulieu.*

Today, GECO properties continue to change hands, with new owners ignorant of the rich, poignant stories that linger in the air, as they raze, renovate, or reduce to rubble what is left of GECO. What's more, with time and progress's unrelenting drive for new and more, owners are sealing up and filling in the old maze of tunnels, a treasured artifact literally beneath their feet. It seems that Reeve Campbell, posthumously, might just get his wish.

What does the future hold for GECO? Oddly, the same relentless drive for change and progress for which the old war plant was a catalyst, will erase this munitions plant from history, as aging citizens of Scarborough, the generation touched by a world war, eventually pass away.

Is GECO worth saving? Perhaps Reeve Campbell was right — wipe the blight from the city's landscape. Pave the way for new growth and development, for revitalization. But then we are left with a troubling prick of conscience: how do we honour the memory of countless men and women who made the ultimate sacrifice, paid with their lives so that the city of Scarborough and the country of Canada could live in freedom? Who will pay tribute to the dedication and the toil of the countless on the home front, supporting not only fellow Canadians in the theatres of war, but the Allied forces around the world?

In September 2014, the City of Toronto, through its Underpass Revitalization Program, sponsored the creation of a mural to honour the women of GECO. The mural is located on St. Clair Avenue East, just east of Warden Avenue in Scarborough, within walking distance of the wartime plant. *Courtesy of Lawrence Hicks.*

In September 2014 the City of Toronto commissioned urban muralist Mitchell Lanecki to capture the essence of GECO, creating a fitting tribute to the women of the plant and their magnificent contribution to the Allied war effort.

It will take a nation to teach each man, woman, and child the terrible human toll that war brings. Every child who lives today, as well as every child to come, must not only learn about the colossal human struggle their brave Canadian forebearers undertook on their behalf — both abroad and at home — but they must also pause to remember.

Lest we forget.

GECO arranged group workshop photographs as a memento of their employees' time at the plant after the war ended. Because the Canadian government wrapped up operations quickly, the first round of layoffs took place only three weeks after Germany surrendered. Many shops did not get the opportunity to have their picture taken. In this historic picture, happy smiles tell the story: peace has returned to Canada. Grandmother to June Button and Ivy Faubel, GECOite Ivy Harris is sitting in the front row, far left. *Courtesy of June Button.*

Long Live Scarboro!

It is fitting to salute the critical work carried out by General Engineering Company (Canada) Limited during the Second World War, using their own words to capture their patriotism, perseverance, and passion for Scarboro's Bomb Girls:

> Now we can turn back to thoughts and plans for ultimate peace. Those of us who will continue to work can help make or do things that are constructive rather than destructive — things that make for people's comfort and happiness. There is a staggering amount of constructive work to be done both in a material and spiritual sense. Perhaps if all of us who formed Scarboro's proud company take with us into our new spheres of endeavor the same spirit of loyalty, the same determination to safeguard the things we worked so hard for in the Plant and the same benevolence toward one another — Scarboro will never die. The tradition, outgrowth of the tragedy of war, will live on, a vibrant, shining thing through the happier years of peace to come.
>
> Long live Scarboro![32]

Appendix A

Layout of GECO:
An Engineer's Sketch of GECO[1]

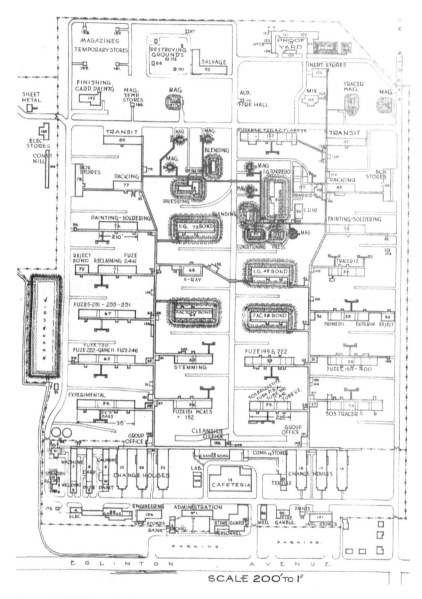

A map of GECO running from Eglinton Avenue (at the bottom of the sketch) to present-day Hymus Road, bordered by Warden Avenue and Birchmount Road. At the Eglinton end of the plant sat the "dirty" side of the facility, where operations that did not involve explosive components were carried out. The "clean" side, where all operations involving explosives were performed, was located south of present-day Civic Road. No object that could cause static electricity or a spark, such as silk, rayon, metal, or chewing gum, could be brought onto the clean side. *Courtesy of Archives of Ontario.*

Appendix B

GECO Management Chart[1]

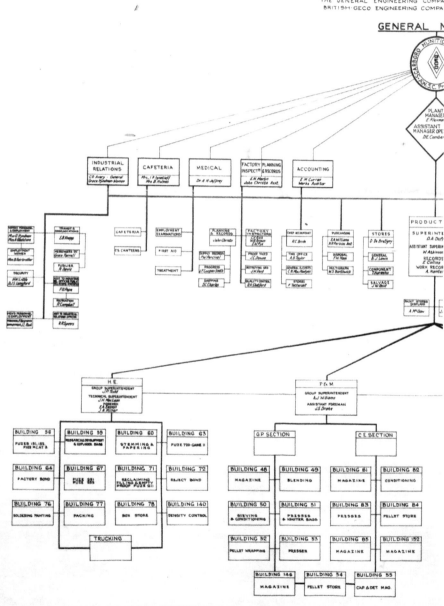

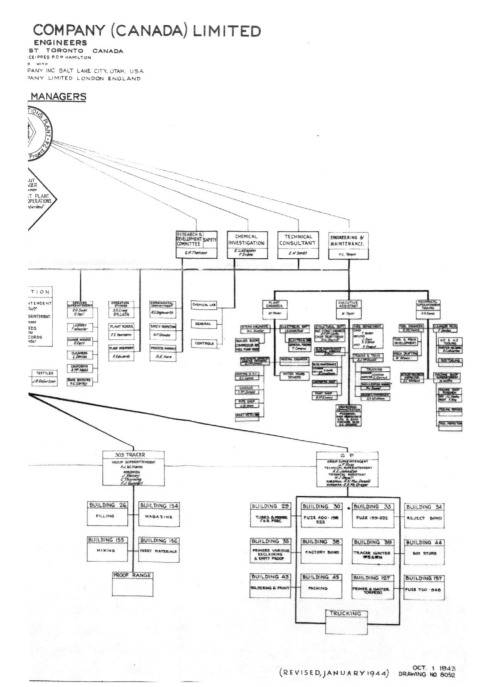

A-2: Organization Chart of GECO at "Scarboro." *Courtesy of Archives of Ontario.*

Appendix C

Typical Workshop Layout:
Fuse 251, Shop 67C

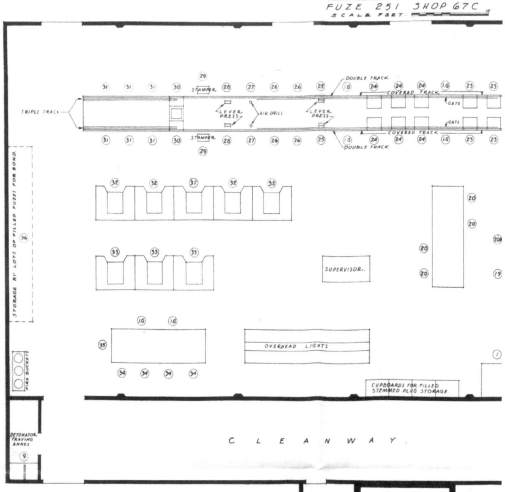

THE GENERAL ENGINEERING COMPANY
SCARBOROUGH, CANADA
TYPICAL LAYOUT OF FUZE FILLING
FUZE 251 SHOP 67C
SCALE FEET.

Operators at GECO filled 13,426,587 No. 251 fuses in Building No. 67 over its tenure — the largest producer of any single fuse in Canada's history. In this diagram, the layout of Building No. 67, Shop "C," where 251 fuses were filled, is depicted. Building No. 67 consisted of three main shops — "A," "B," and "C" — with an annex attached to each

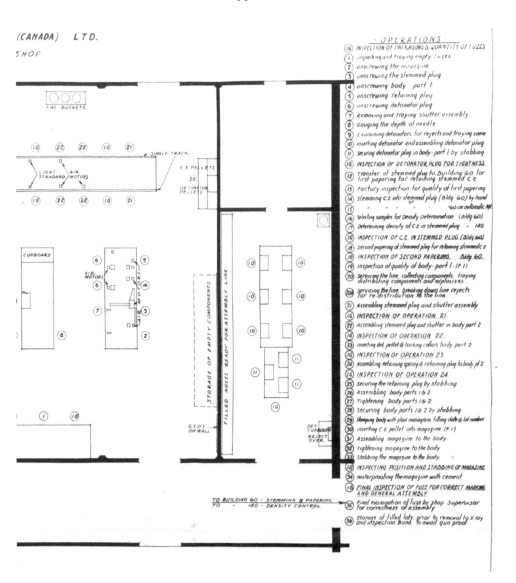

(CANADA) L T D.

SHOP.

- OPERATIONS -

(16) INSPECTION OF PACKAGING & QUANTITY OF FUZES
(1) unpacking and traying empty fuzes
(2) unscrewing the magazine
(3) unscrewing the stemmed plug
(4) unscrewing body part 1
(5) unscrewing retaining plug
(6) unscrewing detonator plug
(7) Removing and traying shutter assembly
(8) Gauging the depth of needle
(9) examining detonators for rejects and traying same
(10) inserting detonator and assembling detonator plug
(11) securing detonator plug in body - part 1 by stabbing
(16) INSPECTION OF DETONATOR PLUG FOR TIGHTNESS.
(12) Transfer of stemmed plug to Building 60 for first papering for retaining stemmed c.e.
(13) Factory inspection for quality of first papering
(14) stemming c.e. into stemmed plug (Bldg 60) by hand
(15) " " " " - 60 c.e. automatic m/c
(16) selecting samples for Density Determination (Bldg 60)
(17) Determining density of C.E. in stemmed plug " 140.
(16) INSPECTION OF C.E. IN STEMMED PLUG (Bldg 60)
(18) Second papering of stemmed plug for retaining stemmed c.e
(16) INSPECTION OF SECOND PAPERING. Bldg 60.
(19) inspection of quality of body - part 1. (F.1)
(20) Servicing the line, collecting components, traying distributing components and explosives
(20a) servicing the line, breaking down line rejects for re-distribution to the line
(21) Assembling stemmed plug and shutter assembly
(16) INSPECTION OF OPERATION 21.
(22) Assembling stemmed plug and shutter in body part 2
(16) INSPECTION OF OPERATION 22.
(23) inserting det. pellet & locking collars body part 2
(16) INSPECTION OF OPERATION 23
(24) Assembling retaining spring & retaining plug to body pt 2
(16) INSPECTION OF OPERATION 24.
(25) securing the retaining plug by stabbing
(26) Assembling body parts 1 & 2
(27) Tightening body parts 1 & 2
(28) securing body parts 1 & 2 by stabbing
(29) Stamping body with plant monogram, filling date & lot number
(30) inserting c.e. pellet into magazine (F.1)
(31) Assembling magazine to the body
(32) tightening magazine to the body
(33) stabbing the magazine to the body.
(16) INSPECTING POSITION AND STABBING OF MAGAZINE
(34) waterproofing the magazine with cement
(16) FINAL INSPECTION OF FUZE FOR CORRECT MARKING AND GENERAL ASSEMBLY
(35) Final examination of fuze by shop Supervisor for correctness of assembly
(36) storage of filled lots, prior to removal to X-ray and inspection Bond, to await gun proof

FIRE BUCKETS.

(1G) (22) (22) (1G) (21)

E. SINGLE TRACK.

LIGHT STANDARD / AIR. MOTORS

C.E. PELLETS
20
DETONATOR PELLETS

(1G) (22) (22) (1G) (21)

CUPBOARD

A.R. MOTORS

(6) (5)
(6) (4)
(7) (3)
(8) (2)

STORAGE OF EMPTY COMPONENTS

FILLED NOSES READY FOR ASSEMBLY LINE

(10) (10)
(10) (10)
(10) (10)
(11)
(11)
(1G)

G.S.D'S ON WALL

DET CUPBOARD
REJECT OVER.

(1) (1G)

TO BUILDING 60 - STEMMING & PAPERING
TO " 140 - DENSITY CONTROL

shop. During the summer of 1943, staff switched Shop "C" over from English production methods to a bulk assembly production line. Each operator performed a single step in filling the fuse. The new assembly line consisted of worktables, extending almost the entire length of the shop. *Courtesy of Archives of Ontario.*

Acknowledgements

The book you are holding is a labour of love that took over a decade to research and write. A book humbly offered from a fiercely proud Canadian's heart, its pages seek to commemorate the daring determination of countless thousands of women who fought on the home front doffing aprons for ammo during the Second World War. A book such as this takes a huge amount of work, research and devotion. Its publication would not have been possible without the support of many individuals and organizations. The following tributes are not listed in order of importance. Everyone mentioned here helped bring *Bomb Girls* to fruition.

I would like to extend my heartfelt gratitude to John McLean Parsons Hamilton, son of Robert McLean Prior Hamilton, and Judy Patton Hamilton, daughter-in-law to Philip Dawson Prior Hamilton, for affording me the honour in telling the incredible story of the Hamilton brothers' tenure at GECO in Scarborough, Ontario, during the war years. You have enriched GECO's story through your generous support and endorsement. I especially wish to express my sincere thanks to the late Philip Henry Banfill Hamilton, son of P.D.P. Hamilton, who wrote the Foreword to *Bomb Girls*. May his written words be a loving legacy to his father's tangible contribution to the war effort.

A special note of appreciation is extended to Florence Ignatieff's children, Paul and Mika, for bringing an intimate, human perspective to their mother's noteworthy GECO story.

Nancy Haines, throughout my many years of research, helped track down information on my behalf. Nancy was always responsive, thorough, and happy to accommodate every seemingly small request, and I offer her my grateful thanks. Thanks also go to Rick Schofield, archivist for the Scarborough Historical Society, for his time, patience, and helpfulness. The folks at the Archives of Ontario, the City of Toronto Archives, the Toronto Reference Library, the Canadian War Museum, and the Imperial War Museum helped me in numerous ways, particularly to my countless archival requests. In every instance, the staff was professional, efficient, and understanding.

To the many professional associations who invited me to share GECO's amazing story, I offer my sincere thanks. You graciously granted me the opportunity to share Scarborough's story in helping to win the war.

I am especially indebted to Dr. J. Patrick Boyer, Q.C. who shared my passion for *Bomb Girls*, and pursued its publication with his colleagues at Dundurn.

To Colin D'Mello of CTV News, who arranged for the production of a GECO TV vignette, sparking public interest in Scarborough's tunnels and its war days. Your interest in our city's history helped spread the word, opening doors towards the publication of *Bomb Girls*.

To Sam and Peter, who kindly welcomed me and granted me access to the old tunnels that run beneath their car repair shop on Manville Road. With a smile and a kind word, they received me – sometimes with fifteen or twenty eager GECO enthusiasts in tow. And to Sheila Crowe, who in the early days of exploration, graciously allowed me to tour the well-preserved tunnels under her property.

A special thank you is offered to Trace Hill and Tony Aus of Prologix on Sinnott Road, for granting me the incredible opportunity to not only tour their GECO tunnels, but to document the demolition of one of GECO's largest fuse-filling workshops, Building No. 67.

I am deeply thankful to Councillor Michelle Berardinetti, Ward 35, Scarborough Southwest, who immediately recognized the value in celebrating the tireless, dedicated work of the women at GECO. With an enthusiastic heart for her community, Michelle and her team helped make a mural for GECO possible: a lovely, lasting tribute for decades to come. Thank you, Michelle.

I must also say thank you to Ryan Hicks, my technical assistant, who came through for me when time was critical.

To the hundreds of GECO enthusiasts who I've met along the way — too many to mention but you know who you are (shout-outs to Mike, Mike, and Peter.) Your enthusiasm and curiosity and generosity in sharing treasured artifacts of Scarborough's wartime history pushed me ever onwards to completing the book.

I extend my deepest heartfelt gratitude to the many war workers I met and interviewed, who, even in their golden years, graciously shared their experiences at GECO, and of life during the Second World War. To the families of GECO employees who have passed away, I thank you for sharing your loved one's stories and pictures, and for wanting to help capture a unique time, not only in your family's history, but in Canada's history too. I would like to make special mention of several cherished GECOites who have passed away since they were initially interviewed for this book: Molly Danniels, Carol Knight, Bill Howe, Philip Henry Banfill Hamilton, Peter Cranston, and Rena O'Hagan. May this book be a lasting tribute to their memory.

Finally, I wish to thank my family: to David for his love and steadfast support; to Kathleen, Rebeccah, and Emily for their love and encouragement, for being proud of their mom; and to Joshua, Jacob, and Noah for their infectious joy — for no matter how mired in citations or editing I became, a simple, chocolate-covered smile instantly grounded me, reminding me of what truly is to be treasured.

Notes

To keep this book to a manageable size the Notes have not been included in the print edition. They are included in the electronic version, and may also be accessed at the author's website at *www.barbaradickson.ca/geco/* or at the publisher's website *www.dundurn.com.*

Bibliography

BOOKS AND BOOKLETS

Ammunition Saves Lives. Toronto: Employment and Selective Service, April 1, 1944.

Bagnell, Kenneth. *The Little Immigrants: The Orphans Who Came to Canada.* Toronto: Macmillan of Canada, 1980.

Bonis, Robert R. *A History of Scarborough.* Scarborough: Scarborough Public Library, 1968.

Craig, John. *The Noronic Is Burning!* Don Mills: General Publishing, 1976.

Employee's Guidebook. Toronto: General Engineering Company (Canada) Limited, 1943.

Employment Booklet for Prospective Employees. Toronto: General Engineering Company (Canada) Limited, February 15, 1943.

The General Engineering Company (Canada) Limited — British Counterpart to Sc/C. circa 1919.

Hibbert, Joyce. *Fragments of War: Stories of Survival of World War II.* Toronto: Dundurn Press, 1985.

Insurance Plan of the City of Toronto. Vol. 9, Sheets 948-1 to 978. Toronto and Montreal: Underwriters' Survey Bureau Limited, 1956.

Kennedy, J. de N. *History of the Department of Munitions and Supply: Canada in the Second World War.* 2 vols. Ottawa: King's Printer, 1950.

MacDowell, Laurel Sefton, and Ian Radforth. *Canadian Working-Class History: Selected Readings.* Third Edition. Toronto: Canadian Scholars' Press, 2006.

Regulations of the Scarboro Plant: Clean Workers. Toronto: General Engineering Company (Canada) Limited, September 30, 1941.

Regulations of the Scarboro Plant: In Case of Accident. Toronto: General Engineering Company (Canada) Limited, 1941.

Roberts, Leslie. *Noranda.* Toronto: Clark, Irwin, 1956.

Rules and Regulations for Plant Guards, A.W.S.C. Project No. 24, Scarboro, 1943. Toronto: General Engineering Company (Canada) Limited, 1943.

Schofield, Richard, Meredyth Schofield, and Karen Whynot. *Scarborough Then and Now (1796–1996).* Scarborough: Scarborough Board of Education and Scarborough Historical Society, 1996.

Stacey, C.P. *History of the Canadian Army in the Second World War, Six Years of War.* Vol. 1. Ottawa: Queen's Printer, 1955.

Stevens, John A., and Harold Pfeiffer. *The Man Who Makes Heads with His Hands: The Art and Life of Harold Pfeiffer, Sculptor.* Burnstown, ON: General Store Publishing, 1997.

Stone, Gilbert, ed. *Women Workers of World War I.* Glasgow: Mansion Field, Zeticula, 2007.

What the M.W.A. Can Do. Scarboro, ON: The Munition Workers' Association, G.E.CO. Scarboro, circa 1941.

JOURNALS

"Absenteeism." *Review of Industrial Relations* Article 29 (July 1943): 61.

"Employees Associations ('Munition Workers Association')." *Review of Industrial Relations* Article 21 (July 1943): 43.

Hall, Jean. "What Production Management Needs to Learn about Women!" *Manufacturing and Industrial Engineering,* July 1943.

Ignatieff, Florence. "Cafeteria and Canteen Service." *Review of Industrial Relations* Article 16 (July 1943): 29.

"Medical." *Review of Industrial Relations* Article 17 (July 1943): 32, 33.

Morrow, L.C. "Industrial Relations: Key to Canadian Plant Success." *Factory Management and Maintenance* Volume 103 (1945): 105.

Official Bulletin of Toronto East Medical Association (February 1944): 1.

Pitcher, W.H. "... and Pass the Ammunition — Review of Fuse-Filling Operations at General Engineering Co. (Canada) Limited, Scarboro." *Canadian Chemistry and Process Industries* (May 1944).

"Service Recognition." *Review of Industrial Relations* Article 24 (July 1943): 46.

"Sick Benefit Plan." *Review of Industrial Relations* Article 20 (July 1943): 41.

"Suggestion Plan." *Review of Industrial Relations* Article 23 (July 1943): 45.

"Transportation." *Review of Industrial Relations* Article 28 (July 1943): 50.

"Vacation with Pay." *Review of Industrial Relations* Article 18 (July 1943): 34.

MAGAZINES

Bradley, La Verne. "Women at Work." *National Geographic,* 1944.

NEWSPAPERS

GECO Fusilier

"800,000 Canadian Men and Women Now Employed in War Industries." August 1, 1942.

"A 'Break' For GECO Softball Players." May 9, 1942.

"A Farm — A Construction Job — A War Plant — And 236 Days." April 11, 1942.

"A Praiseworthy Safety Record..." June 5, 1944.

"A Tribute from a Son." January 16, 1943.

"After V-Day Comes R-Day." April 16, 1945.

"All Those in Favor Say 'Aye.'" June 11, 1945.

"Ammunition." June 5, 1944.

"Attention All Ye Maidens Fair Fame and Fortune Ye May Share." June 20, 1942.

"Awards Given for Good Suggestions." December 12, 1942.

"Baseball Teams — Sing a Song of Softball." July 4, 1942.

"Battle of the Century." July 18, 1942.

"Beware Ye Men of GECO and Restrain Thy Mirth." November 6, 1943.

"Bingo Encore." April 25, 1942.

Brimicombe, F.G. "To Those Women of All Ages." January 30, 1943.

"Bus Transportation Establishes Record." August 29, 1944.

"Cascade of Runs Features Softball." July 18, 1942.

"Charming Taxi Driver Selected by Paramount." November 20, 1943.

"Christmas Dinner Story..." January 10, 1944.

"Col. Clapham Concludes Big Job..." August 14, 1943.

Davis, Ross. "Editor's Column." April 11, 1942.

Davis, Ross. "Editor's Column." August 1, 1942.

Davis, Ross. "Editor's Column." November 28, 1943.

"Day Nursery Scheme Developing Expected to Solve Big Problem." August 15, 1942.

"East End Day Nursery at Dawes and Dentonia." February 27, 1943.

"Eighth Victory Loan Goes Over..." May 14, 1945.

"Employees Thanked by S.A. Official." June 5, 1943.

"Facts and Figures." July 31, 1945.

"Fingers." Cartoon. April 30, 1945.

"Five Thousand at Xmas Dinner..." January 8, 1945.

Flexman, Major E. "Magnificent Contribution to War Effort Made by Scarboro People." July 31, 1945.

"For Health and Beauty's Sake..." November 20, 1943.

"From Farm to Munition Plant." July 31, 1945.

"GECO Canteen One the Finest...Operates on Non-Profit Basis." May 9, 1942.

"GECO Car Stickers." August 1, 1942.

"GECO Contestants Selected..." July 3, 1944.

"GECO Fusilier — A Powder Magazine." March 28, 1942.

"GECO Glamor Girls on Parade..." June 19, 1944.

"GECO Transport Big Business..." October 23, 1944.

"GECO War Loan Campaign More than Doubles Quota." March 28, 1942.

"Goodwill Towards All." December 18, 1942.

Hamilton, R.M.P. "Another Scarboro Victory." November 20, 1944.

Hamilton, R.M.P., and P.D.P. Hamilton. "To All GECO Scarboro Employees." July 31, 1945.

"Healthy, Happy, and Safe." July 31, 1943.

"Hitler's Helpers?" April 11, 1942.

"Impressive Total for B.W.V.F. Donations." November 20, 1943.

"Intriguing Expansion Underway in Recreation Club's Program." January 16, 1943.

"Jack Be Nimble." April 16, 1945.

"Just in Case." October 17, 1942.

"K. Russell Finalist in Beauty Contest." August 1, 1942.

"Let's All Pull ... Together." October 17, 1942.

"Let's Give It Everything We've Got." October 31, 1942.

"List of 'Shortages' Daily Grows Lengthier." March 28, 1942.

"Lively Interest Aroused by MWA Rep. Nominations." January 30, 1943.

"Loan Quota Reached First Day." April 30, 1945.

"Meat Shortage Felt by Canteen: Meatless Days Looming Ahead." September 26, 1942.

"Mixed Feelings Greet Closing ..." May 28, 1945.

"Mobile Canteen Officially Presented." June 5, 1943.

"Mobile Canteens Playing Big Part." April 10, 1943.

"More and More Ammunition Is Needed to Save Lives." June 5, 1944.

Morgan, Joyce. "Cleanside Visit Opens Stenogs' Eyes." March 27, 1943.

"Munition Workers' Association Nominations Getting Underway." January 16, 1943.

Neville, Laura. "'Piston Packin' Moma' Joins GECO Fleet." November 20, 1943.

"New Bus Route Starting Monday." March 27, 1943.

"New Shift Schedule." October 31, 1942.

"Nothing Else Will Do." July 4, 1942.

"One Thousandth Blood Donation Reached by GECO Clinic." March 12, 1943.

"Our Barrier Lady." July 31, 1945.

"Our Front Cover." July 31, 1945.

"Over Two Thousand Youngsters Coming to GECO Christmas Party." December 12, 1942.

"Pin-up Girl Idea Popular." March 13, 1944.

Pope, F.G. "Well Done 'Scarboro'!" May 22, 1943.

"Proper Use of Salt Tablets." August 1, 1942.

"PUTT — PUTT." July 31, 1943.

"Pyjamas — House Dress?" November 20, 1944.

Read, Lieut.-Col. H.R.A. "Good Ammunition Corner-Stone of United Nation's War Effort." January 24, 1944.

Robbins, Ruth. "Scarboro Girls Prize-Winners…" July 31, 1943.

"Rustle of Spring." April 2, 1945.

"Saga of a Man." September 26, 1942.

"Saga of a Woman." October 17, 1942.

"Santa Claus Revisits Scarboro." January 8, 1945.

"Sawdust Brigade Play Part in Passing the Ammunition." February 27, 1943.

"Scarboro Beauties Selected …" July 3, 1943.

"Scarboro Blood Donors Flock to Perform Patriotic Service." December 12, 1942.

"Scarboro Building Number Nine Sends 'Em Back White and Fine." September 12, 1942.

"'Scarboro' Bus Transportation Establishes Enviable Record." August 29, 1944.

"Scarboro Defies Storm King …" December 18, 1944.

"Scarboro in the Beginning." July 31, 1945.

"Scarboro Takes V-Day Calmly." May 14, 1945.

"Scarboro's Most Exclusive Club…" March 19, 1945.

"Scarboro's Tool Hospital Plays Important Part in Production." August 15, 1942.

"Sculptor Models 'War Worker'." July 3, 1943.

"Skating and Sleighing Parties." January 10, 1944.

Taylor, Bill. "Lest We Forget." October 23, 1943.

"Ten Thousand Dollars Collected for B.W.V.F." April 2, 1945.

"The Fourth Arm of the Service." March 28, 1942.

"The Last 119." July 31, 1945.

"The Real Meaning of Sc/C." June 20, 1942.

"Thirty." July 31, 1945.

"To All Geco Scarboro Employees." July 31, 1945.

"Today's the Day for Scarboro Beauties — Honour, Reward Await 'Miss War Worker'." July 18, 1942.

"Tribute." August 1, 1942.

"Turkey 'n Everything All for 'Two Bits'." January 2, 1943.

"United for Victory." May 22, 1943.

"Victory Gardeners Eager to Commence." May 22, 1943.

"Victory Loan." November 6, 1944.

"Visitors Remember Women of Scarboro." January 2, 1943.

"Volunteers and Parents Invade Canteen to See Santa Claus." January 2, 1943.

"War Loan Committee." September 11, 1943.

"War Very Real to Mrs. Peggy MacKay." March 27, 1943.

"Watchfulness the Price of Safety." July 4, 1942.

"We Did It Once — We'll Do It Again." October 10, 1942.

"Weekly Meetings of Workers with Management Resultful." May 23, 1942.

"Whispering Gallery." March 28, 1942.

"You Are Doing a Grand Job for Us Chaps." August 28, 1944.

Other Newspapers

"16 Families To Be Given Living Unit." [*Toronto*] *Evening Telegram*, July 10, 1946.

"18 War Workers Injured When Bus, Truck Collide." *Toronto Daily Star*, January 27, 1945.

AN R.E.L. MAN. Letter to the Editor. "Pape Avenue Buses." *Toronto Daily Star*, February 14, 1942.

"Athlone Says Workers Score Greatest Victory." *Globe and Mail*, March 25, 1944.

Carrick, J.J. "A Ton of Books." Publication unknown. Circa 1943.

"City Area to Supply 4,000 for Arms Plant." *Toronto Daily Star*, November 1, 1940.

Currell, Harvey. "Born of War II Geco Near End." [*Toronto*] *Telegram*, January 21, 1957.

Dunwoody, Derm. "Proud Of GECO Homes Bid Aldermen Come, See." *Toronto Telegram*, June 16, 1950.

"Eight in 4 Rooms Tight Fit, But GECO Quarters Aid Evicted." *Toronto Evening Telegram*, July 15, 1946.

Fairhurst, Lt.-Colonel Annie. "Home League Notes." *The War Cry*, May 1, 1954.

Filey, Mike. "Rediscover Echoes of GECO's Past." *Toronto Sun*, April 7, 1991.

"Find Meals Better Here in Industrial Cafeterias." *Toronto Daily Star*, April 26, 1944.

Gamester, George. "Wartime Toronto's Lost City." *Toronto Star*, January 13, 2002.

"GECO, Ajax Need Girls to Put Kick in Shells." *Toronto Daily Star*, July 4, 1944.

"GECO Housing." *The War Cry*, June 14, 1952.

"Geco Needs 3,400 Women To Feed Monty's Barrage." *Toronto Daily Star*, June 28, 1944.

"GECO New Year's Riot Is 'Worst,' Man Knifed Can't Find Assailant." *Toronto Daily Star*, January 12, 1952.

"GECO Spotless Heaven, Women Like Job There." *Toronto Daily Star*, June 30, 1944.

"Hold the Shell Line, Save Canadian Lives." *Toronto Daily Star*, June 28, 1944.

Hornby, Lance. "Former Leaf Star Gaye Stewart Dies." *Toronto Sun*, November 19, 2010.

"Man Dead, Schools Closed, War Plant Shut — The Storm." *Toronto Daily Star*, December 12, 1944.

"Mighty Chain of Munitions Complete — Fuses Pass Test." *Toronto Daily Star*, June 7, 1941.

Milley, Danielle. "Queen Visited Golden Mile Plaza in 1959." *Scarborough Mirror*, July 22, 2009.

"POW Survived Black Christmas." *National Post*, May 30, 2007.

"Scarboro Council Approves Plan to Purchase GECO." *Enterprise*, September 30, 1948.

Schofield, Rick. "Scarborough's GECo Plant Holds Many Memories." *Scarborough Mirror*, March 18, 2010.

Schofield, Rick. "Tunnels Serve as Reminder of Munitions Plant." *Scarborough Mirror*, November 14, 2003.

"Thriving Outpost." *The War Cry*, March 15, 1952.

CORRESPONDENCE

Carr, David. E-mail correspondence with author, April 2013.

Cranston, Peter. E-mail correspondence with author and letter. April 2012.

Eden, Jackie. E-mail correspondence with author. 2012.

Elstone, Mary. E-mail correspondence with author. August 2014.

Farer, Mika. E-mail correspondence with author. September 2014.

Hamilton, Louise. E-mail correspondence with author. August 2014.

Knight, Carol. Letter to author. June, 15, 2007.

MacDonald, Stanley B. Letters to author. July 26, 2014.

Murray, Barbara. E-mail correspondence with author. 2013, 2014.

Pickles, Ernie. Letter to author. July 31, 2014.

Roberts, Brian. E-mail correspondence with author. Various dates, 2012–2014.

Szydlik, Sue. E-mail correspondence with author. Various dates, 2012.

INTERVIEWS AND TELEPHONE CONVERSATIONS

Byrne, Heather. Telephone call. August 2014.

Clements, Sharon. Interview by author. Markham, 2012.

Danniels, Molly. Interview by author. Scarborough, 2009.

Drake, Victoria. Interview by author. Scarborough, 2012, August 2014.

Elstone, Mary. Telephone call. August 2014.

Everest, John. Interview by author. Scarborough, 2012, July 2014.

French, Hartley (Anthony). Interview by author. Scarborough, various dates, 2009, 2010.

Greenwood, Audrey. Interview by author. Scarborough, February 2013.

Hamilton, John McLean Parsons. Interview by author. Elora, Ontario, February 2013.

Hamilton, Philip H.B. Interview by author. Montreal, July 2012, August 2012.

Hamilton, R.M.P. Interview with Hartley McVicar. *Let's Visit*. Radio recording. Toronto, c. 1945.

Harris, John Alan. Interview by author. Scarborough, 2012.

Hermann, Tamara. Interview by author. Scarborough, 2012.

Howe, William. Interview by author. Scarborough, 2012.

Ignatieff, Paul. Interview by author. Telephone call. France, August, September 2014.

Knight, Carol. Interview by author. Scarborough, 2007.

Knight, Leonard. Telephone call. July 2014.

Langfeldt, Barbara Holmes. Interview by author. Toronto, 2013.

Ledson, Sidney. Interview by author. Scarborough, January 2012.

Lorimer, Cal. Interview by author. Oshawa, October 2011.

Lowcock, Stella. Interview by author. Oshawa, October 2011.

MacDonald, Phillip. Interview by author. Picton, November 2012.

MacDonald, Stanley, Interview by author. Telephone call. Gravenhurst, August 2014.

McRae, Dorothy. Interview by author. Scarborough, various, undated.

O'Hagan, Rena. Interview by author. Newmarket, 2012.

O'Hagan, Barry. Interview by author. Newmarket, 2012.

Parkin, Anne. Interview by author. Telephone call. Vancouver, 2013.

Pickles, Ernest Herbert. Interview by author. Scarborough, January 2013.

Reay-Laidler, Ronald. Interview by author. Scarborough, April 2012, July 2014.

Shearer, Maimie. Interview by author. North York, January 2013.

Simerson, Greg. Interview by author. Scarborough, 2012.

Sullivan, Jim. Interview by author. Newmarket, January 2013.

Sullivan, Kerry. Interview by author. Newmarket, January 2013.

Waddell, John and Priscilla. Interview by author. Scarborough, 2009.

Warner, Elizabeth. Interview by author. Scarborough, 2012.

Wood, Ronald. Interview by author. Scarborough, 2012.

ARCHIVES OF ONTARIO, GECO FONDS

F2082-1-1-2. *The General Engineering Company (Canada) Limited — British Counterpart to Sc/c.* c. 1919.

F2082-1-1-5. *Department of Munitions and Supply, Defense Projects Construction Branch, the General Engineering Company (Canada) Limited, A.W.S.C. Project No. 24, Scarboro, Ontario.*

F2082-1-1-6. *Construction and Maintenance Costs.*

F2082-1-1-7. *Decontamination and Desensitizing, 1945–1946.* 1946.

F2082-1-1-8. *Desensitizing Scarboro Plant, 1945.* 1945.

F2082-1-1-9. Downing, I.N., I.O. (P). Letter to E.N. Martin, General Engineering Co., (Canada) Limited, June 27, 1945.

F2082-1-1-11. *GECO Fusilier* Collection. March 28, 1942–April 15, 1942, May 23, 1942–July 4, 1942, August 1, 1942–August 29, 1942, September 26, 1942–October 31, 1942, November 28, 1942–January 16, 1943, February 13, 1943, March 27, 1943–May 22, 1943, June 19, 1943, July 31, 1943–September 25, 1943, October 23, 1943–November 20, 1943, December 21, 1943–January 24, 1944, April 24, 1944–May 8, 1944, September 11, 1944, November 20, 1944–December 4, 1944, January 8, 1945–February 19, 1945, April 30, 1945–July 31 1945.

F2082-1-1-21. *Review of Industrial Relations.* July 1943.

F2082-1-1-25. *Plant Review Appendices.* 1945.

F2082-1-1-26. *Department of Munitions and Supply, Defense Projects Construction Branch, The General Engineering Company (Canada) Limited, A.W.S.C. Project No. 24, Scarboro, Ontario.*

F2082-1-1-30. *Wage and Salary Rates — 1942, 1943, 1944.* 1944.

F2082-1-1-32. Hamilton, R.M.P. Letter to John H. Fox, Esq., April 1981.

F2082-1-1-32. Kennedy, J. de N. Extracts from *Official History of the Department of — Munitions and Supply — Canada in the Second World War.*

F2082-1-2-10. Mary Pickford with GECO workers. Photograph. Circa June 1943. AO 648.

F2082-1-3. Hamilton, R.M.P. Interview with Hartley McVicar. *Let's Visit.* Radio recording. Toronto, c. 1945.

F2802-1-1-10. *Disposition of Records — 1946.* 1946.

F2802-1-1-18. *1945 Final Summary, History of Scarboro, Canada, 1941–1945.* 1945.

F2802-1-1-32. *Employee's Guidebook.* Toronto: General Engineering Company (Canada) Limited, 1943.

F2802-1-1-32. *Employment Booklet for Prospective Employees.* Toronto: General Engineering Company (Canada) Limited, February 15, 1943.

SCARBOROUGH HISTORICAL SOCIETY. GECO COLLECTION

Brimicombe, F.G. "To Those Women of All Ages." January 30, 1943.

Davis, Ross. "Lively Interest Aroused by MWA Rep. Nominations." January 30, 1943.

CITY OF TORONTO ARCHIVES.

"Laminated Beam Construction." Textual Records of GECO — 1941–1945. Fonds 2, Series 1243, Subseries 5, File 1.

Nordstrand, Sylvia. "Letters from Sylvia Nordstrand about Geco." Fonds 594142-9, Series 89, File 87, 1988–1989.

Skuce, Lou. Lou Skuce Cartoons for Wartime Posters. Fonds 70, Series 858, File 83.

PHOTOGRAPHS

Captioned photo: "Almost eighty percent of our security guards are old Army men." *GECO Fusilier,* April 10, 1943.

Captioned photo: "During its relatively brief span of life Scarboro has had many visitors..." *GECO Fusilier,* July 31, 1945.

Captioned photo: "Every day somewhere in the neighbourhood of eighteen thousand dishes go through the process..." *GECO Fusilier,* April 24, 1943.

Captioned photo: "From the outside looking in — any day of the working week around 5.30 p.m." *GECO Fusilier,* April 10, 1943.

Uncaptioned photo. *GECO Fusilier,* April 16, 1945.

Uncaptioned workshop photographs, *GECO Fusilier,* June 11, 1945.

Photo of Mary Pickford, actress with GECO workers, circa June 1943.

Captioned photo: "Parading the guards, a daily institution at the Plant." *GECO Fusilier,* April 10, 1943.

Captioned photo: "Since Mrs. Richards of Change House 17..." *GECO Fusilier,* November 28, 1943.

Captioned photo: "Views from the 'Miss War Worker' contest at Exhibition Park..." *GECO Fusilier,* July 31, 1944.

WEBSITES

www.ancestry.ca.

"Bofors 40 mm gun." Wikipedia.org. http://en.wikipedia.org/wiki/Bofors_40_mm_gun (accessed August 2014).

"George VI — An Act Respecting Official Secrets." History of Rights. www.historyofrights.com/ statutes/federal/Official_Sec.pdf (accessed August 2014).

"History, The Salvation Army International." salvationarmy.org. www.salvationarmy.org/ihq/ history (accessed September 2014).

"Introduction, Annual Review 2013–2014." salvationarmy.ca. www.salvationarmy.ca/annualreview2013-2014/ (accessed September 2014).

"The Official Site of the Hockey Hall of Fame." Legends of Hockey.net. www.legendsofhockey.net/ LegendsOfHockey/jsp/SearchPlayer.jsp?player=1445 (accessed August 2014).

"Tetryl — Frequently Asked Questions: Delaware Health and Social Sciences." http://dhss.delaware. gov/dph/files/tetrylfaq.pdf (accessed August 2014).

Tobias, Conan. "The Art of Sport." *Taddle Creek.* www.taddlecreekmag.com/the-art-of-sport (accessed August 2014).

"US Inflation Calculator." www.usinflationcalculator.com (accessed September 2014).

OTHER SOURCES

Display. Barracks Sector, Parc De-L'Artillerie, National Parks and Historic Sites of Canada, Old Quebec City, Quebec.

Engineer's sketch. *General Engineering Co. (Canada) Ltd. Scarboro Campus.* 1942.

GECO matchbook. Eddy Match Co. Limited Canada. Courtesy David Carr.

Hamilton, R.M.P. "A Short History of the General Engineering Company Inc." (June 1976).

Identification card for R.M.P. Hamilton. GECO Fonds. Archives of Ontario. F2802-1-1-32.

Identification card, issued from the *Inspection Board of the United Kingdom and Canada,* to GECOite Roxaline Wood. Courtesy Mary Elstone.

Insurance Plan of the City of Toronto (Underwriters' Survey Bureau Limited, January 1956). Vol. 9, Sheets 948-1 to 978.

Keast, Hilda. "Ping Pones." Written note on reverse of a collage of GECO employee photos with names, circa 1944.

Keast, Hilda. Written note on reverse of a GECO shop photo. Courtesy of her son, John, and Alan Harris, circa 1944.

Minister of Finance. Letter to Canadians. "Canada Must Borrow for Victory — A Statement."

Poster. "The Minister of Everything." W.W.II exhibit, Canada War Museum Ottawa, Ontario.

Poster. "Canada's Other Army." W.W.II exhibit, Canada War Museum, Ottawa, Ontario.

The General Engineering Company Canada Ltd. Scarboro Munitions Plan A.W.S.C. Project 24, 1941– 1945. DVD. Ontario: Arrow Films, 1945.

Van Iterson, Bill. "Biographical Summaries of Bob and Betty Hamilton." (November 20, 2010).

Index

7th Calvary Field Ambulance, 134

absenteeism, 62, 170, 176, 177, 184
accidents, 19, 29, 39, 45, 50, 54, 71, 79, 100, 111, 135, 156, 168, 170, 171, 172, 186, 205, 231, 235, 242
Adelaide Street West, 36, 39, 149
advertisement, 38, 103, 116, 179
Africa British Royal Engineers, 119
air conditioning, 7, 43, 77, 162, 163, 165, 182, 185, 202, 230
air raid precautions, 158, 166
Ajax, Ontario, 115, 116, 129
Alice, Princess, 166, 225, 227
"All Clear," 7, 71, 76, 77, 142, 143, 165, 172
Allied War Supplies Corporation (A.W.S.C.), 18, 26, 29, 34, 35, 55, 57, 198
    ambulance. See transportation
    anti-aircraft, 81, 131
    anti-sabotage, 65, 158
Athlone, Earl of, 166, 225, 226
Avery, C.R., 28
awards, 176, 177
Ayr, Scotland, 110, 112

baby boom, 241
badges
    blue chevron (attendance), 177

GECO Diamond (service), 8, 103, 104, 207, 208, 212
bank, 39, 42, 158
Barnardo, Thomas John, 112, 113, 134
Barnardo's Home for Orphans, 112, 134
barrier, 7, 70, 71, 76, 78, 86, 138, 142, 143, 183, 237
Bartley, T. Holmes, 26, 27, 245
baseball. See softball
beauty pageant, 140, 143, 215. See also Miss War Worker
Benato (ship), 107
bench leader, 104, 118, 196
Benson, Fire Chief Tom, 159, 232
berm, 43, 161, 165
Birchmount Road, 31, 102, 136, 141, 159, 233
Bismarck (ship), 18, 57
blitz, 26, 107, 224, 228
blood drives, 60, 61, 91, 108, 115, 220, 230, 240, 244
"Blue Goose," 125, 126, 203
Board of Agriculture and Fisheries, 115
Bofors, 81, 131
Bollert, Grace, 214, 215
Bombing and Gunnery School, No. 4, 25, 55
Bosely, W.H., 247
bowling, 140, 141, 212, 248
Box, Jean, 234

boxes, munition, 129, 143, 144, 164, 202, 204, 229
Bray, Col. W.J., 224
Brimicombe, F.G., 8
British Admiralty Technical Mission, 57
British Columbia, 30, 88, 122, 178
British Land Army, 111, 115
British War Victims' Fund (B.W.V.F.), 109, 224, 244
Brown, Agnes, 81
"brown school," 249
Building No. 67, 78, 81, 82, 265, 266, 267
    workshop layout, 41, 266
    buildings
    life expectancy, 161
    maintenance, 42, 48, 166, 167, 182, 201, 202, 232, 239
Burke, Elizabeth Jane, 31
buses/bussing, 38, 66, 67, 68, 86, 90, 91, 94, 101, 106, 114, 116, 120, 123, 131, 138, 145, 158, 184, 189, 190, 217, 232, 234, 237, 235, 244, 247, 249

cafeteria, 42, 45, 48, 49, 50, 74, 79, 84, 85, 94, 95, 97, 98, 108, 109, 176, 186, 187, 201, 207, 212, 216, 230, 232, 233, 237, 239, 244
Calgary Highlanders, 97
Campbell, Alma, 214
Campbell, L.H., Jr., 226
Campbell, Reeve Albert, 253, 254
Campbell, Walter, 51
Canada Customs, 125
Canada National Museum of Man, 131
Canada Wire, 92
Canadian Chemistry and Process Industries, 17
Canadian National Exhibition, 114, 120, 214, 215
Canadian National Railways, 151
Canadian Pacific Railways, 151
Canadian Red Cross, 220, 244
canteens, 111, 187
    clean-side canteen, 44, 84
    mobile canteen, 39, 108, 224, 244
Carrick, J.J., 150
cartoons, 79, 164, 168, 208, 209, 211
Certificate for Farm Work Efficiency, 115
change house, 7, 37, 42, 43, 44, 45, 69, 70, 76, 77, 84, 86, 116, 120, 138, 143, 146, 158, 169, 170, 176, 182, 184, 188, 224, 225, 246,
Cheesman, Dorothy (Mrs. Dorothy McRae), 35, 39, 85, 89, 90, 167, 175, 183
childcare, 62, 78, 147, 177, 178, 217, 218

children, 20, 86, 88, 89, 91, 99, 112, 114, 115, 125, 132, 133, 136, 142, 174, 175, 186, 216–218, 221, 237, 241, 244, 248–251
Christmas, 59, 117, 118, 129, 150, 216, 217, 226, 231, 234, 244
Christo, John, 28
City of Toronto, 254
Civic Road, 19, 42, 102, 259
clean side, 7, 41, 42, 43, 44, 67, 70, 72, 75, 77, 79, 80, 84, 89, 98, 102, 131, 137, 138, 142, 143, 158, 160, 161, 163, 165–167, 171, 174, 183, 191, 219, 226, 230, 236, 237, 246, 259
cleanway, 43, 44, 51, 86, 160, 165, 166. See also gallery
Clements, Hilda, 133
clock house, 42, 44, 67, 86, 181, 237
coal, 42, 215, 244
Commissioner of Provincial Police, 157
Conboy, Mayor, 226
contraband, 69, 70, 71, 167
    bobby pins, 49, 50, 71, 77, 146
    cigarettes, 70, 85, 159, 167, 224
    gum, 138, 167, 259
    jewellery, 71, 77, 138, 167
    matches, 72, 73, 138, 159, 167
    nail polish, 71
    playing cards, 168, 212, 232
    rayon, 74, 75, 259
    silk, 74, 75, 167
    wool, 74, 75
Controller General, 20, 123
Cost of Living Adjustment (COLA), 175
Craig, J.C., 28
Cranston, Peter, 143, 144
Crichton, Alexander S., 31
Crockford, Reeve Oliver, 250, 251
Cumberland, D.E., 28
Currell, Harvey, 247

dance, 112, 115, 132, 140, 212
Danforth Avenue, 35, 38, 39, 64, 89, 91, 116, 118, 122, 131, 138, 145, 189, 190, 233, 240, 248
danger zone, 41, 51, 67, 69, 74, 84, 101, 160, 162, 174, 253
Danniels, Molly, 85, 89, 100, 101, 168, 228, 232, 241
Darnborough, Florence, 134
Darnbrough, Walter, 133–136
Davis, Ross, 65, 130, 171, 208, 221, 224, 229, 236, 237, 245
Dawes Road, 114, 118, 119, 131, 138, 145, 189, 233

day nursery. *See* childcare

deaths, 19, 29, 100, 156, 171, 185, 191, 207, 210, 228, 232

decontamination, 246

Defence Industries Limited (D.I.L.), 19, 115, 116, 129, 139, 178

Beloeil, Quebec, 27

Pickering, Ontario 19, 30, 47, 139, 193, 203

Defensively Equipped Merchant Ships (D.E.M.S.), 92

Dentonia Park United Church, 217

Department of Munitions and Supply, 16, 24, 57, 64, 238

Department of National Defence, 27

depth charge, 16

desensitization, 152, 240, 246

destroying ground, 193, 247

detonator, 56, 72, 82, 100, 118, 134, 136, 164, 193, 199, 204, 228,

diamond badges. *See* badges

Dieppe, France, 146, 211

dirty side, 41, 42, 45, 68, 70, 72, 84, 89, 142, 159, 174, 183, 188, 219, 236, 246, 258

Division of Industrial Hygiene, Ontario Department of Health, 185

doctor, 39, 91, 105, 112, 145, 147, 148, 169, 182–184, 217

document of understanding, 26, 32

Dominion Arsenal, 15

Dominion Engineering Works, 152

Don Valley, 67, 90, 247

Downsview AFB, 148

Drew, George, 119

Drew Plan, 119

Duff, D. A., 28, 50, 89

Dunwoody, Derm, 250

dynamic duo (Bob and Phil Hamilton), 25, 147, 156

Eastern Commerce, 89, 131

Eaton's. *See* T. Eaton Company

Eglinton Avenue East, 30, 38, 42, 43, 44, 64, 67, 69, 91, 137, 141, 142, 189, 212, 213, 215, 233, 234, 247–249, 252, 258

elections, M.W.A., 219

Elementary Flying Training School, No. 1, 24, 55

Ellis, Elizabeth (Mrs. Elizabeth Warner), 71, 85, 90, 91

emergency housing, 20, 107, 142, 247, 250, 251

employee newspaper, 34, 36, 65, 72, 76, 79, 107, 164, 173, 207, 215, 221, 222, 223

Employee's Guidebook, 80, 176, 177

Employment

booklets, 63, 69, 80, 176, 177

campaign, 64, 142, 169, 178, 206

offices

Danforth Avenue, 35, 36, 38, 61, 89, 91, 240

Scarboro, 61, 89

Yonge Street, 64

empties (fuses), 44, 46, 47, 56, 57, 82, 102, 137, 175, 193, 195, 204

Engineering Heritage Records Foundation, 20

engineer's sketch, 258

engineers and engineering, 25, 27–29, 32–34, 36–39, 42–45, 48, 49, 53, 58, 89, 90, 97, 111, 145, 149, 151–153, 160, 162, 163, 166, 174, 194, 198, 199, 201, 214, 223, 232

Everest, John, 136, 137

executive plant council, 219

explosion doors, 78, 138, 160, 163, 166, 172

explosives

general, 16, 17, 19, 26, 46, 62, 73, 88, 106, 111, 133, 162, 175, 193, 194, 199, 205, 206, 227, 228, 259

handling of, 49, 65, 69, 72, 80, 83, 100, 130, 131, 137, 156, 198, 202, 247

high explosives (H.E.), 19, 41, 43, 44, 47, 54, 65, 69, 74, 105, 117, 120, 121, 131, 133, 158, 162, 169, 170, 172, 194, 199, 205, 206, 227, 237

quantities, 45, 46, 80, 156, 161, 204

storing of, 37, 41, 44, 45, 156, 160, 161, 204, 205

expropriation, 31, 33, 35, 136, 142, 252

Fairey Swordfish torpedo bombers, 18

Farer, Mika (Ignatieff), 95–100, 154

fatigue, 62, 168, 169, 177, 219, 232

Faubel, Ivy, 255

federal treasury, 57

fence patrol, 157, 158, 239

fencing, barbed-wire, 51, 137, 157, 252

fingerprinting, 36, 68, 89, 100, 158

fire

brigade/department, 39, 159

doors, 78, 160, 166, 172

drills, 159

extinguishers, 158, 159, 167

fighting, 65, 123, 159, 201

hall, 29, 42, 159, 201

hoses, 29, 158, 159

hydrants, 49, 159

trucks, 126, 159, 203
walls, 78, 132, 160
fire insurance plan, Toronto, 48, 167
first aid, 44, 167, 184, 235
Flexman, Major Ernest, 28, 50, 53, 54, 171, 172, 176, 178, 197, 215, 235
Food and Agriculture Organization (FAO), 98, 99
Ford, Henry, 98
foremen, 65, 125, 127, 130, 191, 219
Fox, John H., Esq., 21
Fragments of War: Stories of Survival in World War II, 97
Fraser, Helen (Miss Helen Gray), 92, 93
French, Hartley "Tony," 38, 39, 48, 144, 145, 228
fuse. *See* munitions

gaine, 7, 11, 18, 54, 204. *See also* munitions
gallery, 39, 43, 44, 46, 47, 70, 77, 78, 84, 138, 157–159, 163, 165–167, 226, 230
Gayford, Ernest, 24, 149
GECO Fusilier, 34, 51, 65, 72, 76, 79, 86, 107, 108, 109, 145, 168, 171, 173, 175, 208–211, 215, 221, 224, 229, 238, 240, 245
George VI (King), 31, 32, 35, 142, 252
Getty, Honourable Donald R., 142
Golden Mile, 92, 142, 249, 251, 252
government inspectors. *See* inspection
Great Depression , 37, 61, 90, 115, 118, 129, 134, 149, 151, 228
"green" school, 249
grounding rod, 81, 118, 162, 163
guard house, 42, 76, 86, 120
guards. *See* security guards
Gulf Oil, 132
gun-cotton, 193
gunpowder (G.P.), 19, 36, 37, 43, 44, 47, 54, 57, 69, 74, 84, 105, 137, 138, 140, 147, 169, 193, 201, 205, 230, 238, 246

Hamilton, Barbara, 154
Hamilton, Edward, 150
Hamilton, Elizabeth "Betty" (Miss Elizabeth Parsons), 21, 94, 149, 150, 153, 154
Hamilton, Evelyn (Miss Evelyn Banfill), 149, 150
Hamilton, John McLean Parsons, 95, 149, 151, 153, 154
Hamilton, Judy (Miss Judy Patton), 152
Hamilton, Philip Dawson Prior, 20, 21, 24–28, 33, 35–39, 43, 48–51, 53, 55, 58, 61, 67, 69, 71, 89, 97, 98, 100, 145, 147–152, 155, 156, 165, 169, 175–178, 181, 182, 194, 201, 207, 213, 218, 219, 221, 230, 246
Hamilton, Philip Henry Banfill, 50, 149, 151, 152
Hamilton, Robert, 147
Hamilton, Robert McLean Prior, 20, 21, 24–29, 33, 35–39, 43, 48–51, 53, 55, 58, 61, 67, 69, 71, 89, 94, 97, 98, 100, 130, 145, 147–153, 155, 156, 165, 168, 169, 172, 174–178, 180, 181, 182, 186, 194, 201, 207, 213, 218, 219, 221, 230, 233, 237, 238, 246
Harris, Ivy, 255
Harris, John Alan, 102, 103
Harris, W.T., 31
Harris, Walter, 102
Harrison, Eunice, 214, 215
Hayes, No. 7 Munitions Plant, 29, 41, 156, 160, 165, 169
Head, Eliza/Edith (Mrs. Edith Reay-Laidler), 112, 113
Head, Lieutenant-Colonel, R. A., 17, 57
head frame. *See under* mining
Hermann, Tarama, 141
Hermann, William, 140, 141
Hibbert, Joyce, 97
high explosives. *See under* explosives
"Hitler's Helpers," 210
hockey, 142, 153, 212, 248
Hollinger Bus Lines, 91, 184, 188, 232, 234
Hollywood on Parade, 92
Holmes, Barbara (Miss Barbara Mary Jarman, Mrs. Barbara Langfeldt), 93, 94, 95, 154, 187
Holmes, Hartley, 93, 94
hospital, 24, 102, 148, 185, 201
Hough, John, 31, 141, 142
housing, 20, 30, 107, 112, 142, 241, 247–252
Howe, Honourable Clarence Decatur (C.D.), Minister, Munitions and Supply, 16, 24, 25, 123
Howe, William, 123–125
humidity, 69, 156, 161–164, 199, 230
hydro-electric power, 30, 47, 151
hygrometer, 199
Hyndman, Grace, 28, 62, 94,

identification (ID) passes, 67, 68, 158, 176
igloo, 43, 161, 172
Ignatieff, Count Vladimir "Jim," 96, 98, 99
Ignatieff, Florence (Miss Florence Hargreaves), 28, 50, 62, 85, 94–100, 154, 176, 186, 216, 232, 268

Ignatieff, Katharine, 99
Ignatieff, Paul, 96–99, 100, 154
Ignatiev, Count Pavel Nikolayevich, 96, 99
industrial relations, 173, 176
inspection
    duties, 47, 57, 82, 83, 136, 156
    Inspection Board of the United Kingdom
        and Canada, 20, 44, 57, 104, 122,
        193–197, 207, 242
    inspector general (I.G.), 74, 122
    of war materials, 123
Inter-American Commission on Human
    Rights, 100
Irwin, Sybil, *81, 83*

Jarman, John Wallace, 93
Jeffrey, A.H., 28, 50, 62, 169, 176, 182, 185, 235
Johnston, A.E., 28

Keast, Hilda Eileen June (Mrs. Hilda Harris),
    101, 102, 103
Kennedy, Jack deNavarre, 63
King, William Lyon Mackenzie, 23, 24

laminated beam. *See* super structure
Lancaster bomber, 98
Lanecki, Mitchell, 137, 255
laundry, 39, 42, 49, 76, 77, 90, 147, 169, 182,
    187, 188, 201, 248
Laurentian Mountains, 12, 152
Lavalin Inc., 151
Lawrence Avenue, 101, 117, 122, 132, 144, 149,
    254
Le Cateau, France, 134
LeCappelain, Carol (Mrs. Carol Knight), 71,
    85, 103–105, 122, 207, 228, 231, 240
Ledson, Sidney, 137, 138, 139
Leslie, Helen (Miss Helen Gertrude Browes),
    105, 106, 107, 247, 248, 250
Leslie, Howard, 105, 250
Leslie, Howard Wayne "Harry," 250
Leslie, Jacqueline (Mrs. Jackie Eden), 105, 106
Leslie, Maggie, 106
Letitia (ship), 108
Little, H.W., 28
Little, T.B., 28
Littlejohn, E., 28
Local No. 1, 218
London, England, 24, 112, 224
London, Ontario, 25, 26, 55
Lorimer, Stella, 107–110
Lumina Resort, Muskoka, Ontario, 154

MacDonald, Donald Francis, 125
MacDonald, Donald John (D.J.), 125–127
MacDonald, Phillip, 125–127
MacDonald, Stanley, 125, 126
MacDonald Construction, 126
MacDonald-Sullivan Construction, 128
MacKay, Barbara, 107
MacKay, Margaret "Peggy" (Miss Margaret
    Ferguson Wallace), 107–110, 130, 224, 228
MacKay, Private Peter, 107
MacKay, Sergeant William, 107
MacLean, J.H., 28
magazines, 44–47, 82, 83, 161, 205
Main Street, 114
maintenance, 42, 48, 166, 167, 182, 201, 202,
    232, 239
Malton, Ontario, 24, 117, 120
Martin, E.N., 28
Massey Harris, 115, 119
McGill University, 147–149, 152
McGregor, Norma (Miss Norma Turner),
    118–120
McLean, Margaret, 147
McLellan, Chief Wilfred, 250
McNaughton, Lieut. General A.G.L., C.B.,
    C.M.G. D.S.O., 225–226
Meaham, P.W., 168
medical department, 42, 91, 159, 181–186, 230,
    235, 239, 240, 244, 249
medical examination, 217
medical officer, 50, 74
medical team/staff, 73–74, 131, 176, 231–232
mining
        GECO, 24, 26, 29, 69, 149–151, 153, 154
        head frame, 29
        mineshaft, 29
        Pre-Cambrian Shield, 149
Minister, Munitions and Supply. *See* Howe,
    C.D.
Minister, National Defence. *See* McNaughton,
    Lieut. General A.G.L., C.B., C.M.G. D.S.O.
Miss War Worker, 140, 143, 213–215
Montreal, Quebec, 11, 12, 29, 34, 120, 138, 145,
    147, 148, 151, 152, 216
Munition Workers' Association, 218–220
munitions
    components, 36, 44, 45, 47, 56, 58, 82, 83,
        137, 138, 143, 169, 192, 193, 197, 201,
        204, 244, 258
    design, 17, 197
    filling, 8, 16–18, 26–28, 32, 34, 36–39, 41,
        43–45, 47, 49, 53, 56–58, 64, 65, 70,

77–80, 82–84, 91, 94, 97, 104, 107, 116, 118, 121, 123, 124, 135, 138, 143, 156, 160, 162, 163, 165, 166, 169–171, 178, 182, 192–197, 202, 204, 218, 233, 238, 240, 242, 266

flame tracer bullet .303 G II, 54, 137, 197, 242, 243

fuses, specific
base fuse, 243
Fuse 119, 54, 121, 240, 242
Fuse 152, 54
Fuse 199, 54, 57
Fuse 251, 54, 56, 78, 81, 82, 131, 243, 256–267
Gaine 7, 11, 18, 54, 204
nose fuse, 243
percussion, 54, 204, 243
primers (Nos. 1, 11, 12, 15 Mark II, etc.), 7, 18, 31, 36, 54, 56, 72, 107, 118, 137, 192, 196, 204, 243
storage, 42–45, 47, 156, 193, 244
shipping, 18, 31, 44, 47, 54, 56, 68, 82, 83, 129, 139, 198, 202, 203, 204, 229, 242
Tracer-Igniter No. 12, 54, 168, 243
tube (tracer, vent percussion 0.5"), 7, 18, 54, 168, 204

mural, 254, 255

"Naffi", 111
National Filling Factory No. 7, 29
National Hockey League 142
National Selective Service, 143, 178
National War Labour Board, 176
Needham, Eva, 240
Neufeld, Margaret (Mrs. Margaret Hermann), 139–141
Newman, Alice, 214, 215
Niobe, HMCS, 124
No-Man's Land, 148
Noranda (Roberts), 150, 151
Noronic, S.S., 110
Norstrand, Sylvia, 71, 78, 84, 85, 170, 219, 226
North Bay Nugget, 103
nursing, 170, 178, 183, 184, 232
nutrition, 98, 186–187, 212

oath of secrecy, 36, 68, 89, 114, 120, 129
Official Secrets Act 1939, 68
Old Boys' Association, 240
Old Girls' Association, 240
Olga Alexandrovna, Grand Duchess, 96

Operating Stores, 124
ordnance depot, 25, 26, 55

papering, 82
Parkes, M., 185, 234
Parkin, Anne (Miss Anne Wilmot), 120
pellet and magazine, 44, 84, 204, 205, 212, 220
Pfeiffer, Harold, 107, 108, 130–131
Pickering, Ontario, 19, 30, 47, 139, 193, 203
Pickford, Mary, 93, 226
Pickles, Ernest, 131, 160
"Ping Pones," 102
"Piston Packin' Moma," 125, 126
Pitcher, W.H., 17, 18, 157, 164
Plain, Mary "Maimie" (Mrs. Mary Shearer), 110–112
Poems
"And It Came to Pass," 222
"Jack Be Nimble," 164
"Our Barrier Lady," 76, 77
"To Those Women of All Ages," 7
"Untitled," 72, 168
"Young Canadian Died, A," 210
post-war housing, 20, 30, 107, 112, 142
pregnancy, 94, 108, 117, 119, 133, 147, 169,
primer. See under munitions.
Project No. 24, 11, 18, 20, 25, 26, 28, 30, 34–36, 53, 89
proof
gun, 193
load, 25
proofing, 56, 83, 168, 193–195, 247
range, 192–193, 198, 203
yard, 44, 45, 47, 83, 105, 159, 168, 193–197, 203, 247

quality control, 45, 104, 168, 196, 197

rail, 28, 30, 151, 198
Read, H., Lieutenant-Colonel Rear Admiral, 17–18, 57, 58
Reay-Laidler, Edith (Miss Eliza Head), 112–115, 134
recreation club, 176
Red Baron, 148
Regional War Labour Board, 176
regulations, 20, 65, 68, 69, 71, 72, 79–81, 100, 167–168, 176, 197. See also under security
Research Enterprises Limited (R.E.L.), 124, 189, 190
Richards, Ruth, 224
rifle cartridge, 16

Roberts, Leslie, 150, 151
rock wool, 247
Royal Air Force (R.A.F.), 109, 148
Royal Canadian Air Force (RCAF), 24, 68, 93,
 116, 122, 138, 140
Royal Canadian Army Service Corps, 102
Royal Canadian Dragoon, 134
Royal Canadian Navy, 92, 119, 133, 142
Royal Flying Corps, 148
rumours, 26, 63, 64,169, 185, 229–230
Russell, Kathleen "Kitty," *214*, 215
Rutherford, George, 238

sabotage, 36, 65, 158, 253
safety, 47, 49,54, 62, 63, 65, 69,73, 74,79, 80,
 83,100, 102,155, 156,157, 159, 162, 164,
 166, 167, 168, 171, 172, 176, 191, 193, 194,
 199, 201, 205, 208, 239
 standards, 25, 28, 65, 76, 154, 178, 194, 195,
  197, 199, 252
saltpeter, 229
Salvation Army, 108, 224, 244, 249
Sawdust Brigade, 129, 202–204
"Sc/C" (Scarboro/Canada), 19, 26, 197, 198
Scarboro Township, 31, 136, 158–159, 248
Scarborough Fire Department, 123, 143, 159
secrecy, 20, 26, 34, 36–39, 45, 51, 52, 67, 68, 89,
 90, 114, 120, 124, 129, 156, 158, 175, 176,
 199, 204, 229, 238, 244, 245, 252, 253
 military, 175
 oath. *See* oath of secrecy
 Official Act 1939, 68
security
 guards, 39, 70, 157–159, 203, 232
 regulations, 20, 65, 68, 69, 72, 79, 80, 81,
  167, 176, 197
 special security observers, 158
Segsworth, R.S., 28
sentencing, 56, 194
sewage/sewers, 28, 30, 47, 49, 136
Shelburne, HMCS, 133
shifting houses. *See* change houses
shifts, 16, 44, 60, 62, 67–70, 78, 79, 84, 85, 86,
 88, 97, 102, 106, 111, 114, 115, 116, 132,
 138, 142, 147, 157, 158, 162, 168, 170, 177,
 178, 183, 184, 188, 189, 194, 203, 207, 215,
 219, 220, 231, 233, 234, 236, 237, 238, 240
Simerson, Fran, 143
Simerson, Mary "Zaida," 141–143, 232, 233
Sinclair, G., 234
singing, 116, 146, 173
Sinnott Road, 123, 142, 252, 268

Skuce, Lou, 79, 209, 211
Skuce's Goose, 79, 209, 211
Smith, Edward (Ted) H., 27, 28, 37, 38, 176
smokestack, 157, 213
smoking, 159
snowstorm (of 1944), 98, 101, 122, 132, 184,
 189, 231–234
social activities, 173, 212
sodium sulphite, 188, 246
softball, 39, 91, 124, 212, 213, 248
St. Clair Avenue, 48, 67, 102, 136, 137, 212, 254
static electricity, 41, 70, 74, 75, 118, 156,
 162–164, 166, 259
stemming, 7, 82, 170, 199, 200
Stewart, Winifred (Miss Winifred Dady),
 115–116
stores, 42, 44, 45, 47, 65, 124, 193, 212, 244
striking, 199, 219, 220, 230
suggestion program, 135, 136, 174, 175
Sullivan, James Joseph "Joe," 125, 127–128
super structure, 25, 52, 161, 162, 166, 172, 214
Sweetman, Rena (Mrs. Rena O'Hagan), 116
Szydlik, Sue,134, 136, 170

T. Eaton Company
 Georgian Room, 95, 97
 store, 93, 121, 130
Tamplin, H.L., 28, 29, 49
Taylor, William, 28, 37, 58, 210, 223
tetryl, 169–171, 193, 199, 204, 246
 dust, 43, 71, 75, 82, 83, 91, 105, 118, 121,
  130, 131, 144, 147, 157, 169, 170, 182,
  188, , 199, 200
 poisoning/toxic jaundice, 29, 156, 169, 170,
  171, 181
 precautions, 43, 82, 118, 130, 157, 169, 170,
  171, 182, 184, 199, 200
 rash/respiratory effects, 122, 131, 170, 184
 yellow/orange/coppery stain of, 71, 75, 91,
  103, 105, 121, 124, 144, 147, 169, 170,
  171
textiles, 42, 204
time
 clock house, 7, 42, 44, 67, 86, 181, 237
 motion, 42, 89
Todd, J.P., 28
"Ton of Books, A" (Carrick), 150
tooling, 27, 57, 199
Toronto Daily Star, 26, 38, 85, 97, 178, 189, 231
Toronto Police Amateur Athletic Association,
 213, 214
Toronto Telegram, 60, 247, 250

Tracer-Igniter No. 12, 18, 54, 86, 87, 100, 137, 168, 170, 193, 197, 242, 243. *See also under* munitions

training, 18, 20, 24, 28, 54, 65, 175, 176, 191, 194

transformer vaults, 45, 47, 48, 160

transportation, 188–190:
   ambulances, 42, 111, 126, 203
   "Blue Goose," 125, 126, 203
   buses. *See* buses/bussing
   fire trucks, 126, 159
   munitions trucks, 126, 128, 198, 202, 203, 233
   taxis, 126, 202
   truckerettes, 47, 101, 102, 103, 139
   tube
   various, 7, 18, 168, 204
   tracer, vent percussion 0.5", 54. *See also under* munitions

tuberculosis, 147, 185, 230

tunnels, 20, 38, 42, 43, 45, 47, 48, 51, 91, 98, 102, 105, 114, 123, 124, 138, 144, 157–161, 165–167, 202, 252, 253, 254, 268

turban. *See* uniform

Turner, Norma, 118, 119

Underpass Revitalization Project, 254

unemployment, 37

uniform, 8, 67–76, 86, 103, 116, 120, 124, 138, 142, 146, 158, 167, 169, 170, 177, 178, 182, 187, 188, 207, 244, 246
   brassieres, 71, 116, 118, 121
   name tag, 68
   turban, 7, 71, 74, 75, 104, 116, 120, 124, 188
   underwear, 49, 50, 71, 116, 120, 143

unions, 218–220

United Nations, 98, 107, 177, 200

United States, 24, 88, 149, 160, 169, 239

victory bond, 136, 187, 230, 241, 244

victory gardens, 101, 150, 153, 215–216, 248

victory loans, 221–225, 230, 236

visitors, 69, 225

Waddell, Alex Licorice, 128–130, 203

Waddell, Bessie, 128–130

wages, 89, 121, 124, 136, 144, 152, 173, 175, 218–220, 223, 243

Walsh, Lottie, 215

War Assets Corporation, 247

War Industry Average (WIA), 177

War Identification Transit Plan, 189

War Worker, Miss. *See* Miss War Worker

war savings certificates, 20, 221

Warden Avenue, 31, 101, 137, 143, 247, 248, 252, 254, 258. *See also* Wardin Avenue

Wardin Avenue, 30, 31, 38, 212, 213, 215

washrooms, 44, 45, 62, 111, 167, 182, 248, 249, 251

water
   reservoir, 42, 158
   supply, 30, 49, 158, 166, 182, 248
   tanks, 42, 158

Whispering Gallery, 229

Williams, A.J., 28

Williams, E.A., 28

Wilmot, Anne (Mrs. Anne Parkin), 120–122

windows, 43, 78, 91, 138, 163, 164, 165, 172, 185, 230, 234, 248, 252

Wolffers, R., 234

Wood, Roxaline, 122, 123

wood truss, 25

Woolwich, England, 26, 27

work record cards, 191, 218

X-ray (building), 44, 83, 102, 130

X-ray (chest), 130, 185

York, Stan, 234

flash, 141, **142,** 156, 178–84, **179, 193,** 347, 348, 351
flat, 347
front, 344, 345–46, **346**
indoor, 352–58
outdoor, 348–52
portrait, 352–58
side, 344, **346,** 347, **347**
soft, 348, **349**
top, 350, 379
types of, 344–47
Lighting ratios for fill flash, 183–84, **184**
Light meters, *see* Exposure meters
Light output, flash, 148, 164–65, **174,** 176–77, 181, 379, 390
Light spots or streaks on pictures, 474–75
Linear polarizing filter, 236, 237
Loading film into developing tank, 446–48, **447**
Loading the camera, 23–28
  autoload cameras, 23–25, **24,** 298
  infrared films, 385, 387
  manually, **25,** 25–26
Locking wheel, flash, 154
Loupe, 449, 479, **494**

Macro adapter ring, *see* Reversing ring
Macro flash, 135, 147, 379
Macro lenses, 108–109, **109,** 133–36, **134, 370,** 370–72, **371,** 377, 378, **378**
Macro mode, compact camera, 280
Magazine:
  film, 7, 24
  slide, 490
Magazines, photography, 498–99
Magicube, flash, 143
Magnifier, 449, 478–79, **494**
Mail-order photofinishers, 216
Main light, 352, **353, 358**
Maintenance of camera, 18–19
Manual exposure mode, 66, 68
Manual flash control, 158
Manual flash exposures, figuring, 173–77
  for bounce flash, 186, **187**
Manual focus lenses, 115
Marine aquariums, photographing at, 410–11
Matrix metering, *see* Multizone metering
Mats, for framing, 481, **481,** 483

Maximum lens aperture, 108, 111, 126
Medium-format cameras, 5–7, **6**
Medium speed films, 33, 207
Memory lock, exposure, 73–74, 88, 282
Metric conversion tables, 550–52
Microfiber lens cleaning cloth, 19, 229, 291, 427
Micro lenses, *see* Macro lenses
Microprism focusing collar, 50
Microscope, photographing through a, 414–15
Middle (gray) tone, exposure readings for, 92, 98, 99–100
Mid-roll change, 28–30, 292
Minimum focusing distance, 48, 280
Mirror telephoto lenses, **128,** 129
Mirror lock-up, viewfinder, 23
Modeling lights, flash, 357, **358**
Model releases, 503
Moon, photographing the, 367, 392–93
Motor drives, 270–72, **271,** 391–92
Mounting of enlargements, 480–82, **481**
Multifunction back, camera, 269, 270
Multigrade/multicontrast photo papers, *see* Variable contrast photo papers
Multimode exposure cameras, 45–46, 66–68, **67**
Multiple exposure control, 30–31, **31,** 191, 288, 387, **390,** 392
Multiple exposures, 30–32, **31,** 258, 387–95
  multiple flash and, *see* Multiple flash
Multiple flash:
  repetitive flashes on single film frame, 166–67, **189,** 190–91, 390–91, **391**
  use of more than one flash unit, 167, **188,** 188–90
Multiple-image lens, 95, 254, **254**
Multizone metering, 71–73, **72,** 95–97, **96,** 156, 365, **365**

Natural light, 344
Nature Photographer, 499
Negatives, 199–200, 442
  processes for, 442–43
  developing of, 443–49, **446, 447**
  printing of, 449–55, **450,** 459–60, 463, 466–69, **467**

Neutral density (ND) filters, 233, **238,** 238–41, **240,** 379, 494
Newsletters, photography, 499
Newton's rings, 490
Night mode of compact camera, 282
Night photography:
    shooting with existing light and at night, 360–69
        fast films for, 360–64, **364**
        film for, 368
        trial exposure guidelines, chart of, 362–63
Nikonos underwater cameras, 399, 400–01, **402, 406**
    See also Underwater photography
Nonglare glass, framing with, 483
Non-TTL (through-the-lens) autoflash, 156–58
    bounce flash and, 186
    fill flash and, 180
Normal lenses, 103–104, **104**
Normal sync, shutter, 166

Off-camera flash, 163, **167,** 171–73, 188, 258, **358**
Off-center subject, composition:
    focusing on, 119, **120,** 291
    rule of thirds, 318, 319, **319**
Off-the-film (OTF) flash metering, 71, 155
On-camera flash, 184
One-time-use cameras, *see* Single-use cameras
One-touch zoom lens, 123
On/off power switch, flash, 158–59
Open-aperture metering, 73
Open flash, **189,** 190, 258
Open flash button, flash, 159–60, 186, 190, 390
Opening up the lens, 43
Optical quality of lenses, 110–12, **111,** 129
"O" rings, for camera strap, 16
Outdoor Photographer, 499
Overexposure, 92, 238, 472–73
    intentional, 65, 74–76, **75**

Painting with light, open flash, **189,** 190
Pan head, tripod, 263
Panning, 334–36, **336, 337, 342**
Panoramic format, 276, 288, **289,** 294–95, **296**
Panoramic single-use cameras, 298
Paper grades, enlarging, *see* Graded contrast photo papers

Paper safe, for photo papers, 465–66
Parallax correction/compensation, 13, 368
Parallax error, 13, 139, 280–81, **281,** 376
Passive phase detection autofocus system, 119–20, 278–79
PC cords for flash, 172–73
Pellicle mirror, in SLR viewfinder, 12–13
Pentaprism, in SLR viewfinder, 12
Periodicals, photography, 498–99
Perspective-correction (PC) lenses, 133
Petersen's PHOTOgraphic, 499
Photo CD, 216, 307, **484,** 484–85, 500
Photocells, exposure meter, 69–70, 79–81, **80**
Photo credit line, 503
PEI, PHOTO > Electronic Imaging, 504
Photoflood bulbs, **355,** 355–56, 381
Photograms, darkroom, 471
Photographer's Market, 503
Photographic copying, 380–83
Photographic gray card for exposure readings, 97–98
Photographic terms, foreign, 439
Photographic umbrella, 187, 352
Photography books, 440, 497–98
Photography, definition of, 344
Photomacrography, 370
Photomicrography, 370
Photo paper:
    for contact prints, 451, 455
    for enlarging, 451, 455–59, **456, 457,** 479–80
Photo players, 295
Photo scanners, 295, 307, 484
PhotoStockNotes, 499
Photo Techniques, 499
Photo vest, 269
Physiograph, 394
Pistol grip for cameras, 264
Pixels, 310, 313
Plane of focus, 377
Point-and-shoot cameras, *see* Compact cameras
Point of focus indicator, lens, 51
Point of reference, composition, 332–34
Polarizing filters, **225,** 227, 233, **234,** 234–48, **236, 237,** 397
Polaroid instant cameras, *see* Instant cameras

Popular Photography, 112, 499
Portraits, 189, 291, 351, 504–505
    lighting for, 352–58
Power-saving circuitry, flash, 169
Predictive autofocus, 116
Preflash, 163, 287
Prepaid film processing mailers,
    216–17, 433
Primary colors, in photography, 249,
    249, 390
Print dryer, 451
Printing filters, for black-and-white
    photo papers, 456–57
Print sizes, 459, 479–80
Print tongs, **450,** 454
Print washer, 451
Processing films and prints, 214–17,
    440–476
    analyzing faults in your
        photographs, 472–76
    chemicals, 442–45, 448–49,
        450–51, 453–55
    contact proof sheets, making, 444,
        445, 449–55, **450**
    developing film, 442–49, **446,
        447**
    equipment for, 445–447, 450–54,
        456–57, 459–65
    enlargements, making, *see*
        Enlargements, making
    self-processing, 440–76
    steps for developing film, 444,
        445–49, **446, 447**
    when traveling, 432–33, **434**
Professional film, 198
Professional Photographer, 504
Professional Photographers of
    America (PPA), 504
Professional photography, 504–505
Programmed exposure mode, 46, 66,
    67, **67**
Projecting slides, *see* Slide shows
Projection screens, **492,** 492–93
Projector bulbs, 487
Projector lenses, 488–89, 496
Projectors, *see* Slide projectors
Proof prints/sheets, 444, 445, 449–55,
    450
Property releases, 503
Protecting the camera, 16–19, 290–91,
    422–24, **423**
Push processing, 209, 361–64

Quartz-halogen bulbs, 356–57
Quick release, tripod, 263–64
Quick-return mirror, 9–12

Radio slave signal device, 168, 173
Rainbows, photographing, 352
Random access memory (RAM), 311,
    312
Rangefinder cameras, 27, 37, 103,
    139, 366–67
Ready light, flash, 159
Real image viewfinders, 281
Rear-curtain sync, shutter, 166, 394
Reciprocity effect, film, 211, 369
Recycle time, flash, 168–70
Red-eye, flash, 146, **163,** 163–64,
    287, 476
Red-eye reduction pen, 164
Reflected-light exposure meter
    readings, **85,** 86, **86,** 87
Reflectors, light, 347, 348, 351, 352,
    355–57, **355,** 379
Reflex-type telephoto lenses, **128,** 129
Release priority, autofocus, 116
Remote controls for camera, 272, 288
Remote cord, 39, 259, **260,** 366, 378,
    390, 427
Remote flash sensor, 173, 189–90
Remote sensor cord, flash, 172
Remote slave flash, 167–68, 173
Repeating flash mode, *see* Multiple
    flash
Reproduction ratio, for close-ups,
    133, 371, 372
Resolution of digital images, 309–11
Resolution/resolving power of film,
    307
Reversal film, *see* Black-and-white
    film, reversal (slide); Color
    reversal (slide) film
Reversing a normal or wide-angle lens,
    135, 372, 377
Reversing ring, 135–36, 372–73, **373,**
    426
Rewind crank/knob, 24, 32
Ring light, flash, 135, 147, 379
Roll film, 212, 448
Rule of thirds, composition, 318–19,
    319

Sabattier effect, darkroom, 471
Safelights, *see* Darkroom safelights
Sandwiching images, 395, 471
Schools of photography, 501
Screw-in filters, 226–27, 229
Screw mount, for lenses, 114
Seamless paper, for background, 354
Secondary colors, in photography,
    249, **249,** 390
Secondary flash head, 160

Second curtain sync, shutter, 166, 394

Selective contrast photo papers, *see* Variable contrast photo papers

Selenium cells, exposure meter, 79

Self-timer, 23, 258–59, 288, 366, 378

Selling photographs, 503–505, **504**

Series filters, 227

Set-screw filter adapter, 227

Shadows, **345,** 348, 350–51, 379
    exposure for, 92–100, **93, 94, 96, 99**
    flash photography and, 193–94

Sharpness of a lens, **111,** 111–12

Sheet film, 213

Shift lenses, 133

Shoe-mount flash, **145,** 146
    features of, **153,** 153–68

Shoulder brace (for cameras), 264

Shutterbug, 499

Shutter-preferred cameras, 68

Shutter-priority exposure mode, 46, 66, **67,** 67–68

Shutters, types of, 13–14, **14**
    see also Focal-plane shutter; Leaf shutter

Shutter speed control dial, 37

Shutter speeds, 13–14, 36, 37–40
    B shutter setting, 38–39, 190, 282, 360, 366, **388,** 390
    compact cameras and, 283
    f/stops and, **44,** 44–45, **45**
    interrelationship of, **39,** 40–41
    macro lenses and, 134
    setting of, 37, 43–44
    stop-action and, *see* Stop-action
    telephoto lenses and, 126
    T shutter setting, 38, 190, 360, 366, 390
    see also specific photographic conditions and effects

Shutter synchronization with flash, 149–52, **152,** 189–90, 337

Side lighting, 344, **346,** 347, **347**

Silhouettes, 68, 91, 171, **331,** 347

Silicon blue cell, exposure meter, 79

Silicon photo diode, exposure meter, 79

Silver halides, film coating, 444

Single focal length lenses, 107, 283–84

Single frame advance, 116

Single lens reflex (SLR) cameras, 4, **4**
    comparison to compact cameras, 6–16, **8,** 277–78

features and controls, example of, **10–11**
    manual control of, 9
    underwater, 401–11
    see also specific features and functions of single lens reflex cameras

Single shot focus, of lens, 49, 115

Single-use cameras, 4, 276, **297,** 297–300, **299**
    waterproof, 298, **299,** 399, **407**

Size indicators, composition, 327, **328**

Skylight (1A) filter, 132, 234, 397

Slave flash, 167–68, 173, 188–89

Slide duplication, 382–83

Slide film, *see* Black-and-white film, reversal (slide); Color reversal (slide) film

Slide mounts, 205, 289–90, 291

Slide projectors, **486,** 486–92, **487, 490**
    bulbs for, 487
    lenses for, 488–89, 496
    special features and accessories, 491–92

Slide shows, 421, 486–96

Slide sorter, 493–94, **494**

Slide tray/magazine, 490, **486, 490**

Slip-on adapter, for filters, 227

Slow-speed films, 33–34, 207, 208, 209

Slow sync, for flash, 165, **165**

SLR, *see* Single lens reflex (SLR) cameras

Small-format cameras, 4–5

Snoot, for studio lights, 353–54

Soft-focus filters, **230,** 253, 471, **472**

Soft lighting, 348, **349**

Software for photo editing, 308, 500

Solar-powered compact camera, 289–90

Special effects filters, 251–52, **252**

Specialized preprogrammed exposure mode, 46, 68

Spirit level, tripod, 264

Split-field lens, 254

Split-image rangefinder, for focusing, **49,** 50

Spot area autofocusing, 119

Spot filter, 253

Spot exposure meter, hand-held, 88, **89**

Spot metering, 71, **72,** 74, **94, 96,** 97, 365, **365**

Standard lenses, 103, **104**

Star effect without a filter, 252–53, 351
Star filters, 251–52, **252**
Stars, photographing, 413–14
Step-up ring, for filters, 227
Stop-action, **38,** 45, 332–37, **335, 336,** 361
Stop bath, film, 444, 445, 449
    photo paper, 450, 451, 454, 467
Stop-down metering, 73
Stopping down the lens, 43
Strobe, flash, 143
Stroboscopic flash, 166–67
Studio cameras, 7
Studio lights, **145,** 147, 352–358, **358**
Sufficient light indicator, flash, 159, 186
Sunsets, photographing, **351,** 352, 392
Synchronization, flash, *see* Flash synchronization
Synchro-sunlight flash, *see* Fill flash

Tabletop tripod, 264
Teleconverter, *see* Tele-extender
Tele-extender, 127–29, **128,** 375, 377
Telephoto flash adapter, 161
Telephoto lenses, **104,** 105, 124–29, **125,** 207
    filter attachment to, 227
    supporting, 22, 124–26, **128,** 257
Telescope, photographing through a, 412–14, **413**
Telescope camera adapter, 413
Television screen, photographing images on, 367–68
Temperature conversion chart, 552
Temperature's effect on cameras, 17, 422–24
Test print, **467,** 467–68
Texture screen, for enlarging, 471
Thermometer, darkroom, 445
35mm cameras, 3–16
    compact cameras, *see* Compact cameras
    half-frame, 4–5
    point-and-shoot cameras, *see* Compact cameras
    single lens reflex (SLR) cameras, *see* Single lens reflex (SLR) cameras
Through-the-lens (TTL) metering, 70, **70,** 71, 155, 377
    filters and filter factor, 210, 232–33, 238

with flash, 71, 85, 155–58
Tilting and rotating flash head, **158,** 160
Time exposures, 38–39, **211, 257,** 257–59, **260,** 282, 360, 420
Time-lapse photography, 258, 271–72
T shutter setting, 39, 190, 282, 360, 366, 390
Timer, darkroom, 445, 448
Timing, composition, 338–40
Toners, for photo papers, 471
Top lighting, 350, 379
Tours, photo, 502
Trailing sync, for flash, 166, 394
Transparency film, *see* Black-and-white film, reversal (slide); Color reversal (slide) film
Trap focus, 121
Travel photography, 416–39
Tray siphon, darkroom, 451
Tripods, 22, 124–26, **128,** 134, **135,** 256–65 **257, 263,** 361, **364,** 366, 378, 381, 427
    brands of, 259–60
    multiple flashes and, 190, 191, 390
    parts and features, 260–65
    positioning, **261,** 265
TTL (through-the-lens) autoflash, **152, 153,** 155, 156, **156,** 171, **172,** 178, 186, **187**
TTL sync/remote cord, 172, **172**
Tungsten color slide film, 192, 200–202, **201**
Tungsten-halogen bulbs, 356–57
Tungsten light, 200, 354–55, **355, 369**
Two-for-one films, 206–207
Two-touch zoom lens, 123–24

Ultraviolet (UV) filters, 20, **20,** 132, 233–34, 397, 425
Ultra-wide-angle lenses, 105
Umbrella, photographic, **145,** 187, 352
Underexposure, 92, 473
    intentional, 65, 74–76, **75**
Underwater cameras:
    amphibious, 399, 400–401, **402, 406**
    Nikonos models, 399, 400–401, **402, 406**
    waterproof 35mm compacts, 290, **290,** 399
    waterproof housings for, 399–404, **400, 402, 403**

Underwater cameras *(cont.)*
  waterproof single-use, 297, 298,
    299, 399, **407**
Underwater photography, 398–411
  backscatter, **404,** 406, **406**
  camera care, 408–409
  composition, 409
  film for, 408
  special concerns:
    color absorption, 405–406
    color balance, 408
    exposure, 405
    flash use, **404,** 405
    focusing, 408
    lens focal length, 406–407
Unipod, 265
U.S. Customs, 435–37
Used camera equipment, buying,
    272–73
"Use flash" signal, 168
UV filters, *see* Ultraviolet (UV) filters

Variable contrast photo papers,
    456–57
Variable focal length lenses, 122–23
  close up, 375–376
Variable power control, *see* Light
    output, flash
Variable self-timer, 288
Vibration reduction, camera, 283
Video photography, 307
Video processors, 484
Videotapes, instructional, 500–501
View cameras, **6,** 7
Viewfinder:
  of compact cameras, 48, 279, **279,**
    280, 281
    single-use cameras, 298–99
  of single lens reflex (SLR) cameras,
    9, 48, 52–53
Viewfinder coverage, **51,** 52

Viewfinder magnification, 52
Viewing system:
  of single lens reflex (SLR) cameras,
    9–13, **12, 15,** 48
  of 35mm compact cameras, 13, 48
Vignetting, 229–30, 375

Warming filters, 244
Warranties, 438
  lens, 113, **113**
Washing negatives, 449
  prints, 455, 468
Waterproof cameras, *see* Underwater
    cameras
Weatherproof cameras, 290, **290**
Weights and measures, tables of,
    550–52
Wide-angle flash adapter/diffuser, 161
Wide-angle lenses, **104,** 105, **107,**
    130, 130–33
  for underwater photography,
    407–408
Wide area autofocusing, 118–19
Wireless remote flash, 167–68, 173
Workshops, photographic, 501
World Wide Web, photography sites,
    499–500, **500**

Zero adjustment of hand-held
    exposure meter, 89
Zone focus, 48–49
Zone system for determining
    exposure, **99,** 99–100
Zoom adjustment button, 161–62
Zoom flash head, 148, 181–82
Zooming, for action effects, **2,** 338,
    338
Zoom lenses, 107–108, 110, 121–24,
    122, 123, 394, 425, **426**
Zoom lens reflex (ZLR) cameras, 8, **8,**
    110, 285